DICTIONARY OF INTERNATIONAL HUMAN RIGHTS LAW

Dictionary of International Human Rights Law

Connie de la Vega

Professor of Law and Academic Director of International Programs, University of San Francisco School of Law, USA

Edward Elgar
Cheltenham, UK • Northampton, MA, USA

© Connie de la Vega 2013

All rights reserved. No part of this publication may be reproduced, stored in a retrieval system or transmitted in any form or by any means, electronic, mechanical or photocopying, recording, or otherwise without the prior permission of the publisher.

Published by
Edward Elgar Publishing Limited
The Lypiatts
15 Lansdown Road
Cheltenham
Glos GL50 2JA
UK

Edward Elgar Publishing, Inc.
William Pratt House
9 Dewey Court
Northampton
Massachusetts 01060
USA

A catalogue record for this book
is available from the British Library

Library of Congress Control Number: 2012952650

This book is available electronically in the ElgarOnline.com
Law Subject Collection, E-ISBN 978 1 78254 070 0

ISBN 978 1 84980 377 9 (cased)

Typeset by Servis Filmsetting Ltd, Stockport, Cheshire
Printed by MPG PRINTGROUP, UK

CONTENTS

Acknowledgements vii
Guide to the dictionary ix
List of abbreviations xi

Definitions 1
Appendix 177

ACKNOWLEDGEMENTS

I would like to thank a number of people without whom this project would not have been possible. First, I would like to thank Professor David Weissbrodt, University of Minnesota School of Law, and my co-author of *International Human Rights Law: An Introduction* (Penn Press 2007). I would not have considered his suggestion for this project without having had the experience of having written that book with him. Besides helping me get a start on a list of words, the book was a useful research tool at all stages of this project. Also useful was his textbook, *International Human Rights: Law, Policy, and Process* with Joan Fitzpatrick and Frank C. Newman. I also appreciate his willingness to answer both research and substantive questions throughout the project.

Second, I would like to thank my intern, Ann Kam, and research assistant, Marie Vincent. Ms Kam spent the summer of 2010 at the Frank C. Newman International Human Rights Law Clinic. Among the tasks she worked on was starting the list of words for this book. She did an excellent job starting the process on what words to include. Marie Vincent was my research assistant for two years and without her the Appendix would not have been possible. Ms Vincent is very thorough in everything she undertakes. She has excellent organizational skills and her ability to pay attention to detail resulted in the vast compilation of instruments in the Appendix. She also assisted me with some of the definitions in the dictionary itself.

Third, I would like to thank my friend and colleague Dan O'Donnell who provided me with input at various stages of this project and drafted a number of definitions. His wise advice and knowledge are truly appreciated.

I would like to thank a number of other people who assisted me by commenting on the list or assisting me with specific areas of the law. Among this group were my colleagues at the University of San Francisco School of Law who were the first to comment on the draft list of words and what categories should be included. Other persons who gave me input on the list or specific words were: Sandra Coliver, Julie Dorf, Eva Herzer, Shannon Minter, Professor Naomi Roht-Arriaza, University of California at Hastings School of Law, Professor Dinah Shelton, George Washington University School of Law, Professor Jordan Paust and Julianne Traylor.

Finally, I would like to thank Tara Gorvine at Edward Elgar Publishing who was always available to give me input on the numerous questions that came up throughout this project.

GUIDE TO THE DICTIONARY

This dictionary includes two major sections. The first one consists of the definitions. Because there are numerous human rights instruments, I decided it would be useful to include an Appendix with short descriptions of the instruments and references on how to locate them. In order to avoid duplication, I only included the major human rights treaties and documents in the main part of the dictionary. Thus, instruments in general will be found in the Appendix, but in the case of major treaties there will also be a definition. Those treaties are emboldened in the Appendix. In determining what name to use in listing instruments, I used the official title unless a particular document is well known by a shorter name.

This has been a challenging project on various levels including the determination of what words to include, how to include them and how to define them. The decision of how to include the various rights involved not only whether to list them as the "right to ___" or by the name of the right. I made the decision that it would be easier to find each right under its name rather than under a long list of "right to ___". However, this determination also involved how to characterize those entitlements that are listed as "freedom of ___" or "right to freedom of ___". Since there were fewer rights in that category, I have listed them as "freedom of ___" without the designation of right, though many do appear in the treaties that way. It might be helpful to note that the distinction between rights and freedoms is not clear or consistently treated in the various human rights instruments, as the definitions of those terms indicate.

Many human rights include sub-categories of concepts. So, for example, criminal justice includes a number of separate rights and freedoms. I had to decide how many to define separately. I based the ultimate decision on whether they are stand-alone concepts and how the treaty bodies have addressed them. This may mean that a particular right being looked for could be included in broader concepts.

I tried to avoid usage of gender based words unless the rights necessarily involve the use of those words. However, since many of the human rights treaties use the male gender in their language, there are some definitions that include that usage.

ABBREVIATIONS

ATCA/ATS	Alien Tort Claims Act/Alien Tort Statute
CAT	Convention Against Torture; Committee Against Torture
CEDAW	Convention on the Elimination of All Forms of Discrimination Against Women; Committee on the Elimination of Discrimination Against Women
CERD	International Convention on the Elimination of All Forms of Racial Discrimination; Committee on the Elimination of Racial Discrimination
COE	Council of Europe
CRC	Convention on the Rights of the Child; Committee on the Rights of the Child
CSD	Commission on Sustainable Development
CSW	Commission on the Status of Women
ECJ	European Court of Justice
ECOSOC	Economic and Social Council
EU	European Union
FAO	Food and Agriculture Organization
GATT	General Agreement on Tariffs and Trade
GRULAC	Grupo Latinoamericano y del Caribe
HRC	Human Rights Council; Human Rights Committee
IACHR	Inter-American Commission on Human Rights
ICC	International Criminal Court
ICCPR	International Covenant on Civil and Political Rights
ICESCR	International Covenant on Economic, Social and Cultural Rights
ICJ	International Court of Justice
ICRC	International Committee of the Red Cross
ICTR	International Criminal Tribunal for Rwanda
ICTY	International Criminal Tribunal for the Former Yugoslavia
IDPs	Internally Displaced Persons
IGO	Intergovernmental organization
ILO	International Labor Organization
IMF	International Monetary Fund
IPEC	International Programme on the Elimination of Child Labor
NGO	Non-governmental organization
NHRI	National Human Rights Institution

OAS	Organization of American States
OHCHR	Office of the High Commissioner for Human Rights
OIC	Organization of the Islamic Conference
OSCE	Organization for Security and Cooperation in Europe
R2P	Responsibility to protect
TRIPS	Agreement on Trade-Related Aspects of Intellectual Property
UDHR	Universal Declaration of Human Rights
UN	United Nations
UNESCO	United Nations Educational, Scientific, and Cultural Organization
UNHCHR	United Nations High Commissioner for Human Rights
UNHCR	United Nations High Commissioner for Refugees
UNICEF	United Nations Children's Fund
UNMIK	United Nations Mission Interim Administration in Kosovo
UNODC	United Nations Office on Drugs and Crime
UNTAET	United Nations Transitional Administration in East Timor
UPR	Universal Periodic Review
WEOG	Western European and Others Group
WHO	World Health Organization
WTO	World Trade Organization

A

Acceptance

One of the ways a country can become a party to a treaty. It is one of four such procedures mentioned in the Vienna Convention on the Law of Treaties whereby a State establishes at the international level that it consents to be bound by a treaty.

Accession

One of the ways a country can become a party to a treaty. It is one of four such procedures mentioned by the Vienna Convention on the Law of Treaties whereby a State establishes at the international level that it consents to be bound by a treaty. Accession involves a process of becoming party to a treaty without first having signed it or attended the drafting conference.

Act of State Doctrine

Doctrine enunciated by the United States Supreme Court designed to show respect for co-equal sovereigns in the late 1800s. Essentially, the Court determined that courts of one country should not sit in judgment on the acts of another government done within its own territory. More recently, the Court has indicated that it is a consequence of domestic separation of powers limiting the Judicial Branch's review of the conduct of foreign affairs, but has questioned whether its use should be expanded.

Additional Protocols I and II to the Geneva Conventions

See **Protocol I and Protocol II Additional to the Geneva Conventions of 12 August 1949, and relating to the Protection of Victims of International Armed Conflicts**.

A Declaration of the Rights of Man (Sankey Declaration)

A document written by British novelist H.G. Wells and his colleagues based on a letter he wrote to *The Times* in October 1939 that spoke of rights to food, medical care, education, access to information, freedom of discussion, association and worship. He also discussed rights to work, freedom of movement and protection from violence, compulsion and intimidation. The declaration was widely distributed in Britain and translated into ten languages. Many human rights pioneers commented on the Declaration including Jan Christian Smuts who later drafted Articles 55 and 56 of the UN Charter.

Ad Hoc Tribunal

A tribunal created to address a specific situation involving gross violations of human rights where no other mechanism exists for prosecuting those responsible for the violations. Among those created by the Security Council as an enforcement measure under Chapter VII of the UN Charter are the International Criminal Tribunal for the Former Yugoslavia, and the International Criminal Tribunal for Rwanda.

Administration of Justice

See **Criminal Justice**.

Advisory Jurisdiction/Opinion

The term given to jurisdiction that a human rights body may have to issue opinions without having the consent of a party or without having a specific complaint before it. Generally, it can involve giving an opinion about the interpretation of a particular term in an instrument. An example is the Inter-American Court of Human Rights which can issue decisions about the interpretation of the American Convention on Human Rights or other treaties that members of the Organization of American States are party to. It can also issue opinions regarding the compatibility of domestic laws with those instruments.

Affirmative Action

A remedy for discrimination or lack of equality included in the International Convention on the Elimination of All Forms of Racial Discrimination and the Convention on the Elimination of Discrimination Against Women. Both treaties refer to affirmative action as "special measures" and mandate that they are required for ending discrimination and attaining equality with respect to various rights. Both treaties also specify that such measures do not constitute discrimination but should be limited in time. The Human Rights Committee which oversees compliance with the International Covenant on Civil and Political Rights has referred to the need to take remedial steps to address *de facto* as well as *de jure* discrimination and has urged States Parties to take remedial steps to guarantee protection against practices with discriminatory effects, not only those that are discriminatory on their face. Generally, affirmative action is raised in relation to education and employment rights, though in theory it can apply to all the rights included in the treaties. See also **Special Measures**.

African [Banjul] Charter on Human and Peoples' Rights

Treaty adopted by members of the African Union in Banjul, Africa in 1981 and entered into force on 21 October 1986. As of 2006, 53 countries had ratified the Charter. It contains many clauses comparable to other human rights instruments, but while it covers civil and political rights it stresses economic, social and cultural rights. It was innovative for including the right to development and various duties of the individual, as well as duties of the State to strengthen national independence and contribute to its own defense.

African Commission on Human and Peoples' Rights

Body created by the African Charter on Human and Peoples' Rights to oversee compliance with the Charter. It consists of 11 members who serve in their individual capacity and are nominated and elected by parties to the Charter. Under the Charter, the mandate of the Commission includes taking measures to promote human rights such as researching specific situations, on-site missions, organizing seminars and conferences, giving recommendations to States, setting out human rights principles and co-operating with other international organizations.

African Court on Human and Peoples' Rights

Established by a Protocol to the African Charter which came into force in 2004. The 11 judges are elected in their individual capacity from countries that are party to the African Charter. It has both advisory and contentious jurisdiction and is expected to hear cases brought by African Union Member States and African intergovernmental organizations as well as NGOs. Individuals can bring a case only with the agreement of the country that is party to the case or through the African Commission for Human and Peoples' Rights. In 2004, the African Union Assembly of Heads of State and Government decided to integrate the African Court on Human and Peoples' Rights into the African Union Court of Justice. This restructuring has created a number of problems that have made it difficult for the Court to carry out its work.

African Group (UN)

One of the informal five regional groups at the United Nations. It consists of 54 African countries, which makes it the biggest of the groups. See also **Regional Groups (UN)**.

African Union

The regional intergovernmental organization created in 2002 to replace the Organization of African Unity. Two of the objectives of the African Union are to encourage international co-operation, taking into account the Charter of the United Nations and the Universal Declaration of Human Rights, and to promote and protect human and peoples' rights pursuant to the African Charter on Human and Peoples' Rights.

African Union Court of Justice

At present, this Court consists of the melding of the prior African Union Court and the African Court on Human and Peoples' Rights. It has 17 judges who are nationals of Member States to the African Union and the African Charter on Human and Peoples' Rights. The Protocol setting up the latter provides for "adequate gender representation". The Court has a very broad mandate to address disputes under the African Union and all treaties under the Union. Numerous problems have arisen from the joining of the two bodies because of the legal authority in setting each up, as well as the fact that the African Union Court was designed to address intra-State conflicts and the African Court on Human and Peoples' Rights was supposed to focus on human rights issues and cases.

Agenda 21

Part of the program of action along with the Rio Declaration passed by the United Nations Conference on Environment and Development in Rio de Janeiro, Brazil in 1992. Agenda 21 provided a framework of meeting the substantive challenges of sustainable development, such as protecting various elements of the environment such as air and land, and instituting mechanisms for safe use of toxic chemicals and managing hazardous waste. See also **Commission on Sustainable Development**; **Rio Declaration**.

Aggression

See **Crimes of Aggression**.

Agreement for the Prosecution and Punishment of the Major War Criminals of the European Axis (London Agreement)

Agreement by the Allied governments of the Soviet Union, United Kingdom, United States and provisional government of the French Republic to create the International Military Tribunal to sit in Nuremberg to address the numerous reports of Nazi atrocities involving civilians after World War II. It set forth the Tribunal's jurisdiction for individual responsibility for crimes against peace, war crimes and crimes against humanity. It provided that official positions of persons as heads of State or other government officials would not shield them from trial or punishment.

Agreement on Trade-Related Aspects of Intellectual Property (TRIPS)

Agreement resulting from the Uruguay Round of the General Agreement on Tariffs and Trade (GATT) held in 1994. TRIPS requires that States

Parties to the World Trade Organization (WTO) protect intellectual property through national legislation and regulation. It created an enforcement mechanism through the WTO that includes reciprocal trade sanctions. In 2000, the UN Sub-Commission on the Promotion and Protection of Human Rights adopted a resolution expressing concern that TRIPS did not adequately recognize and protect human rights norms, in particular those involving economic, social and cultural rights, including the right to food, patenting of genetically modified organisms, infringement of certain communities' (especially indigenous communities') control over their own genetic and natural resources and cultural values and the implication of patents on the right to health.

AIDS/HIV

The Human Immunodeficiency Virus (HIV) and Acquired Immunodeficiency Syndrome (AIDS), diseases that have appeared since the major human rights treaties were drafted. Nonetheless, AIDS/HIV invokes several aspects of human rights protections. First, it could be considered one of the categories of non-discrimination under the Universal Declaration of Human Rights and the two International Covenants as a health status that would be covered under a prohibited category of discrimination under "other status". Second, it can be considered as an aspect of the right to health. The Committee on Economic, Social and Cultural Rights took note of AIDS/HIV in its General Comment 14 on the right to health. The World Health Organization has programs and standards for treating and preventing AIDS/HIV. The United Nations Development Programme (UNDP) included efforts to combat AIDS/HIV in its 2004 report.

Aliens

Also referred to as non-citizens and refugees, these individuals were one of the first topics to be discussed under international law outside of the nation-State that had been the sole subject of discussion under that concept during the eighteenth and nineteenth centuries. Early steps included diplomatic efforts to protect the rights of aliens abroad, which initially were in the form of reprisals but gradually were replaced by negotiations between governments. The right of a government to intervene on citizens' behalf rested on two principles: the right of aliens to be treated in accordance with international standards of justice and to be treated equally. Numerous treaties now address the rights of aliens.

Alien Torts Claims Act (ATCA or Alien Tort Statute, ATS)

Statute included in the United States Judiciary Act of 1789, which was not widely litigated until the 1980s, when growing interest in protecting human rights and an increase in the number of lawyers familiar with international law led to an increase in litigation based on it. The use of the statute has been upheld by the United States Supreme Court as an important measure to promote accountability for human rights for serious human rights violations occurring in other countries.

Alternative Care

The right of children who are deprived of a family environment, including abandoned children, orphans and children removed from their home due to abuse or neglect, to "special protection and assistance". This right is recognized by Article 20 of the Convention on the Rights of the Child, which mentions four kinds of alternative care: foster placement, adoption, placement in children's homes. (The fourth is *Kafalah*, a sort of permanent placement of orphans or homeless children in a new family recognized by Islamic Law, which prohibits adoption.) Article 20 indicates that placement in institutional care should be used only if "necessary", i.e. that placement in a family is, in principle, more compatible with the rights of children.

American Convention on Human Rights

Regional treaty approved by members of the Organization of American States which entered into force on 18 July 1978. Most of the countries of North and South America are parties with the notable exception of the United States. It covers civil and political and economic as well as economic, social, and cultural rights. Individuals of States Parties may submit petitions alleging violations of the Convention to the Inter-American Commission on Human Rights. Only States Parties and the Inter-American Commission on Human Rights have the right to submit a case to the Inter-American Court for Human Rights, which is the final arbiter regarding compliance with the Convention.

American Declaration of the Rights and Duties of Man

Resolution adopted by the Organization of American States (OAS) in 1948 to protect human rights. It covers both civil and political rights as well as economic, social and cultural rights. It is notable that Chapter Two covers duties that individuals have to do such things as to educate themselves, vote and pay taxes. The Inter-American Commission on Human Rights has held that all members of the OAS are bound by the Declaration. The Inter-American Court of Human Rights ruled in 1989 that the Declaration "is the text that defines the human rights referred to in the Charter of the Organization".

Amnesty

Concept of protecting human rights violators from prosecution for human rights violations, generally adopted by regimes following gross violations of human rights. The passing of amnesty laws is thought to be helpful for assisting governments to transition to democracy, but has been increasingly condemned by treaties such as the American Convention on Human Rights and both of its oversight bodies as well as the governments of a number of countries.

An Act Declaring the Rights and Liberties of the Subject and Settling the Succession of the Crown

One of the early documents addressing individual rights. Following the revolution of 1688 in England, Parliament enacted the Declaration to protect citizens from violations by the monarchy. It is also known as the English Bill of Rights 1689, An Act Declaring the Rights and Liberties of the Subject, and Settling the Succession of the Crown.

Apartheid

A system that existed in South Africa from 1960–1994 that established separate laws for the treatment of whites, blacks and colored people in that country. It led to a call for boycott of South Africa by the international community which eventually resulted in a change of government that ended the discriminatory system. The term has since been included in the definition of crimes against humanity under the statute of the International Criminal Court.

Approval

One of the ways a country can become a party to a treaty. It is one of four such procedures mentioned in the Vienna Convention on the Law of Treaties whereby a State establishes at the international level that it consents to be bound by a treaty.

Arab Charter on Human Rights

Treaty adopted by the League of Arab States in 1994, which was revised in 2004 and entered into force in 2008. It provides for civil and political rights as well as economic rights, including education, equality, fair trial, health, life, property and travel, but offers a more limited range of rights than the International Bill of Human Rights. It has created controversy by including a condemnation of Zionism, along with racism and foreign occupation. The Charter establishes a Committee of Experts on Human Rights for oversight of the treaty obligations.

Arab Organization for Human Rights

An organization created by the Declaration of Tunis Conference of 1983 to protect civil and political rights. It acknowledges the Universal Declaration of Human Rights and calls for freedom of thought and expression and freedom from torture and violence.

Arbitrary Detention

Term referring to situations when detention violates human rights norms. Article 9 of the Universal Declaration of Human Rights prohibits arbitrary arrest or detention. The Working Group on Arbitrary Detention has developed three categories for determining what constitutes arbitrary detention: Category I – if it has no legal basis; Category II – if it is in response to the exercise of a human right such as the exercise of the right to freedom of expression; and Category III – if the individual was deprived of fair trial procedures. See also **Liberty and Security of Person, Right to**.

Arbitrary Killing or Execution (Summary Execution and Extrajudicial Killings)

The prohibition against arbitrary killing or execution is not specifically addressed by the Universal Declaration of Human Rights but is part of the right to life. The prohibition involves killings by governments where due process or other procedural protections are not followed. The Principles on the Effective Prevention and Investigation of Extra-Legal, Arbitrary and Summary Executions is a prominent non-treaty human rights instrument that attempted to address prevention of this violation.

Asian Human Rights Charter

Completed by the Asian Human Rights Commission, a non-governmental organization, in 1998. Other Asian NGOs have since adopted the Charter, but it has not been adopted by any governments.

Asia-Pacific Group (UN)

One of the informal groups at the UN. It consists of 53 countries in Asia and the Pacific, excluding Australia and New Zealand which are part of the Western European and Others Group. See also **Regional Groups (UN)**.

Assembly and Association

See **Freedom of Peaceful Assembly and Association**.

Association of Southeast Asian Nations (ASEAN)

A sub-regional organization that is primarily focused on political, economic and security issues. However, the ASEAN Charter of 2008 does include reference to either democracy and the rule of law, or promotion of human rights and fundamental freedoms as some of its purposes in Article 1(7). Article 14 calls for the creation of a human rights body, although that has yet to materialize. ASEAN has also adopted a Declaration on the Promotion and Protection of the rights of Migrant Workers and the ASEAN Convention on Counter-Terrorism.

Asylum

The right to seek relief from persecution in other countries recognized by the Universal Declaration of Human Rights. It is also recognized in a number of treaties, including the Convention Relating to the Status of Refugees, which includes relief from persecution based on race, religion, nationality, membership in a particular social group or political opinion. Most countries have ratified the Protocol relating to the Status of Refugees that removes the geographical and temporal limitations of the Convention. The asylum applicant is present in the country it is seeking this right from, whereas a refugee applies for this relief while abroad.

Atlantic Charter

A document agreed to by the Allies in 1941 that stated the goals of World War II. It included a number of concepts that went on to become codified in human rights instruments after the war. In addition to protection of territorial and self-governance rights, and abandonment of the use of force, it included freedom from fear and want. The latter had been included as one of the "four essential human freedoms" identified by President Roosevelt in his State of the Union Address to Congress in 1941.

B

Basic Principles for the Treatment of Prisoners

One of the instruments elaborating on the rights of detained persons. These principles were adopted in General Assembly Resolution 45/111 1990. While not directly binding as a treaty, the principles are part of the more than 30 documents interpreting the rights of detainees, which include the following basic protections: the right to a fair trial, the presumption of innocence, the right to appeal, the prohibition against torture, the right to equal protection of the law and the right to freedom from arrest or detention.

Basic Principles on the Independence of the Judiciary

Adopted by the Seventh United Nations Congress on the Prevention of Crime and Treatment of Offenders in 1985. While not binding as a treaty, they are part of the global standards that constitute the soft law on the right to a fair trial.

Basic Principles on the Role of Lawyers

Adopted by the Eighth United Nations Congress on the Prevention of Crime and Treatment of Offenders in 1990. While not binding as a treaty, they are part of the global standards that constitute the soft law on the right to a fair trial.

Beijing Declaration and Platform for Action

The outcome documents from the UN Fourth World Conference on Women convened in Beijing, China in 1995. Among its many provisions, the Beijing Declaration reaffirms governments' commitments to "the equal rights and inherent human dignity of women and men and other purposes and principles enshrined in the Charter of the United Nations, to the Universal Declaration of Human Rights and other international human rights instruments" (para. 8); the notion that "women's rights are human rights" (para. 14). Further, governments pledge that they are determined to work with international organizations and institutions at all levels to "ensure the success of the Platform for Action. . ." (para. 36). According to its Mission Statement, the Beijing Platform for Action is an agenda for women's empowerment. It reaffirms the fundamental principle "that the human rights of women and of the girl child are an inalienable, integral and indivisible part of universal human rights". In Chapter 3, it calls on ". . . Governments, the international community and civil society including non-governmental organizations and the private sector" to take strategic action in 12 Critical Areas of Concern: poverty; education and training; health; violence; armed conflict; the economy; power and decision-making; mechanisms for women's advancement; human rights; media; environment; and the girl child. In Chapter 4, it identifies problems, strategic objectives and concrete actions that need to be taken to improve the situation of women in each of these critical areas of concern. See also **World Conferences on Women**.

Beijing Rules

See **Standard Minimum Rules for the Administration of Juvenile Justice**.

Bible

Made up of the Old Testament and New Testament, this is the holy book of Christianity which serves as the core of Christianity. It includes concepts of fairness, equality and human dignity. It includes the Ten Commandments, one of the early religious codes that form the basis for human rights principles. The Old Testament also forms part of the Jewish holy book See also **Golden Rule**; **Ten Commandments**; **Torah**.

Body of Principles for the Protection of All Persons under Any Form of Detention or Imprisonment

One of the instruments elaborating on the rights of detained persons. These principles were adopted in General Assembly Resolution 43/173 in 1988. While not directly binding as a treaty, the principles are part of the more than 30 documents interpreting the rights of detainees, which include the following basic protections: the right to a fair trial, the presumption of innocence, the right to appeal, the prohibition against torture, the right to equal protection of the law and the right to freedom from arrest or detention.

Business, Human Rights Obligations

Businesses are considered private actors under international law and have come under increasing scrutiny for the role they can play in human rights violations. The attempt to impose international legal responsibility on business has increased as the state-oriented model of human rights has not adequately addressed the range of abuses. Theories under which it has been argued that business and corporations can be held liable include aiding and abetting and *respondeat* superior, but often they have been difficult to implement in the context of criminal responsibility because they arguably lack the mental capacity required for such responsibility. Various international organizations, including the International Labour Organization and the Organization for Economic Cooperation and Development have attempted to establish human rights standards for business. In 2003, the UN Sub-Commission on Promotion and Protection of Human Rights unanimously approved the Norms on the Responsibilities of Transnational Corporations and Other Business Enterprises with Regard to Human Rights. Those prompted the establishment of the mandate of the UN Special Representative of the Secretary General on Transnational Corporations and other Business Enterprises with Regard to Human Rights who drafted the Guiding Principles on Business and Human Rights that were adopted by the Human Rights Council in 2011 and led to the establishment of a Working Group on human rights and transnational corporations and other business enterprises.

C

Cairo Declaration on Human Rights in Islam

Declaration adopted by the Organization of Islamic Conference (OIC) in 1990. It includes a variety of rights such as life, equality, property, travel, fair trial, health and education, but is more limited than the Universal Declaration of Human Rights which has been endorsed by the OIC.

Charter of the Fundamental Rights of the European Union

Part of the Constitution for Europe which includes 46 articles setting forth rights to civil, political, economic, social and cultural rights, as well as other less commonly accepted rights such as those to access to services, environmental protection, consumer protection, political participation, good administration and access to documents. It also provides that the meaning and scope of the rights in the Charter shall be the same as those in the Convention for the Protection of Human Rights and Fundamental Freedoms, but that the European Union may still provide for more extensive protection.

Charter of the International Military Tribunal for the Far East (Tokyo Tribunal)

Document setting up the International Military Tribunal for the Far East following World War II. Its 17 articles set forth the procedures for the tribunal as well as the rights of the defendants. See also **International Military Tribunal for the Far East (Tokyo Tribunal); Special Proclamation, Establishment of the International Tribunal for the Far East**

Charter of the International Military Tribunal of August 8, 1945 (Nuremberg Charter)

Agreement entered into following World War II addressing the international crimes that were committed by the Nazi regime. It defined terms such as war crimes, genocide and crimes against humanity and was the basis for the tribunal held at Nuremberg from 1945–1956. It was signed by France, the Soviet Union, the United States and the United Kingdom.

Charter of the Organization of American States

The Charter for the countries in the Western Hemisphere was opened for signature in 1948 and entered into force in 1951. It has been amended in 1970, 1988, 1996 and 1997. One of the most notable of the amendments with respect to human rights was the adoption of the American Declaration of Rights and Duties of Man by the Ninth International Conference of America States in 1948. The Charter itself, however, contains many provisions that pertain to human rights, most notably in relation to economic, social and cultural rights, including equality of opportunity, equitable distribution of wealth and income, the elimination of extreme poverty, and the full participation of peoples in decisions relating to their own development.

Charter of the United Nations

Multilateral treaty adopted on 26 June 1945 which entered into force on 24 October 1945, creating the United Nations. The Charter was promulgated following World War II to maintain international peace and security; to develop friendly relations among nations based on respect for the principle of equality and self-determination; and to achieve international co-operation in solving problems of an economic, social, cultural or humanitarian character. It established human rights as a matter of international concern, specifically referring to equality for all without distinction as to race, sex, language or religion in Article 1. While Article 2(7) provides that the United Nations should not intervene in the domestic jurisdiction of any State, Article 51 provides for the "inherent right of individual or collective self-defence if an armed attack occurs against a Member of the United Nations". Article 55 includes the promotion of "conditions of economic and social progress and development; solutions of international economic, social, health, and related problems; and the international cultural and educational cooperation; and universal respect for, and observance of, human rights and fundamental freedoms all without distinction as to race, sex, language, or religion" among its mandates. Article 56 calls for joint and separate action to achieve the purposes of Article 55. Article 7 provides that the principal organs of the United Nations are a General Assembly, a Security Council, an Economic and Social Council, a Trusteeship Council, an International Court of Justice and a Secretariat. Human rights procedures set up under these bodies are called the "Charter based procedures".

Child Labor

A practice prohibited by numerous treaties, including those of the United Nations, the International Labor Organization, and the United Nations Children's Fund. Despite the universal prohibition, the practice continues in many parts of the world and is the subject of numerous campaigns to eradicate it.

Child, Rights of

The rights of children, generally considered those who are under the age of 18, are covered in numerous treaties, declarations and resolutions of the United Nations and regional bodies. It is one of the groups or categories of individuals at risk who have been identified as requiring protection by a specific treaty – the Convention on the Rights of the Child, which includes 40 articles listing protection for children in a wide range of political, civil, economic, social and cultural rights.

Civil and Political Rights

One of two major groupings of human rights together with economic, social and cultural rights. This group of rights was included in the Universal Declaration of Human Rights, but when it came time to drafting an enforcement treaty, the two groups of rights were separated in part as a result of differing views of rights between the United States and the Soviet Union. The other reason for separating them was that it was argued that it was easier to enforce civil and political rights directly whereas economic, social and cultural rights would require implementing legislation, although this is not the case necessarily with all the rights in the two groupings. Nonetheless, numerous resolutions of the General Assembly and other human rights bodies have emphasized the interrelationship of both sets of rights. This grouping includes rights such as those to self-determination, family, life, nationality, liberty and security of person, protections during detention and equal protection; prohibitions against torture, cruel, inhuman or degrading treatment or punishment and slavery, liberty and security of person; criminal justice; freedoms of thought, conscience and religion, expression, peaceful assembly and association.

Civil Society

This term encompasses the sector of society that is distinct from government and business. It includes non-governmental organizations that can officially participate in the UN, but encompasses a much broader set of organizations that can interact with the UN bodies in a number of ways. These organizations include professional organizations, religious groups, and labor unions. The Department of Economic and Social Affairs (DESA) has developed the Civil Society Organizations body to facilitate interaction between it and civil society. See also **Non-governmental Organizations**.

Clothing, Right to

This right is mentioned in Article 25 of the Universal Declaration of Human Rights as part of the right to an adequate standard of living. It is also specified in the International Covenant on Economic, Social and Cultural Rights (ICESCR) as one of the rights emanating from, and indispensable for, the realization of that right. The right to clothing is more than a physical necessity as it is also a manifestation of culture and custom. The General Comments issued by the Committee overseeing the ICESCR have interpreted the right in the context of the right to health, minimizing risk of occupational accidents, rights of the elderly and disabled persons. The Convention on the Rights of the Child also includes clothing as part of an adequate standard of living.

Color

One of the prohibited enumerated grounds of discrimination in the Universal Declaration of Human Rights, the two international covenants and numerous other human rights treaties. UN bodies responsible for applying these norms have largely ignored this specific form of discrimination. In the eighteenth century, when the concept of human racial groups was developed by European scientists, they were defined in terms of color: White, Black, Red, Yellow and, later, Brown. Today, although many would argue that race is a social construct more than a biological reality, UN human rights bodies continue to focus on racial discrimination. In some countries, however, increasing attention is being paid to "colorism", that is, discrimination by some members of a racial group against others of the same group, on the grounds of their skin color. This kind of discrimination has been documented in many parts of the world, in different racial groups.

Command Responsibility

The criminal responsibility of commanders for the acts of their subordinates. The Rome Statute of the International Criminal Court is one of the first international instruments to include a provision regarding the responsibility of commanders and other superiors. Article 28 of the Rome Statute provides that military commanders or persons acting in that capacity can be held responsible for crimes under the statute as a result of failure to exercise control over forces when the commander knew or should have known that the forces were about to commit such crimes, and the commander failed to take necessary and reasonable measures to prevent their commission or to submit them to investigation and prosecution. Superiors can be held responsible when they knew or consciously disregarded information that their subordinates were about to commit such crimes, the crimes were within the effective control of the superior, and the superior failed to submit the matter for investigation and prosecution.

Commission on Crime Prevention and Criminal Justice, UN

Commission established in 1992 by ECOSOC to replace the Committee on Crime Prevention and Control, one of its subsidiary organs. As an expert body the Committee had been a source of international standards in regard to the administration of justice and human rights including the Standard Minimum Rules for the Treatment of Prisoners and the UN Rules for the Protection of Juveniles Deprived of Their Liberty. The Commission, which is made up of 40 governmental members, has not been effective in standard setting, but has considered issues related to fighting corruption, international crime, assistance to victims of crime, abuse of power, and implementation of UN standards.

Commission on Human Rights, UN

Created by the Economic and Social Council under the Charter of the United Nations, Article 68 to do the principal work on human rights. It consisted of 53 government members elected by ECOSOC on a regional basis and reporting directly to it. It drafted numerous documents including the Universal Declaration of Human Rights, the two human rights Covenants and numerous treaties. It continued to elaborate on those norms as well as develop enforcement – both country specific and thematic – procedures. The former included both confidential procedures such as that created by Resolution 1503 as well as public procedures created by Resolution 1235. From 1946 to 1999 the expert body, Sub-Commission on Promotion and Protection of Human Rights, reported to it. The Commission held its last meeting on 27 March 2006 and was replaced by the Human Rights Council.

Commission on Sustainable Development (CSD), UN

Created by the General Assembly in 1992 as a functional commission of the Economic and Social Council (ECOSOC) to ensure that there was follow-up to the UN Conference on Environment and Development. It consists of 53 members elected on a regional basis by ECOSOC. It is responsible for reviewing progress on Agenda 21 and the Rio Declaration on Environment and Development. It also provides guidance on the Johannesburg Plan of Implementation for achieving sustainable development at the international, regional, national and local level. It focuses on promoting dialogue between governments, the international community and major groups identified in Agenda 21 as being key actors for addressing sustainable development. The major groups include: women, youth, indigenous peoples, non-governmental organizations, local authorities, workers and trade unions, business and industry, the scientific community and farmers.

Commission on the Status of Women (CSW), UN

Created by ECOSOC in 1946, first as a sub-commission for a year but then as a full commission. The CSW consists of 45 government members elected on a regional basis by ECOSOC. It prepares reports and recommendations to ECOSOC on women's rights in civil, economic, educational, political and social fields. It can also address problems that require immediate attention and has a petition procedure for addressing violations similar to Resolution 1503. It only meets for two weeks a year and rotates agenda items so has been useful for addressing ongoing problems but less effective at following up on its outcome document, the Agreed Conclusions. It also adopts yearly resolutions on a number of topics. It has served as a preparatory body for UN world conferences on women and since 2005 the CSW has held a review conference at its annual session every five years. It drafted the Optional Protocol to the Convention on the Elimination of Discrimination Against Women that set up an individual petition mechanism.

Committee Against Torture (CAT)

Oversight body for the Convention Against Torture. It consists of ten experts in the field covered by the treaty who serve in their individual capacity. They are elected by the States Parties for a term of four years. Like the other treaty bodies, it reviews periodic reports from States Parties and adopts Concluding Observations with recommendations for them to address areas of concern. It also issues General Comments interpreting the treaty provisions. Unlike other treaty bodies, the Committee is authorized to initiate an inquiry where there are well-founded indications that torture is being systematically practiced. Also, the 2002 Protocol to the Convention establishes a procedure for regular visits by international and national bodies to countries that ratify it.

Committee on Economic, Social and Cultural Rights

Oversight body for the International Covenant on Economic, Social and Cultural Rights. The Covenant initially gave oversight of the treaty to the Economic and Social Council (ECOSOC) which is made up of government delegates. This was the result of a lack of State commitment to an effective enforcement mechanism under the treaty. In 1986, however, the United Nations created this Committee superseding the enforcement bodies under ECOSOC. The Committee is now made up of 18 experts serving in their personal capacity for four year terms. It reviews States Parties' reports and issues Concluding Observations, as well as General Comments interpreting the Covenant's provisions.

Committee on Enforced Disappearances

Oversight body for the International Convention for the Protection of All Persons from Enforced Disappearance. It consists of ten experts serving in their personal capacities and elected by States Parties for a term of four years. Like other treaty bodies, it reviews reports from States Parties and adopts Concluding Observations with recommendations. It can also consider requests from relatives or legal representatives regarding disappeared persons and can make request that a State Party take all appropriate measures to locate the person and inform the Committee within a certain period of time. If can also consider individual communications from victims from States Parties who have made a declaration under Article 31 to accept the competence of the Committee to accept such communications.

Committee on the Elimination of Racial Discrimination (CERD)

Oversight body for the International Convention on the Elimination of all Forms of Racial Discrimination. It consists of 18 experts serving in their personal capacity elected by States Parties for terms of four years. Like the other treaty bodies, it reviews reports from States Parties and adopts Concluding Observations with recommendations for them to address areas of concern. It issues General Recommendations interpreting the treaty's provisions.

Committee on the Protection of the Rights of All Migrant Workers and Members of Their Families

Oversight body for the International Convention on the Protection of the Rights of All Migrant Workers and Members of their Families. It consists of ten experts (14 after it enters into force for the 41st State Party) serving in their individual capacity elected by the States Parties for terms of four years. Like other treaty bodies, it reviews reports from States Parties and adopts Concluding Observations with recommendations. The Convention specifically provides for the participation of the International Labour Office regarding those matters that fall within its competence.

Committee on the Rights of Persons with Disabilities

Oversight body for the Convention on the Rights of Persons with Disabilities. It consists of 12 experts (18 after it enters into force for an additional 60 parties) serving in their individual capacity elected by States Parties for terms of four years. Like other treaty bodies, it reviews reports and adopts Concluding Observations with recommendations. It can also receive petitions from individuals living in States that have ratified the Optional Protocol to the Convention.

Committee on the Rights of the Child (CRC)

Oversight body for the Convention on the Rights of the Child. It consists of ten experts serving in their individual capacity elected by the States Parties for terms of four years. Like other treaty bodies, it reviews reports from States Parties and adopts Concluding Observations with recommendations. It also adopts General Comments interpreting the provisions of the Convention.

Common Article 3

An article shared by the four Geneva Conventions of 1949. The article calls for protection for victims of both international and internal armed conflict.

Communications

Formal name given to petitions and complaints filed under various UN human rights procedures. These include petitions pursuant to the various treaties as well as complaints under procedures of the Commission on Human Rights and its successor body the Human Rights Council. A Working Group on Communications screens complaints under the latter.

Complementarity

A principle enunciated in the Rome Statute that created the International Criminal Court that allows a State with a legitimately functioning legal system to investigate allegations itself, as long as the State's interest in the case is not for "the purpose of shielding the person concerned from criminal responsibility".

Conference on Security and Cooperation in Europe (Helsinki Process)

See **Organization for Security and Cooperation in Europe**.

Conscientious Objection

The right to refuse to perform military service. The Human Rights Committee has recognized that the right is derived from freedom of religion and belief. A number of States have laws exempting citizens who genuinely hold religious or other beliefs that forbid the performance of military service from such compulsory service and have replaced it with alternative national service.

Constitution of Solon

Constitution adopted by the ruler of the same name in Athens some six centuries BC. Solon repealed the laws adopted by the previous ruler of Athens, Draco, whose name inspired the term draconian. The text of the constitution has been lost, and it is known through the writings of later Greek historians. Although the accuracy of such writings is uncertain, the constitution is credited with giving citizens the right to recall elected officials and prohibiting debts secured by the persons of the debtor, which contributed to slavery. The text of the oath judges were required to take has survived; they swore not to accept bribes and to give verdicts in accordance with the laws adopted by the people of Athens and the legislative council.

Consular Assistance, Right to

Right provided in the Vienna Convention on Consular Relations which provides under Article 36 that non-citizens have a right to be notified of their right to communicate with consular officers of their country when detained. In an Advisory Opinion in 1999 the Inter-American Court of Human Rights ruled that due process guarantees under the International Covenant on Civil and Political Rights include the rights of the accused under other treaties such as those in Article 36 in the Vienna Convention. Thus, the right to information on consular assistance is part of due process protections under the Advisory Opinion.

Contentious or Adjudicatory Jurisdiction

Term given to jurisdiction that a human rights body may have to issue decisions in cases before it. Generally, the treaty establishing the body establishes the prerequisites for it to hear and issue decisions, including who can bring a case before it and what prerequisites must be met for the case to go forward. Under some treaties only cases between parties are allowed. Other treaties provide for complaint procedures by individuals or groups.

Control Council Law No. 10

This instrument following the London Agreement was issued by the Allied Control Council on 20 December 1945 and established several courts to try less visible defendants in Germany for crimes against peace, war crimes and crimes against humanity by the Allies after World War II in the respective occupation zones of the Allies. Based on this law, the US authorities proceeded after the end of the initial Nuremberg Trial against the major war criminals to hold another 12 trials in Nuremberg. The judges in all these trials were American, and so were the prosecutors. In the other occupation zones similar trials took place.

Convention

The most common title used in the names of multilateral treaties, including international human rights treaties.

Convention Against the Taking of Hostages

See **International Convention Against the Taking of Hostages**.

Convention Against Torture and Other Cruel, Inhuman or Degrading Treatment or Punishment

United Nations treaty further addressing the international prohibition against torture and related treatment and punishment. It was approved by the General Assembly in 1984 and it entered into force in 1987. It contains precepts on how governments should prohibit, prevent, investigate, punish, and remedy instances of torture and called for universal jurisdiction over and extradition of suspected torturers. It also created a procedure for review of complaints about the use of torture and other ill-treatment.

Convention and Protocol relating to the Status of Refugees

United Nations treaty dealing with the rights of refugees. The Convention was approved by a special UN Conference in 1951 and entered into force in 1954. It includes 34 substantive articles that define refugees and provide for a number of rights and procedures for addressing expulsion. The Protocol entered into force in 1967 and provides for implementation procedures, including international co-operation and national legislation, and refers disputes regarding interpretation or application of the treaty to the ICJ.

Convention for the Protection of Human Rights and Fundamental Freedoms

See **[European] Convention for the Protection of Human Rights and Fundamental Freedoms**.

Convention on the Elimination of All Forms of Discrimination Against Women

United Nations treaty addressing the rights of women. It was adopted by the General Assembly in 1979 and entered into force in 1981. It includes 16 articles addressing substantive civil, political, economic, social and cultural rights for States Parties to end discrimination and work towards attaining equality. An Optional Protocol which entered into force in 2000 provides for an individual complaint procedure.

Convention on the Prevention and Punishment of the Crime of Genocide

The first human rights treaty adopted by the General Assembly in 1948; it entered into force that same year. It defines genocide and makes it a crime along with conspiracy, public incitement to commit it, attempts to commit it and complicity. The definition focuses on physical acts involving the physical destruction of national, ethnic, racial or religious groups. Its narrow terms requiring intent have caused disputes about its application to even large massacres of people. It does not provide for an enforcement body, but provides that disputes related to interpretation or responsibility for violations can be submitted to the ICJ. The ICJ issued an Advisory

Opinion in 1951 that reservations to the treaty were valid only if they were consistent with the object and purpose of the treaty, which has been applied widely.

Convention on the Reduction of Statelessness

United Nations treaty addressing the right to nationality by focusing exclusively on provisions that are intended to prevent or reduce statelessness. It was adopted in 1961 and entered into force in 1975. It includes 13 substantive provisions that include the requirement that States Parties register children born in their respective countries for ending statelessness. Because it contains fewer specific rights than those under the 1954 Convention Relating to the Status of Stateless Persons, it is sometimes considered to be less protective than that treaty. It refers disputes regarding the treaty to the ICJ.

Convention on the Rights of Persons with Disabilities and Optional Protocol

One of the core UN multilateral human rights treaties passed by the General Assembly in 2006 which entered into force in 2008. It was the most quickly negotiated human rights treaty. It includes 30 articles that provide for the protection of the rights of persons with disabilities, including economic, social and cultural as well as civil and political rights. Unlike other human rights treaties it includes an article with definitions of words such as communication, language, discrimination on the basis of disability, reasonable accommodation and universal design. It includes non-discrimination language as well as protection for certain groups with disabilities such as women and children. Its First Optional Protocol authorizes individuals from States Parties to file petitions. The Committee on the Rights of Persons with Disabilities is made up of 12 experts when the Optional Protocol enters into force, and it will increase to 18 experts after 60 countries ratify it.

Convention on the Rights of the Child

United Nations treaty dealing with the rights of children, which it defines as persons under the age of 18. It was approved by the General Assembly in 1989 and entered into force in 1990, becoming the most quickly adopted human rights treaty. It includes 40 articles that cover a number of civil, political, economic, social and cultural rights. As of 2012, all countries of the world had become party to the Convention with the exception of the United States, Somalia and South Sudan.

Convention relating to the Status of Stateless Persons

United Nations treaty addressing the right to nationality. It was adopted in 1954 by a special Conference convened by ECOSOC, and entered into force in 1960. It is devoted to the protection of stateless persons in its 34 substantive provisions which include a number of rights, including freedom of association, employment, housing and property. It refers disputes regarding interpretation or application of the treaty to the ICJ.

Copenhagen Earth Summit (Climate Change)

The climate change conference held in Copenhagen, Denmark in 2009 that focused on issues related to climate change. While the conference resulted in some agreements regarding action plans by both developed and developing nations to address climate change, there were a lot of concerns that the agreement was very limited. One of the provisions was that nations will work towards a "mitigation target" of two degrees Celsius by cutting carbon emissions. The failure to reach better targets was seen as a result of the conflict between the United States and China.

Core Human Rights Treaties

A term used in the UN human rights system to refer to the nine treaties whose implementation by States Parties is monitored by a committee of international experts. They are: the International Covenant on Civil and Political Rights; the International Covenant on Economic, Social and Cultural Rights; the International Convention on the Elimination of All Forms of Racial Discrimination; the International Convention on the Elimination of All Forms of Discrimination Against Women; the Convention Against Torture and Other Cruel, Inhuman or Degrading Treatment or Punishment; the Convention on the Rights of the Child; the International Convention on the Protection of the Rights of All Migrant Workers and Members of Their Families; the International Convention for the Protection of All Persons from Enforced Disappearance; and the Convention on the Rights of Persons with Disabilities.

Corporal Punishment

Term referring to physical punishment, including sentences or sanctions imposed by a court or traditional authority, such as caning, whipping, amputation or branding; sanctions imposed as disciplinary punishments in schools, prisons or similar institutions; and spanking or similar acts of violence imposed by parents or carers in the home or family. International human rights treaties do not expressly prohibit corporal punishment as such, but international bodies such as the Human Rights Committee and the Committee Against Torture recognize practices such as whipping, amputation and branding as torture or inhumane treatment, which do violate international human rights law (see, for example, General Comment No. 20 of the former). The Committee on the Rights of the Child considers all corporal punishment of children to be a form of cruel or degrading treatment incompatible with the Convention on the Rights of the Child, whether used in schools, the family or any other setting (General Comment No. 8).

Council of Europe (COE)

Body established in 1949 by European nations. Following World War II, European nations wanted a regional mechanism for protection human rights. The COE States approved the European Convention on Human Rights in 1950 and subsequently 14 protocols that added rights, such as those to education, free elections and property, as well as abolishing the death penalty. Implementation procedures have also been established. While COE members were not initially required to ratify the European Convention, all Council members eventually did. After the Cold War when Eastern European countries asked to join the Council, ratification of the Convention became mandatory.

Counsel, Right to

While the Universal Declaration does not provide specifically for the right to counsel, in elaborating on the right to a fair trial, Article 14 of the International Covenant on Civil and Political Rights provides that it includes the right to "communicate with counsel of his own choosing" and to have legal assistance assigned without payment if he cannot afford it.

Covenant

One of the titles used in the names of multilateral treaties. It is used in the title of two basic treaties drafted to implement the Universal Declaration of Human Rights – the International Covenant on Economic, Social and Cultural Rights and the International Covenant on Civil and Political Rights. The majority of human rights treaties use "Convention" in their titles.

Covenant of the League of Nations

The name of the Charter for the League of Nations that was drafted after World War I. Various drafts were started by groups in Great Britain and the United States before the war ended and a commission to draft the Covenant was established at the Paris Peace Conference in 1919 with the overall purpose of the organization being to restrict recourse to war. Various disputes arose during the drafting which included topics such as whether to include racial, as well as religious, equality and whether an international army should enforce the decisions of the League of Nations. It created structures that are similar to those created under the Charter of the United Nations. The Covenant entered into force on 10 January 1920, and some of its provisions were amended in 1924. See also **League of Nations**.

Crime of Aggression

One of the four crimes listed as a violation under the Rome Statute that created the International Criminal Court, but it was the only crime not defined. The State Parties did reach some consensus on the definition at a Conference in Kampala, Uganda in 2010. In the Kampala Convention which was adopted by consensus at the Conference, the crime of aggression is defined as a "leadership crime" where only those who are in control of political or military decisions can be held responsible for violations resulting from the use of force by one State against another. The new definition failed to address a number of issues such as the liability of non-state actors, violations against non-state actors, and interventions based on humanitarian concerns. Further, the terms of Kampala will not enter into force until 1 January 2017 when the States Parties need to decide whether to activate its provisions. Once the Convention enters into force, the International Criminal Court will have jurisdiction to hear cases of individuals accused of the crime.

Crimes Against Humanity

One of the groups of internationally prohibited crimes. It generally takes place during armed conflict, but experts have argued that the link is not necessary. The first time the crime was defined under international law was under the Nuremberg Charter which defined it as murder, extermination, enslavement, deportation and other inhuman acts committed against any civilian population before or during war as well as persecutions on political, racial or religious grounds. The Control Council Law No. 10 added rape to the definition. Other international treaties that have included a definition in the listing of international crimes include the Tokyo War Crimes Tribunal of 1946; the statutes of the International Criminal Tribunal for the Former Yugoslavia; The International Criminal Tribunal for Rwanda; and the International Criminal Court (ICC). The statute of the latter includes torture, rape, sexual slavery, enforced prostitution, forced pregnancy, enforced sterilization, apartheid, forcible transfer of population, severe deprivation of physical liberty and the enforced disappearance of persons. It also defines some terms more precisely, including extermination, enslavement, deportation (or forcible population transfer), torture and forced pregnancy.

Crimes Against Peace

One of the first crimes defined following World War II that initiated the development of international criminal responsibility. In 1945, France, the Soviet Union, the United States and the United Kingdom signed the Agreement for the Prosecution and Punishment of the Major War Criminals of the European Axis and the Charter of the International Criminal Tribunal (Nuremberg Charter). The latter included prosecution of crimes against peace, which it defined as the "planning, preparation, initiation or waging of a war of aggression, or a war in violation of international treaties, agreements or assurances, or participation in a common plan or conspiracy for the accomplishment of any of the foregoing". Seven of the 23 major war criminals at Nuremberg were tried for crimes against peace.

Criminal Justice

This refers to a number of rights related to procedural fairness in the criminal process and the administration of justice. The rights are specified in Articles 8–11 of the Universal Declaration of Human Rights and Articles 14 and 15 of the International Covenant on Civil and Political Rights (ICCPR). The rights include: those related to a fair trial including a public trial; the presumption of innocence; freedoms from arbitrary arrest, torture and cruel inhuman or degrading treatment or punishment and retroactive punishment; right to security of person; minimum guarantees related to the determination of a criminal charge, such as prompt notice of the charges, adequate time to prepare a defense and communicate with counsel, legal assistance when unable to pay for counsel, examination of witnesses, interpreter when needed and not to testify or confess to guilt; and to effective remedy or legal redress. Article 14 also provides for special rights of juvenile persons, which are further elaborated in the Convention on the Rights of the Child in Articles 12 and 37. Many of the criminal justice rights in the ICCPR are considered non-derogable rights under Article 4. Regional treaties also include provisions related to criminal justice.

Criminal Sanctions

The concept of punishment for individual violations of the law. In the context of international law, it focuses on punishment for individuals who violate international criminal law, in particular crimes against peace, war crimes and crimes against humanity. Under the Nuremberg Charter, the sanctions included the death penalty and imprisonment of ten years to life. Subsequent treaties have removed the death penalty as a sanction.

Cruel, Inhuman or Degrading Treatment or Punishment

Along with torture these ill-treatments are prohibited by Article 5 of the Universal Declaration of Human Rights and Article 7 of the International Covenant on Civil and Political Rights. Subsequently a number of treaties have included the prohibition against these ill-treatments. The ill-treatments have not been defined in the treaties but decisions of the treaty bodies that oversee them have found their violations in certain practices used on detainees. Regional treaties have similar though not identical prohibitions and have further defined these ill-treatments. Of note in this regard are decisions of the European Court of Justice. The Special Rapporteurs appointed by the Commission of Human Rights and its replacement body the Human Rights Council have also developed the meaning of these ill-treatments.

Cultural Relativism

National customs or practices which are sometimes used to diminish the impact of human rights norms. The European Court of Human Rights has used the concept of "margin of appreciation" to allow nations the capacity to vary application of their human rights treaties in light of varying national practices. Claims of cultural relativism and religious belief have also been used to avoid positive treaty obligations, especially with respect to women's rights.

Culture, Right to

A right guaranteed in the Universal Declaration of Human Rights, the two Human Rights Covenants and a number of other human rights treaties. It is the least developed of the rights guaranteed under international human rights law, due in part to the many definitions of culture. The basic treaties recognize the right to culture, including everyone's right to take part in cultural life, to enjoy the benefits of scientific progress, and to develop international contacts and co-operation in the area of science and culture. Some of the treaties provide cultural rights to minorities and indigenous peoples. A number of treaties prohibit discrimination based on culture and the Convention on the Prevention and Punishment of the Crime of Genocide has been interpreted to forbid the deliberate destruction of a people and their culture. The right has been further defined in the Universal Declaration on Cultural Diversity adopted by UNESCO in 2001.

Customary International Law

International custom is a source of international law where there is evidence of a general practice accepted as law. It consists of State practice accompanied by *opinio juris* (the sense of legal obligation). The widespread acceptance of human rights treaties, often described as hard law, and declarations, resolutions and other international instruments (often described as soft law) has become a source of evidence of State practice as well as *opinio juris*. Widespread, rather than unanimous, acceptance is needed. A customary international norm binds all governments whether or not they have accepted it so long as they have not expressly and persistently objected to its development.

D

Damages

A monetary award designed to compensate victims for violations of their rights. It has slowly been recognized as a remedy for violations of human rights. The European Court of Human Rights has been one of the human rights bodies to grant damages for human rights violations. It awards pecuniary damages when it can quantify economic harm, and non-pecuniary or moral damages to compensate for emotional suffering or interference with protected rights. The Inter-American Court of Human Rights also has authority to award compensatory damages in accordance with the domestic procedures of the State involved. Punitive damages, which are designed to punish the wrongdoer and are available in national procedures, are generally not available in international procedures.

Dayton Peace Accord

See **General Framework Agreement for Peace in Bosnia and Herzegovina**.

Death Penalty

A punishment imposed for criminal violations under both national and international law. After Nuremberg, the international community moved away from using the death penalty for violations of international criminal law. There has also been a movement to ban the death penalty under national law, but a large number of countries continue to use it. International law does set limits on the use of the death penalty, including that it can only be used for the most serious crimes in accordance with the law at the time of the commission of the crime, it should not be arbitrarily applied, persons sentenced to death shall have the right to seek pardon or commutation of the sentence, and it cannot be imposed on persons who were under 18 at the time of the commission of the crime or on pregnant women.

Declaration of the Rights of Man and of the Citizen

See **French Declaration of the Rights of Man and of the Citizen**.

Declaration of the United Nations Conference on the Human Environment (Stockholm Declaration)

Outcome document of the UN Conference on the Human Environment held in Stockholm, Sweden in 1972. The Stockholm Declaration includes one of the earliest references to concepts such as sustainable development, observing that: "To defend and improve the human environment for present and future generations has become an imperative goal for mankind – a goal to be pursued together with, and in harmony with, the established and fundamental goals of peace and worldwide economic and social development." See also **Sustainable Development, Right to**.

Declaration on the Right to Development

Document adopted by the General Assembly in 1986 with a vote of 146 in favor, one against (the United States), and eight countries abstaining (Northern European countries and Israel). It sets out the right of all human beings "to participate in, contribute to, and enjoy economic, social, cultural and political development, in which all human rights and fundamental freedoms can be fully realized". It also provides that States have duties to formulate policies that will achieve this right. See also **Development, Right to**; **Sustainable Development, Right to**.

Declaration on the Rights of Indigenous Peoples

Instrument drafted by the Working Group on Indigenous Populations from 1985 to 1993, when the Working Group submitted it to the Sub-Commission for Promotion and Protection of Human Rights. The Sub-Commission submitted it to the Commission on Human Rights in 1994, but it was not adopted until 2006 by the newly created Human Rights Council that replaced the Commission that year. The delay in adoption was related to disagreements between States and indigenous representatives over self-determination and the definition of indigenous. The Declaration is an attempt to protect the integrity of indigenous peoples and cultures through protection against land dispossession, population transfers, propaganda and cultural assimilation.

Declaration Relative to the Universal Abolition of the Slave Trade

The first international statement on slavery adopted in 1815 by the Anti-Slavery Society, the first international non-governmental organization, which was focused on ending the Atlantic slave trade. The Declaration was the basis of over 300 multilateral and bilateral agreements passed between 1815 and 1957 implemented to suppress slavery.

Degrading Treatment or Punishment

Ill-treatments that are prohibited along with torture under international law. While prohibited under a number of treaties and instruments, few of them define the term, though its meaning can be inferred from decisions of the Committee Against Torture, the Human Rights Committee and other human rights bodies. The European Court of Human Rights was one of the first international tribunals to define the term. It ruled that in order for a punishment to be degrading, the humiliation or debasement involved must attain more than the normal degradation that results from punishment in general and thus depends on the circumstances of the case, and in particular the nature and context of the punishment and the manner and method of its execution.

Democracy

A system of government that includes the participation of its citizens. While international human rights instruments do not contain provisions guaranteeing democracy, they do provide for public participation in government and voting rights, including fair elections and the right to hold office and have access to public service. While the Human Rights Committee has not guaranteed the right to direct participation, it has issued a General Comment that provides that whatever political system a government has selected, it must ensure the effective participation of minority communities in decisions that affect them.

Derogation

A term involving the possibility that States Parties need not comply with certain provisions of human rights protection in cases where there is a threat to national security. The International Covenant on Civil and Political Rights, Article 4 provides that in time of public emergency that threatens the life of a nation, States Parties may derogate from their obligations under the Covenant to the extent strictly required by the exigencies of the situation as long as the acts are not inconsistent with other international obligations and they do not discriminate. Article 4 also provides that certain rights are non-derogable, including the right to life, the right to be free from torture or cruel, inhuman or degrading treatment or punishment, and the prohibition against slavery. It is thought that the drafters were thinking of armed conflict as the main public emergency that would threaten the life of the nation. Regional treaties contain similar provisions.

Detention

International law places protections and limitations on governments' use of this sanction. Numerous treaties and instruments provide basic protections to persons who are detained or imprisoned. The protections include: the right to be informed of reasons for an arrest and to be promptly informed of charges; the right to be brought promptly (usually defined to be within 48 hours) before a judge or similar person authorized to exercise judicial power to determine the lawfulness of the detention; treatment prior to conviction should take into account the presumption of innocence and this includes being held separate from convicted persons; the prohibition of torture and other ill-treatment while in detention; the right to equal protection of the law; and the right to freedom from arbitrary arrest or detention.

Development, Right to

The Convention on the Rights of the Child makes several references to the right of children to development, sometimes referred to as the right to "physical, mental, spiritual, moral and social development" (Articles 27.1 and 32.1; see also Articles 6.2, 18.1, 23.3 and 29.1(a)). The Preamble of the Convention also refers to the "full and harmonious development of his or her personality". The Convention on the Rights of Persons with Disabilities also recognizes the right to "The development . . . of their personality, talents and creativity, as well as their mental and physical abilities, to their fullest potential . . ." (Article 24.1(b)). The Basic Principles for the Treatment of Prisoners adopted by the UN in 1990 recognizes the right of prisoners to participate in activities aimed at "the full development of the human personality". Recognition of the individual's right to holistic personal development in these instruments implies that it is a right of all persons, albeit one not expressly recognized by earlier human rights instruments. The Commission on Human Rights and its replacement body have passed a number of resolutions on the right to development.

Disabled

One of the groups or categories of individuals who may be at risk and have been identified as needing special protection. The major human rights treaties prohibit discrimination on the basis of group membership, but persons with disabilities also have been identified as requiring protection by treaty – the Convention on the Rights of Persons with Disabilities entered into force in 2008 and provides for special protection in civil, political, economic, social and cultural rights.

Disappearances

A prohibited practice under international law which includes violation of a number of internationally recognized rights that can take place when a governmental body takes a person into custody without providing them with the protections related to detention. The prohibition against enforced disappearances has been listed as a customary international norm. The Commission on Human Rights established a Working Group on Enforced or Involuntary Disappearances in 1980 to address the massive numbers of disappearances that had been taking place. The Working Group's mandate was subsequently expanded by a Resolution of the General Assembly to monitor States' progress and assist them with compliance. The Working Group's mandate has been extended by the Human Rights Council.

Discrimination

A prohibited practice under international law that involves treating groups or categories of people differently and in particular denying them basic rights. The principle of equal rights is one of the foundational underpinnings of the United Nations Charter and numerous treaties since then have not only emphasized equal rights but have prohibited discrimination on a variety of grounds. The Universal Declaration of Human Rights prohibits discrimination of any kind, such as race, color, sex, language, religion, political or other opinion, national or social origin, property, birth or other status. The latter is so broad that it can be argued to encompass any arbitrary discrimination. The prohibition against discrimination has been adopted in numerous treaties and instruments giving rise to a customary international law norm as well as a peremptory norm of international law.

Diversion

Discretionary disposal of criminal charges (or potential charges) against a juvenile by a police officer or prosecutor, before formal criminal proceedings. Diversion often, but not always, involves referral to a non-residential program for the prevention of offending, or voluntary acceptance of certain conditions ("diversion measures"). It allows minor offenses to be disposed of in a way that avoids the potentially adverse consequences of prosecution (trauma, stigma), and is encouraged by the Beijing Rules (Rule 11) and the Convention on the Rights of the Child (Article 40.3(b)).

Draft Declaration of Principles on Human Rights and the Environment

The first international instrument drafted on human rights in the environment. It was prepared by a group of experts in 1994 convened in Geneva, Switzerland by the Sierra Club Legal Defense Fund in co-operation with two environmental groups on behalf of the Special Rapporteur on Human Rights and the Environment who had been appointed by the Sub-Commission on Promotion and Protection of Human Rights in 1989. Drawing upon the Stockholm and Rio Declarations, the Draft Declaration recognizes the relationship between the right to a healthy environment and other fundamental human rights. The Sub-Commission recommended that the Commission on Human Rights establish a thematic rapporteur on the subject based on this, but this was never done. The Commission did appoint a Special Rapporteur to address human rights and the effects of the transport of toxic waste.

Dualist Approach to International Law

An approach to the application of international law at the international level that considers that while international law is binding between governments it may not be asserted by individuals in the national courts of a country unless the legislature or other branch of the government makes it national law or regulation. This approach is followed in particular by those countries that follow the common law tradition, though many of those countries often use a mixture of dualist and monist approaches to the direct application of international law at the national level.

Durban Declaration and Program of Action of the World Conference Against Racism

The name of the outcome document of the World Conference Against Racism, Racial Discrimination, Xenophobia and Related Intolerance held in Durban, South Africa in 2001. The Durban Declaration recognizes concern about anti-Semitism and Islamophobia in various parts of the world and called upon States, United Nations bodies and specialized agencies, international and regional organizations, youth and civil society to take an active part in the process for ending the "scourges of racism, racial discrimination, xenophobia, and related intolerance". The Durban Declaration and Programme of Action note that a victim-oriented approach is an important tool to eliminate racial discrimination and reference is made to a number of groups needing protection, including Africans and people of African descent, Asians and persons of Asian descent, indigenous peoples, migrants, refugees, minorities and the Roma. It includes recommendations for national plans and programs to fight racism, for better treatment of victims, for stronger anti-discrimination legislation and administrative measures, for improving education on this issue, and for implementation of the International Convention for the Elimination of All Forms of Racial Discrimination. The Durban Program has helped develop action at both the UN and national level. See also **World Conference Against Racism, Racial Discrimination, Xenophobia and Related Intolerance**.

Duty/Duties

While most human rights treaties provide for rights and freedoms, reference is sometimes made to the duties that persons have towards others and their communities. Article 29 of the Universal Declaration of Human Rights provides that everyone has duties to the community and that in the exercise of their rights and freedoms everyone is "subject only to such limitations as are determined by law solely for the purpose of securing due recognition and respect for the rights and freedoms of others" and for meeting the requirements of morality, public order and welfare of a democratic society. Most other human rights treaties do not refer to duties, but the American Declaration of the Rights and Duties of Man has a full chapter that lists the duties individuals have. They include the duty to: educate one's minor children; honor and support parents; acquire at least an elementary education; vote and obey the law; render any civil and military service one's country may require for defense and public disasters; co-operate with the State and community with respect to social security and welfare; pay taxes established by law for the support of public services; work as far as one is able to obtain livelihood or benefit the community; and refrain from taking part in political activities if they are reserved for citizens and one is an alien. The African [Banjul] Charter on Human and Peoples' Rights likewise lists the duties that every individual has towards his family and society, the State, and other communities including the international community.

E

Earth Summit

The first Earth Summit was held in Stockholm, Sweden in 1972. It was also called the United Nations Conference on the Human Environment and it produced an action plan which laid out the educational, informational, social and cultural aspects of environmental issues. This is also the name given to the United Nations Conference on Environment and Development held in Rio de Janeiro, Brazil in 1992 and its follow-up conferences in 2002 in Johannesburg, South Africa and 2012 in Rio de Janeiro. The climate change summit held in Copenhagen, Denmark in 2009 is sometimes referred to as the Copenhagen Earth Summit. See also **Rio Declaration on Environment and Development**.

Eastern European Group (UN)

One of the informal regional groups of the United Nations. It is made up of 23 countries from East Europe. See also **Regional Groups (UN)**.

Economic and Social Council (ECOSOC)

One of the principal organs of the United Nations created pursuant to Chapter X of the Charter. It consists of 54 Members of the United Nations elected by the General Assembly, the body it directly reports to. It was created to coordinate economic, social and related work of the 14 UN specialized agencies and oversaw a number of human rights organizations, including the Commission on Human Rights. It is the body that accredits non-governmental organizations to participate in the UN bodies. It was originally directly responsible for oversight of the International Covenant on Economic Social and Cultural Rights. The latter tasks have been taken over by the Committee on Economic, Social and Cultural Rights and ECOSOC's influence has been greatly reduced by the creation of the Human Rights Council which replaced the Commission and reports directly to the General Assembly.

Economic, Social, and Cultural Rights

One of two major groupings of human rights together with civil and political rights. This group of rights was included in the Universal Declaration of Human Rights, but when it came time to draft an enforcement treaty, the two groups of rights were separated in part as a result of differing views of rights between the United States and the Soviet Union. The other reason for separating them was that it was argued that it was easier to enforce civil and political rights directly whereas economic, social and cultural rights would require implementing legislation, though this is not the case necessarily with all the rights in the two groupings. Nonetheless, numerous resolutions of the General Assembly and other human rights bodies have emphasized the interrelationship of both sets of rights. This grouping includes rights such as those to education, health, work, food, housing, social security and cultural life.

ECOSOC Resolution 728F

As part of its attempt to alter the rule that the Commission on Human Rights had no power to take action with respect to violations of human rights from its creation in 1947, ECOSOC passed this resolution in 1959 to consolidate the procedures for handling human rights communications to the UN Resolution 728F provided for the Secretary General to prepare and distribute a brief list summarizing communications it received regarding human rights to the Commission and its expert body the Sub-Commission, in private and without the names of the authors of the communications. The resolution encouraged governments to reply to the communications.

ECOSOC Resolution 1235

In 1967 ECOSOC approved this resolution in response to the Commission on Human Rights' request to be empowered to make recommendations about specific violations brought to its attention. This resolution allowed the Commission to examine allegations of gross human rights violations found in the 728F lists of communications. It also authorized the Commission to make a thorough study of cases revealing consistent patterns of human rights violations, thus weakening the "no power" rule that had governed the Commission from its creation in 1947. This resolution became the basis for the public procedure used by the Commission and its Sub-Commission to address gross human rights violations. It has been replaced by other procedures since the Human Rights Council replaced the Commission.

ECOSOC Resolution 1503 Procedure

In 1970 ECOSOC approved this resolution to provide an analysis of the 728F communications. ECOSOC adopted a three-stage screening process proposed by the Sub-Commission, which gave power to the Sub-Commission to screen the communications that appeared "to reveal a consistent pattern of gross and reliably attested violations of human rights and fundamental freedoms". The Sub-Commission would then refer particular situations that met this standard to the Commission to determine whether a thorough study was required with a report and recommendations to ECOSOC. The investigation was confidential, conducted in co-operation with the State involved, and could only be undertaken if domestic remedies were exhausted and did not relate to other matters being dealt with under other UN procedures. This procedure evolved throughout the years and ultimately involved publication of names of countries under consideration at various stages. The procedure was taken over by the Human Rights Council and was the basis for a similar procedure under the Commission on the Status of Women.

Edicts of Ashoka

These edicts were drafted by the Third King of the Mauryan dynasty in South Asia, also known as King Piyadasi, who ruled from 270 to 232 BC. After leading his country to victory in a war that resulted in 100,000 enemy deaths and the displacement of 150,000 persons he experienced remorse and spent the rest of his life striving to govern in accord with his Buddhist beliefs. His edicts recognize the principle that justice should be fair, independent and impartial, the right of persons sentenced to death to appeal the sentence, and freedom of religion. To further these principles, he appointed officials who travelled the country visiting prisons to ensure that prisoners were treated properly and identify those who deserved to be released on humanitarian grounds, adopted laws restricting the killing of wildlife and burning of forests, and adopted programs to make medicinal plants, shelter and water widely available.

Education, Right to

One of the rights included in the economic, social and cultural grouping. It is covered in Article 26 of the Universal Declaration of Human Rights, Article 13 of the International Covenant on Economic, Social and Cultural Rights, and has been included in numerous other international and regional treaties and instruments. The basic principles of the UDHR include: that elementary education shall be free and compulsory; that technical and professional education shall be generally available; that higher education shall be equally accessible on the basis of merit; that its content shall be directed toward the full development of the human personality and strengthen respect for human rights as well as promote understanding, tolerance and friendship among nations. The Covenant adds the provision that secondary education shall be made generally available, in particular by introduction of free education. It provides the right to attend private schools as long as they conform to the principles of the Covenant and minimum standards set by States. The Committee overseeing the treaty has noted that education can be classified as an economic, social and cultural right but is also an example of the interrelationship with civil and political rights. It has also noted that economic difficulties do not relieve States Parties from complying with their obligations to adopt and report on plans of action for implementing the right.

Environment, Right to Healthy

While this right was not included in the Universal Declaration of Human Rights, it can be inferred as a right emanating from the right to life and the right to a standard of living adequate for health and well-being. Many national constitutions include language recognizing various aspects of the importance of a healthy environment, either as a right, or by placing a duty on the State to protect it. The international community addressed environmental rights for the first time in 1972 at the UN Conference on the Human Environment, where the Stockholm declaration was adopted. It was not addressed again in a meaningful way until the 1992 UN Conference on Environment and Development (UNCED), which produced the Rio Declaration on Environment and Development. The Commission on Human Rights failed to accept a declaration and a thematic rapporteur on human rights in the environment, but it did authorize a Special Rapporteur on the adverse effects of the illicit movement and dumping of toxic and dangerous products and wastes on the enjoyment of human rights in 1995. The right to a healthy environment was again considered by the Human Rights Council in 2011 when it requested the preparation of a study. International treaty bodies have addressed the right to the environment in the context of other rights such as the rights to life and health. The right to a healthy environment has also been considered in several regional human rights instruments.

Equal Protection

One of the basic rights recognized in Article 7 of the Universal Declaration of Human Rights and numerous other international and regional treaties and instruments as well as under the constitutions and laws of most States. The basic provisions mandate that all people are entitled to the various human rights enumerated in the instruments and laws without discrimination. Further, they are entitled to the equal protection of those rights under the law. United Nations documents generally provide that everyone is entitled to the rights and freedoms enunciated therein without distinction of any kind, such as race, color, sex, language, religion, political or other opinion, national or social origin, property, birth or other status. The latter broad standard is said to prohibit any arbitrary discrimination.

Ethnic Cleansing

The United Nations defines ethnic cleansing as "rendering an area ethnically homogeneous by using force or intimidation to remove from a given area persons of another ethnic or religious group". While the term was coined in 1992 following the wars in Bosnia and Croatia in the former Yugoslavia and the discovery of concentration camps in that region, the practice of widespread and systematic acts of persecution against opposing populations forcing them to flee has been known throughout history. In 2005 the UN General Assembly adopted an initiative called the "responsibility to protect" (R2P) which focused on preventing genocide, war crimes, crimes against humanity and ethnic cleansing.

European Commission Against Racism and Intolerance (ECRI)

A body created under the European regional human rights system. This body reviews Member States' laws, policies and measures to combat racism and intolerance.

European Commission of Human Rights

One of the enforcement bodies created under the European Convention for the Protection of Human Rights and Fundamental Freedoms in 1953. Under the treaty, all cases went first to the European Commission, which would determine if the case was well-founded. If it was, it would launch a case in the European Court of Human Rights on behalf of the individual. Protocol 11 came into force in 1998 and abolished the Commission. After that cases were brought directly to the European Court which now determines both admissibility and substantive issues.

European Committee for the Prevention of Torture (CPT)

A body created under the European regional human rights system. This body makes visits to places of detention to assure compliance with the European Convention for Prevention of Torture and Inhuman or Degrading Treatment or Punishment.

[European] Convention for the Protection of Human Rights and Fundamental Freedoms

A treaty enacted by the members of the Council of Europe which entered into force in 1953, emphasizing civil and political rights. It applies to every individual within the jurisdiction of States Parties, including non-citizens. Fourteen Protocols have added provisions and procedures to the treaty. Rights that have been added include those to property, education, free elections, a general prohibition against discrimination, and travel. One protocol abolished the death penalty. The Convention originally had three main enforcement mechanisms: the European Commission of Human Rights, the European Court of Human Rights and the Committee of Ministers. In 1998 Protocol 11 abolished the European Commission. The European Convention allows for both individual and inter-State complaints. It is the only regional system that has adjudicated a large number of inter-State complaints. Forty-seven countries are Parties to the European Convention.

European Court of Human Rights

One of the enforcement bodies created under the European Convention for the Protection of Human Rights and Fundamental Freedoms in 1953.

Under the treaty, all cases went first to the European Commission, which would determine if the case was well-founded. If it was, it would launch a case in the European Court of Human Rights on behalf of the individual. Protocol 11 went into force in 1998 and abolished the Commission and enlarged the Court. After that individuals brought cases directly to the European Court which would decide both admissibility and substantive issues. The Court oversees both individual and inter-State complaints and is the only regional body that has adjudicated a large number of the latter.

European Court of Justice (ECJ)

The ECJ sits in Luxembourg and interprets and applies European Union law and general principles of national and international law. It has established human rights doctrines as a matter of European Community law, and in 1974 began to cite the European Convention on Human Rights as a guideline to be followed under that framework. Rights it has affirmed include protection against gender and other discrimination, the right to be heard and the right to a fair hearing.

European Ombudsman

This position was established under the Maastricht Treaty to investigate maladministration in any European Union institution. This includes complaints of administrative irregularities, unfairness, discrimination, abuse of power, failure to reply, refusal of information or unnecessary delay. Most of the complaints involve the European Commission and while the Ombudsman does not have enforcement powers, most of its decisions are complied with.

European Social Charter

In the early 1960s the Council of Europe adopted the European Social Charter to complement the civil and political rights guarantees of the European Convention of Human Rights. It entered into force in 1965. The Charter guarantees economic and social rights, including housing, health, education, employment and social protection. In 1999, the European Social Charter (Revised) entered into force, updating and adapting substantive provisions of the Charter including broader non-discrimination and employment termination protections. The revised Charter will eventually replace the original Charter.

European Union (EU)

The body resulting from European efforts towards integration. It consisted of 15 Member States until 2004, when they were joined by ten Central and Eastern European States. Additional countries have joined since. The basic treaties for integration ratified in the 1950s have been amended as the organization has grown. Starting with the Single European Act (SEA) of 1986 which established the free internal market and mentioned human rights, each successive treaty has elevated human rights among the basic principles of the organization. In the SEA, Member States agree to promote the European Convention for the Protection and Rights and Fundamental Freedoms, and the European Social Charter. Human Rights were also emphasized in the Maastricht Treaty on European Union in 1992. The EU has issued directives and developed policies on human rights, including those on topics related to education, employment discrimination, equality, fair application of the law, freedom of association and migrant workers.

European Union Agency for Fundamental Rights (FRA)

Advisory body of the European Union established in 2007 by Council Regulation to provide Member States with assistance and expertise relating to fundamental rights. Based in Vienna, Austria the FRA collects data about the situation of fundamental rights in the 27 Member States of the European Union. Candidate countries and countries which have concluded a stabilization and association agreement with the European Union can also be invited to participate following a special procedure. The FRA issues conclusions and opinions to policy-makers and stakeholders. The Agency produces an annual report on fundamental rights in the European Union and thematic reports on key fundamental rights issues within its mandate, such as racism, homophobia, rights of the child, immigration and access to justice. The FRA also organizes an annual Fundamental Rights Conference, and develops information resources in order to raise awareness and bring knowledge of fundamental rights to specific target groups and to the European citizen in general.

Exhaustion of Remedies

A common admissibility requirement for most international human rights procedures, both those created under the United Nations Charter and treaties as well as regional systems. The requirements generally provide that petitioners or complainants first exhaust the domestic remedies where the violations took place before they are able to file a claim before the international or regional body. An exception to the requirement can be made if the domestic procedures are ineffective or unreasonably prolonged.

Expert Mechanism on the Rights of Indigenous Peoples

A thematic mechanism created by the Human Rights Council in 2007 to replace the Working Group on Indigenous Populations.

Expression, Freedom of Speech

Article 19 of the Universal Declaration of Human Rights provides that: "Everyone has the right to freedom of opinion and expression; this right includes freedom to hold opinions without interference and to seek, receive and impart information and ideas through any media regardless of frontiers." The right is subject to certain restrictions such as respect for the rights or reputations of others and protection of national security. Nearly all national constitutions protect freedom of expression or freedom of speech and the press. Freedom of expression problems often arise in the context of national security, public morals, protection of the justice system, hate speech and defamation since the need to place limitations often arises in these contexts. If governments use national security as a reason to limit this right, they generally bear the burden of proving the threat as well as the manner in which the limitation will have the effect of reducing or removing the threat. With respect to the other limitations, courts and treaty bodies mention the need to balance the various rights involved. With respect to hate speech, international bodies tend to emphasize that restrictions on the dissemination of ideas based on racial superiority or hatred are compatible with the right to freedom of opinion and expression. On the other hand, some national courts such as the United States Supreme Court have interpreted their constitutions to be more protective of freedom of expression even where hate speech is involved.

Extradition

This concept entails sending persons from a country where they are physically present to a country that has requested that they be returned to, usually to face criminal charges for actions committed there. International human rights law provides that persons should not be extradited to a country where that individual has substantial grounds for believing that he or she would be in danger of being subjected to torture if returned there. Various treaties have been interpreted to protect against forcible return or "refoulement" of persons facing a substantial risk of torture.

Extrajudicial Killings

This term refers to violations of the right to life where the government kills or executes someone outside the context of the usual criminal justice system. See also **Arbitrary Killing or Execution (Summary Execution and Extrajudicial Killings)**.

F

Fact-finding

The name given to the activities involved in getting information regarding human rights in specific countries or locations. The investigations can be done on site and involve methods such as interviewing witnesses, observing trials, visiting prisons and meeting with government officials. Investigations can also be done off site when access is not available to a particular country or location or for financial reasons. Methods in such cases include interviewing refugees or persons who have visited the site of the inquiry, reviewing legal documents, telephone interviews and email and other correspondence. Fact-finding can be carried out by the United Nations or regional human rights bodies and by non-governmental organizations. The permission of the government is usually needed for onsite fact-finding, especially for visits to government facilities. The goals of fact-finding include documentation of various human rights situations but sometimes the fact-finding activity can result in ameliorating human rights violations.

Fair Trial

One of the basic rights included in the Universal Declaration of Human Rights, which is also included in the International Covenant on Civil and Political Rights. Article 14 of the latter provides that the right includes "equality to a fair and public hearing by an independent tribunal" in the determination of criminal charges brought against a person. Other aspects of the right include the presumption of innocence, public trial, guarantees necessary for a defense and the right to be free from retroactive punishment. Other rights related to a fair trial include the prohibition of arbitrary arrest, the right to an effective remedy or legal redress, the right to be free from torture, and the rights to security of person and privacy. See also **Criminal Justice**.

Family

One of the basic rights included in the Universal Declaration of Human Rights which protects the right to establish a family which is entitled to protection by society and the State. It includes non-discrimination in providing for and terminating marriage as well as the requirement that it shall be entered into with free and full consent of both spouses. It is also included in the International Covenant on Civil and Political Rights and the Human Rights Committee that oversees enforcement of that treaty has acknowledged that while the concept of family might vary both between and within States the right must be protected when a group of persons is regarded as a family. However, the Committee has not extended that protection to the rights of homosexuals because the treaty refers to the right of "men and women" to marry.

Female Genital Mutilation (FGM)

This is a cultural practice that involves the removal of part or all of the external female genitalia. It is practiced in many countries in Africa, some Arab countries, parts of Asia and among immigrant communities in Australia, Europe and North America. The practice has been identified as being harmful to women in particular in relation to the right to health and it has been condemned by the World Health Organization.

First Optional Protocol to the International Covenant on Civil and Political Rights

See **Optional Protocol to the International Covenant on Civil and Political Rights**.

Food and Agricultural Organization (FAO)

One of the specialized agencies of the United Nations, also known as an intergovernmental organization since its oversight body comprises government delegates. It has programs and policies related to the right to food with the goal of ending hunger. It was created in 1945 and its headquarters are in Rome, Italy. The Conference of Member Nations meets every two years to review programs and policies. It elects a Council of 49 Member States that serves as an interim governing body and the Director-General.

Food, Right to

This right is identified in Article 25 of the Universal Declaration of Human Rights as a component of the right to an adequate standard of living. The International Covenant on Economic, Social and Cultural Rights emphasizes the right in Article 11 by "recognizing the fundamental right to be free from hunger". The article also requires that States Parties agree to take individual measures and to co-operate at the international level to improve methods of production, conservation and distribution of food. The Committee overseeing that treaty has further defined the right in General Comment 12, which affirms its indivisible link to the inherent dignity of the human person and that it is indispensable for the fulfillment of other human rights. The General Comment further defines the three levels of obligations that States Parties have to respect, to protect and to fulfill the right. The Commission on Human Rights created a mandate of the Special Rapporteur on food, which has been continued by the Human Rights Council, to further address the parameters of the right as well as to address communications regarding violations.

Forced Evictions

The name given to evictions that are carried out either by States or private actors forcing persons out of their homes for discriminatory purposes or without procedural protections or provision of alternate housing. The prohibition of this practice has been based on the right to housing. General Comment 7 of the International Covenant on Economic, Social and Cultural Rights confirms that forced evictions violate the Covenant.

Forced Labour Convention of 1930

See **International Labor Organization Forced Labor Convention of 1930 (ILO Convention No. 29)**.

Forced or Compulsory Labor

An aspect of slavery which is prohibited by numerous international instruments. The elimination of forced labor is specifically addressed by the International Labor Organization as one of its four fundamental principles. The Forced Labour Convention of 1930 provides for the abolition of forced labor which it defines as "all work or service which is exacted from any person under the menace of any penalty and for which the said person has not offered himself voluntarily". This definition distinguishes forced labor from slavery in that it does not include the concept of ownership. However, since forced labor involves a similar degree of restrictions on the individual's freedom it is similar to slavery. Article 8 of the International Covenant on Civil and Political Rights prohibits forced or compulsory labor, and includes situations where it does not constitute a violation, such as work as part of a criminal sentence, military service, service required to address emergencies, and work that is part of normal civil obligations.

Four Freedoms

In January 1941, United States President Franklin D. Roosevelt outlined his vision of the future in his State of the Union address to Congress based on what he called "four essential human freedoms". The four freedoms he identified were: freedom of speech and expression; freedom of religion; freedom from want; and freedom from fear. He noted that all these freedoms should be available everywhere in the world. Freedom from want thus means economic understandings that will secure a healthy peace-time life for all its inhabitants everywhere in the world. Further, freedom from fear means worldwide reduction of armaments so that no nation can commit an act of aggression anywhere in the world. President Roosevelt expanded on these four freedoms in his State of the Union address in 1944. In that speech he emphasized peace and listed inalienable political rights, such as rights of free speech, free press, free worship, trial by jury, freedom from unreasonable searches and seizures, as the rights to life and liberty upon which the United States was based on. He then emphasized that economic security and independence are essential to true individual freedom and listed what he called "a second Bill of Rights" that included: economic, social and cultural rights, such as the right to a remunerative job; the right to earn enough to provide adequate food, clothing and education; freedom from unfair competition; right to a decent home; right to adequate health care; right to protection from economic fears of old age, sickness, accident and unemployment; and the right to a good education. The Four Freedoms are thought to be the foundation for the Universal Declaration of Human Rights, which his wife Eleanor Roosevelt was involved in drafting.

Freedom from Hunger

See **Food, Right to**.

Freedom of Movement and Residence

This freedom is protected in Article 13 of the Universal Declaration of Human Rights as well as Article 12 of the International Covenant on Civil and Political Rights (ICCPR) and in regional treaties. It includes freedom of movement and residence within the borders of each State as well as the right to leave and return to any country. General Comment 27 to the ICCPR provides that the right applies to all parts of federal States as well as the obligation to protect the right from private as well as public interference. It is noted that this is a particularly important issue for women. Forced population displacement constitutes a violation of this right and may also be a violation of international humanitarian law if it occurs during international armed conflicts.

Freedom of Opinion and Expression

This freedom is protected in Article 19 of the Universal Declaration of Human Rights which also refers to the right to impart information and ideas through any media regardless of frontiers and the right to hold opinions without interference. Article 19 of the International Covenant on Civil and Political Rights (ICCPR) distinguishes between the unqualified right to hold opinions and the right of freedom of expression which is subject to limitations that must be provided by law: respect for the rights or reputation of others and those necessary for national security, public order, or public health and morals. The Human Rights Committee has concluded that the prohibition in Article 20 of the ICCPR of propaganda and advocacy of national, racial, or religious hatred that constitutes incitement to discrimination, hostility or violence is compatible with freedom of expression as Article 19 provides that the exercise of that right carries special duties and responsibilities. The Committee on the Elimination of Racial Discrimination reached a similar conclusion in its General Recommendation on hate speech. Freedom of opinion and expression also connotes the right to seek information.

Freedom of Peaceful Assembly and Association

This freedom is protected in Article 20 of the Universal Declaration on Human Rights which also provides that no one may be compelled to belong to an association. The International Covenant on Civil and Political Rights divides these two rights into separate articles. Article 21 recognizes the right of peaceful assembly and notes that it can be restricted only if necessary for national security or public safety, public order, the protection of public health or morals or the protections of rights and freedoms of others. Article 22 provides for the right to freedom of association, which includes the right to form and join trade unions. That right is also protected in Article 8 of the International Covenant on Economic, Social and Cultural Rights and instruments of the International Labor Organization, as well as regional treaties. See also **Labor rights**; **Trade Unions, Right to Join and Form**.

Freedom of Thought, Conscience, and Religion

This freedom is protected in Article 18 of the Universal Declaration of Human Rights which provides that everyone has the right to these three freedoms which include the right to change one's religion or belief. The latter was a controversial concept which was omitted in Article 18 of the International Covenant on Civil and Political Rights, which also included limitations on the right to manifest one's religion as prescribed by law and "necessary to protect public safety, order, health, or morals or the fundamental rights and freedoms of others". The Human Rights Committee has interpreted this to mean that while the right to freedom of conscience and religion is absolute, the right to manifest it can be limited. Also, it has determined that the freedom to choose a religion or belief includes the freedom to replace it.

Freedoms

This is one of the concepts used to describe the different kinds of human entitlements. Other words used to describe them include rights, prohibition, and protections. Freedom connotes the kind of activity that should be free from government interference except in situations necessary for public safety and order and involve more collective concerns, but the distinction is not always clear and treaties do not treat these concepts consistently. Collectively, all the various entitlements are referred to as fundamental freedoms. See also **Rights**.

Freedom to do Scientific Research

Article 15(3) of the International Covenant on Economic, Social and Cultural Rights provides that States Parties "undertake to respect the freedom indispensable for scientific research and creative activity". Article 15(4) provides that States Parties should recognize the benefits derived from co-operation in the scientific and cultural fields. On the other hand, the International Covenant on Civil and Political Rights does place one limit on this freedom by providing in Article 7 that no one shall be subjected to medical and scientific experimentation without his free consent.

French Declaration of the Rights of Man and of the Citizen

A document that resulted from eighteenth-century theories of natural law philosophers who argued that fundamental rights were beyond State control and that individuals were autonomous in nature. Under this theory, individuals retain personal autonomy in the form of inalienable rights even though they are part of society. Those rights include the right to choose and change government. The French Declaration was adopted in 1789 and has been the basis for a number of constitutions, including the Bill of Rights that was added to the United States Constitution between 1789 and 1791, the Netherlands (1798), Sweden (1809), Spain (1812), Norway (1814), Belgium (1831), Liberia (1847), Sardinia (1848), Denmark (1849) and Prussia (1850).

Friendly Settlement

Part of the procedure for complaints filed under the regional human right bodies. For example, the Inter-American Commission on Human Rights is authorized to place itself at the disposal of the parties to a pending petition to assist them with arranging meetings, transmitting communications and mediating negotiations. The Commission reviews agreements reached by the parties to ensure that they are in compliance with the human rights provisions of the American Convention on Human Rights. The European Court of Human Rights has a similar procedure.

Fulfill

See **Responsibility to Respect, Protect and Fulfill**.

G

Gender

This concept refers to the sex of a person and is one of the prohibited types of discrimination in numerous human rights instruments. The Universal Declaration of Human Rights, Article 2 provides that everyone is entitled to the rights in the Declaration without distinction of any kind including sex, whereas both International Covenants require that States Parties undertake to guarantee the rights therein without discrimination of any kind including sex.

Gender Identity

The Yogyakarta Principles define this term as each person's deeply felt internal and individual experience of gender, which may or may not correspond with the sex assigned at birth, including the personal sense of the body and other expressions of gender including dress, speech, and mannerism. Along with sexual orientation, gender identity forms the basis for non-discrimination in the Yogyakarta Principles.

General Agreement on Tariffs and Trade (GATT)

The multilateral agreement signed in 1947 to regulate trade. It was replaced in 1994 by the World Trade Organization (WTO), though most of its provisions continued in force under the WTO. See also **Agreement on Trade-Related Aspects of Intellectual Property (TRIPS)**; **World Trade Organization**.

General Assembly, UN

The main body of the United Nations responsible for overseeing the promotion and protection of human rights. It is the world's most authoritative source of international declarations and treaties, as it is the oversight body for ECOSOC, the treaty bodies, and the Human Rights Council. It is the most representative organ of the United Nations as all members are entitled to vote. It elects the ten non-permanent members of the Security Council, and the members of ECOSOC and the Human Rights Council.

It is the final body for approval of UN human rights treaties, declarations and other instruments.

General Comments

This is the name for the treaty bodies' interpretation of the human rights provisions in the treaties they oversee. They are also called General Recommendations by some treaty bodies. In general, the treaty bodies have issued general comments or recommendations on each article of their particular treaty, but they have also adopted general comments on topics related to country reporting requirements, enforcement topics, or issues that have developed since the adoption of the treaty. More recently the treaty bodies have issued more detailed and comprehensive general comments and recommendations to give States Parties clearer guidance on how the treaty provisions apply in particular situations.

General Framework Agreement for Peace in Bosnia and Herzegovina (Dayton Peace Accord)

This is the agreement that was signed on 14 December 1995 following mass violations of human rights in Bosnia and Herzegovina. The Agreement established a mixed tribunal called the Human Rights Chamber to address civil rather than criminal human rights abuses. The Chamber had the authority to issue cease and desist orders as well as award compensatory damages. The Chamber was made up of 14 members, including four persons from the Federation of Bosnia and Herzegovina, two from the Republic Srpska, and eight international members appointed by the Council of Europe. The mandate of the Chamber expired on 21 December 2003. Cases still pending at that time were taken over by the Human Rights Commission during 2004. The Commission was also a mixed tribunal with two members appointed by the Federation of Bosnia and Herzegovina, one member appointed by the Republic Srpska, and two appointed by the Council of Europe.

General Principles of Law

One of the sources of law described in Article 38(1) of the 1946 Statute of the International Court of Justice (ICJ). The Statute specifically provides that along with treaties and custom, "general principles of law recognized by civilized nations" are one of the sources the ICJ must apply, though they are a lower preference than provisions in treaties. General principles of law are different to customary international law in that they do not require the establishment that the practice is accompanied by *opinio juris* or the sense of legal obligation. Nonetheless it entails a principle that is so basic that it can be found in the legal systems of most countries.

General Recommendations

See **General Comments**.

Geneva Convention for the Amelioration of the Condition of the Wounded and Sick in Armies in the Field (1864)

The first multilateral treaty protecting victims of armed conflict. Its purpose was to protect military hospitals and provided for equal treatment for combatants on both side of a conflict. The International Committee of the Red Cross was instrumental in preparing the initial drafts of this treaty after it was founded in the 1863 Geneva Conference.

Geneva Convention I for the Amelioration of the Condition of the Wounded and Sick in Armies in the Field

The first of the four treaties addressing criminal responsibility for human rights abuses during time of war. This treaty defines the basic principles for the protection of victims in cases of armed conflict or occupation. It established the use of the red cross on a white ground as the emblem of the Medical Services of armed forces. Previous versions of this convention were adopted in 1864, 1906, and 1929.

Geneva Convention II for the Amelioration of the Condition of Wounded, Sick and Shipwrecked Members of Armed Forces at Sea

The second of the four treaties addressing human rights protections during time of war. This treaty defines the basic principles for the protection of the wounded and sick members of armed forces at sea. Convention II adapts the main protections of the First Geneva Convention to combat at sea, and replaces the Hague Convention of 1907 for the Adaptation to Maritime Warfare of the Principles of the Geneva Convention.

Geneva Convention III relative to the Treatment of Prisoners of War

The third of the four treaties addressing human rights protections during time of war. This treaty defines the basic principles for the protection of prisoners of war. The Convention includes labor of prisoners of war, their financial resources, and the relief they receive and the judicial proceedings against them. It also provides that prisoners of war shall be released and repatriated without delay after the cessation of active hostilities.

Geneva Convention IV relative to the Protection of Civilian Persons in Time of War

The fourth of the four treaties addressing human rights protections during time of war. This treaty defines the basic principles for the protection of civilians during armed conflict or occupation. The Convention provides for the protection of populations against certain consequences of war, and sets forth the regulations governing the status and treatment of foreigners on the territory of a party to a conflict and that of civilians in occupied territory.

Geneva Conventions of 1949

These are four treaties that address the treatment of protected individuals during wartime. They also provide for criminal responsibility for human rights abuses during wartime. Together with three protocols, the treaties require that States Parties establish effective penal sanctions for persons committing or ordering any grave breaches of humanitarian law, such as killing or torturing civilians. They provide that soldiers may direct deadly force against an enemy but not civilians, civilian targets, or members of armed forces who have laid down their arms, are wounded, or are otherwise placed out of combat. They call for the investigation, extradition, trial and punishment of violators. The conventions cover both international and internal armed conflict. The four conventions share various terms such as Common Article 3 which provides for protection of victims of armed conflict. See also **Geneva Convention I for the Amelioration of** the Condition of the Wounded and Sick in Armies in the Field; Geneva Convention II for the Amelioration of the Condition of Wounded, Sick and Shipwrecked Members of Armed Forces at Sea; Geneva Convention III relative to the Treatment of Prisoners of War; Geneva Convention IV relative to the Protection of Civilian Persons in Time of War; Protocol I Additional to the Geneva Conventions of 12 August 1949, and relating to the Protection of Victims of International Armed Conflicts; Protocol II Additional to the Geneva Conventions of 12 August 1949, and relating to the Protection of Victims of Non-International Armed Conflicts.**

Genocide

The killing (derived from Latin "cide") of a people (derived from Greek "genos"). Though it has been practiced throughout history, it was added to the English language in 1944 to describe the crimes against humanity involving the deliberate and systematic killing of racial and national groups that took place during World War II. The General Assembly adopted the Convention on the Prevention and Punishment of the Crime of Genocide on 9 December 1948 to define genocide to mean the following acts committed with the intent to destroy national, ethnical, racial or religious groups: (a) killing members of the group; (b) causing bodily or mental harm to the members of the group; (c) deliberately inflicting conditions aimed at the physical destruction of the group; (d) imposing measures to prevent births within the group; and (e) forcibly transferring children of the group to another group.

Globalization

The process of international integration. Most commonly the term refers to the process of international economic integration, though it has also been used in the context of other fields such as sociology, education, technology and culture. The effect of globalization on human rights has been mixed. The positive aspects have included economic development in some regions of the world and the transfer of technology which has facilitated job creation, promotion of rights such as those related to education, and freedom of expression. However, globalization has also had negative effects on several human rights, including the destruction of jobs and thus the right to work in some countries, the lack of property rights for knowledge based in traditional medicines and the right to culture. Concern about the negative effects led the Sub-Commission on

Promotion and Protection of Human Rights to address globalization in the late 1990s. The Commission on Human Rights approved the appointment of two Special Rapporteurs on globalization and its impact on the full enjoyment of human rights. The Special Rapporteurs presented a final report in 2003 which reaffirmed basic human rights principles including non-discrimination and the interrelationship of all rights in the context of globalization. The Annex includes a normative framework regarding the liberalized trading system that includes the following issues: equity and non-discrimination; the right to participation that includes the freedoms of expression, association and assembly; the right to information; the right to participation in public affairs; economic, social and cultural rights including an adequate standard of living and labor rights; the right to life, liberty and personal security; group and cultural rights; and the environment and human rights.

Golden Rule

One of the fundamental human rights principles found in many religions. The basic rule provides: Do unto others as you would wish them to do unto you. Other incantations of the rule include: the Old Testament ("Thou shalt love thy neighbor as thyself"); an ancient teaching of Buddhism ("Hurt not others in ways that you yourself would find hurtful"); the New Testament ("Therefore all things whatsoever ye would that men should do to you, do ye even so to them"); a teaching of Confucius ("Do not to others what you do not want them to do to you"); and Islam ("None of you believes until he wishes for his brother what he wishes for himself").

Good Offices

This is the name given to the prestige of the office of the UN Secretary General that is used when undertaking diplomacy to address international disputes. Often the good offices are backed by the threat of Security Council action. The Secretary General can assign his good offices to special representatives who may perform the same function in preventing international disputes from escalating. Despite the ad hoc nature of these interventions, the office of the Secretary General has been well respected and trusted by world leaders.

Grave Breaches of the Geneva Conventions

The Geneva Conventions of 1949 (Conventions I to IV) and Additional Protocols I and II to the Conventions are the core of International Humanitarian Law. Each of the Conventions contains an article that identifies violations of certain obligations it contains as grave breaches, that States Parties have an obligation to criminalize (Articles 49, 50, 130 and 147 of the I, II, III and IV Conventions, respectively). They also have an obligation to search for and prosecute persons alleged to have committed or ordered the commission of grave breaches. The offenses covered include willful killing, torture or inhuman treatment; willfully causing great suffering or serious injury to body or health; extensive, unlawful and wanton destruction or appropriation of property unjustified by military necessity; compelling a prisoner of war to serve in enemy forces, depriving a prisoner of war of the rights of fair and regular trial; and the unlawful deportation, transfer or unlawful confinement of civilians. These acts constitute grave offenses only if they occur during armed conflict (or occupation), and only if the victims are "protected persons". The definition of protected persons depends on the Convention, each of which is designed to cover different groups. They include sick or wounded members of the forces or auxiliary personnel involved in an armed conflict (I Convention), sick, wounded or shipwrecked members of the armed forces at sea (II Convention), prisoners of war (III Convention) and civilian non-combatants (IV Convention).

Groups at Risk

Human rights concerns may involve groups or categories of individuals who may be at risk as well as the rights of individuals. Some kinds of individuals have been the subject of specific treaties such as racial minorities, women, migrants, and children. Others have been accorded protection by declarations or other non-treaty instruments, such as indigenous persons and religious minorities. Most rights which might be perceived as group rights, such as the right to join trade unions, are expressed in human rights treaties as individual rights. A few rights such as those to a family and self-determination are protected specifically as group rights.

Grupo Latinoamericano y del Caribe (GRULAC)

This is the name of one of the five geographic groups of countries at the UN. GRULAC is the group from Latin America and the Caribbean. The five groups are used for representation purposes on bodies such as the Economic and Social Council and Working Groups. The latter are usually made up of five persons, each one representing one of the five geographic groups.

Guidelines on the Role of Prosecutors

One of the global non-treaty standards issued by the United Nations relating to the right to a fair trial. These guidelines provide standards for the conduct of prosecutors.

Guiding Principles on Human Rights and Business (UN)

The name given to the principles drafted by the Special Representative of the Secretary General on Transnational Corporations and other Business Enterprises with Regard to Human Rights during his six year mandate. The Guiding Principles were adopted by the Human Rights Council in 2011 and led to the establishment of a Working Group on human rights and transnational corporations and other business enterprises. They are designed to provide a global standard for preventing and addressing the risk of adverse impacts on human rights linked to business activity. The Guiding Principles use the "protect, respect, and remedy" framework of the UN to address the responsibilities of States to better manage business and human rights. The framework also addresses the obligations that businesses have to respect human rights.

Guiding Principles on Internal Displacement

Non-treaty standards developed by the United Nations to address the rights of internally displaced persons (IDPs). The Special Representative of the Secretary General on internally displaced persons helped to develop and promulgate the Guiding Principles. The Guiding Principles prohibit discrimination and other grave human rights abuses against IDPs; limit the circumstances in which they can be displaced from their homes; call for humanitarian assistance, and provide for their right to return voluntarily to their homes or to resettle voluntarily elsewhere.

H

Habeas Corpus

A procedure available in common law countries that can be used to test the legality of any detention. In Latin American countries, *amparo* is a procedure that can provide for similar relief.

Hague Conventions of 1899 and 1907

These comprise 15 treaties that emphasized limits on the methods and means of warfare. Among their provisions are included bans of poisonous gases and other weapons that result in unnecessary suffering.

The Conventions identified "violations of the laws or customs of war" that became the basis of individual criminal responsibility for war crimes. The Conventions are now considered part of the customary international humanitarian law applicable to all countries.

Hammurabi, Code of

One of the ancient codes deemed to be the basis for the development of human rights standards. This is the name of the Babylonian law code that dates back to approximately 1700 BC and is attributed to the sixth Babylonian king, Hammurabi. The underlying principle in this code was the use of law to prevent the strong from oppressing the weak. While most of the code covers topics related to contracts, family matters, and military service, there are provisions that address criminal law issues such as the presumption of innocence, that both sides have an opportunity to present evidence, and scaling of punishments based on social status.

Handbook on Procedures and Criteria for Determining Refugee Status **under the 1951 Convention and the 1967 Protocol relating to the Status of Refugees (UNHCR)**

This handbook was published by the office of the UN High Commissioner for Refugees and is deemed to be an authoritative guide for addressing issues related to the rights of refugees. It includes provisions for defining who qualifies as a refugee or asylum seeker. While it recognizes that there is no universally accepted definition of "persecution" it notes that it can be inferred from the 1951 Convention relating to the Status of Refugees and its 1967 Protocol "that a threat to life or freedom on account of race, religion, nationality, political or other opinion or membership of a particular social group is always persecution. Other serious violations of human rights – for the same reasons – would also constitute persecution."

Hard Law

This is the name given to the body of law made up of treaties and formal agreements between countries. The instruments can be multilateral or bilateral and can constitute the basis for the *opinio juris* requirement for establishing customary international law: that countries act in a particular way because they feel obligated to do so.

Hate Speech

Article 20 of the International Covenant on Civil and Political Rights provides that "advocacy of national, racial or religious hatred that constitutes incitement to discrimination, hostility or violence shall be prohibited by law". Statements that fall into this category fall into the kinds of limitations that are allowed on the right to freedom of expression. Article 4 of the International Convention on the Elimination of All Forms of Racial Discrimination also condemns propaganda and organizations based on theories of superiority based on race, color or ethnic origin. The Committee on the Elimination of Racial Discrimination has adopted General Recommendation 15 on hate speech which provides that the prohibition on the dissemination of ideas based on racial superiority or hatred is compatible with the right to freedom of opinion and expression.

Health, Right to

The right to health was recognized by Article 25 of the Universal Declaration of Human Rights as a component of the right to an adequate standard of living. The Covenant on Economic, Social and Cultural Rights in Article 12 recognizes the right to health as separate from that right. It recognizes the "right of everyone to the highest standard of physical and mental health" and identifies steps to achieve the right including the reduction of infant mortality and healthy development of the child; improvement of environmental and industrial hygiene; the prevention, treatment, and control of diseases; and the creation of conditions which would assure everyone medical service and attention in the event of sickness. The Committee overseeing compliance with that treaty issued General Comment 14, which notes the interdependency of this right with other rights and notes that poverty and other obstacles prevent its full realization in many countries. The Covenant on Civil and Political Rights in Article 7 also includes a provision relating to the right to health by including a prohibition on medical and scientific experimentation without prior consent. All major regional human rights systems include the right to health. In 2002, the Commission on Human Rights recognized the right to health and appointed a Special Rapporteur on that right. The mandate has been continued by the Human Rights Council. The right is also addressed by the World Health Organization and has arisen in the context of the World Trade Organization.

High-Level Panel on Threats, Challenges and Change

A panel initiated by UN Secretary General Kofi Annan in 2003 to generate new ideas about the kinds of security policies and institutions required for the UN to be effective in the twenty-first century. It attempted to address the problems related to the failure of the UN to agree to a definition of terrorism which had in turn caused an obstruction to the formulation of counter-terrorism standards. The High Level Panel offered a definition of terrorism which included the following elements: recognition that State use of force against civilians is regulated by the Geneva Conventions and constitutes a war crime or a crime against humanity by the persons involved; recognition of 12 anti-terrorism Conventions and a restatement that terrorism in time of armed conflict is prohibited by the Geneva Conventions and Protocols; reference to the definitions in the 1999 International Convention for the Suppression of the Financing of Terrorism and Security Council Resolution 1566 of 2004; and a description of terrorism that includes acts specified in the Geneva Conventions or Security Council Resolution 1566 that are intended to cause death or serious bodily harm to civilians or other non-combatants with the purpose of intimidating a population or to compel a government or international organization to perform or abstain from doing an act.

HIV/AIDS

See **AIDS/HIV**.

Holocaust

The name given to the crimes against humanity that occurred before and during World War II carried out by the Nazis which included the deliberate and systematic killing of 6 million Jews, 3 million Russian prisoners of war, half a million Roma (Gypsies), as well as thousands of persons with mental illness, Jehovah's Witnesses, homosexuals and Communists. These crimes were prescribed for prosecution in the Charter of the International Military Tribunal (Nuremberg Charter) which was signed by France, the Soviet Union, the United States and the United Kingdom after World War II.

Homosexuality

This term refers to persons who have sexual relations with persons of the same sex. It encompasses terms such as gays and lesbians. Thousands of homosexuals were killed during the Holocaust, and homosexuals still struggle for recognition of their rights as a group at the international level.

Housing, Right to Adequate

The right to adequate housing was recognized as a component of the right to an adequate standard of living in Article 25 of the Universal Declaration of Human Rights. Article 11 of the Covenant on Economic, Social and Cultural Rights does not expand on this right. However, the Committee overseeing that treaty further defined the right in its General Comment 4 in 1991. The General Comment relied in part on the codification of the right in other international and regional human rights treaties, which have identified two components of the right: that it is part of an adequate standard of living and that there can be no discrimination in how it is provided. The General Comment defined seven ways in which housing may be considered adequate: legal security of tenure; availability of services, materials, facilities, and infrastructure; affordability; habitability; accessibility; location; and cultural adequacy. The prohibition against forced evictions has been included in the work of various bodies addressing the right to housing. Beginning in 2000, the UN Commission on Human Rights appointed a Special Rapporteur to focus on adequate housing. The Human Rights Council has continued this thematic mandate.

Human Dignity

Article 1 of the Universal Declaration of Human Rights acknowledges that all human beings are born free and equal in dignity and rights. The Preambles of the two international Covenants recognize that human rights derive from the inherent dignity of the human person, but neither addresses this concept further. The European Committee on Social Rights has noted that human dignity is the fundamental core of positive European human rights law and that health care is necessary for its preservation.

Humane Treatment

Article 10 of the International Covenant on Civil and Political Rights provides that all persons deprived of their liberty shall be treated with humanity and dignity. Specifically, it goes on to provide that accused and convicted persons shall be separated and juveniles shall be separated from adults. Further, the goal of the penal system shall be reformation and rehabilitation of prisoners.

Humanitarian Law

The body of law that addresses human rights issues during time of war which resulted in some of the earliest human rights documents. The International Committee of the Red Cross, which was created in 1863 following the battle of Solférino, helped draft the first multilateral treaty protecting victims of armed conflict – the 1864 Geneva Convention for the Amelioration of the Condition of the Wounded and Sick in Armies in the Field. The 15 Hague Conventions of 1899 and 1907 emphasized limits on means and methods of warfare, including the prohibition of targeting civilians and non-combatants. Under the four Geneva Conventions of 1949 and two Protocols, States Parties are required to establish effective penal sanctions for persons who commit or order to be committed any grave breaches of humanitarian law. Pursuant to the Convention Against Torture and Other Cruel, Inhuman or Degrading Treatment or Punishment and the Geneva Conventions, several governments passed laws establishing universal jurisdiction over war crimes, torture, and other crimes against humanity. The UN Security Council established ad hoc tribunals for trying crimes of genocide, crimes against humanity, and war crimes committed in the former Yugoslavia and Rwanda. And in 1998, the Rome Statute for the International Criminal Court was adopted. That treaty entered into force in 2002.

Human Rights Commission of the League of Arab States

One of the sub-regional human rights bodies set up by the League of Arab States in 1968. The Human Rights Commission adopted an Arab Charter on Human Rights in 1994, and revised it in 2004.

Human Rights Committee, UN

Oversight body created to monitor the International Covenant on Civil and Political Rights (ICCPR). The Committee consists of 18 members from 18 different nations elected by the States Parties to the treaty. Members are experts in the field and act in their personal capacity even though they are nominated by their governments, which makes the Committee less susceptible to accusations of playing politics. The Committee has two main functions: to review compliance reports by States Parties and to adjudicate individual complaints filed by individuals in countries that have ratified the First Optional Protocol to the ICCPR. It also issues General Comments on issues concerning the implementation of the Covenant elaborating the content of the specific rights delineated in the treaty.

Human Rights Council, UN

This body resulted from the substantial changes made to the UN Charter-based human rights machinery in 2006. The changes resulted from a report by the UN Secretary General in 2005 that argued that the Commission on Human Rights suffered from declining credibility and professionalism and should be replaced by a new Human Rights Council. The General Assembly (GA) approved the creation of the Council with a vote of 170–4 on 15 March 2006. To address concerns regarding politicization the resolution creating the Council stresses the importance of non-selectivity in the consideration of human rights issues and the need to eliminate double standards. The Council continued the mandates of all the special procedures of the Commission as well as the 1503 complaint procedure. It also retained procedures for the participation of non-governmental organizations, which was seen as strength of the Commission. However, it did end the existence of the Sub-Commission on Promotion and Protection of Human Rights, the expert body of the Commission, and replaced it with an Advisory Body. The Council enjoys a higher status than the Commission as it reports directly to the GA. It consists of 47 members instead of the 53 members of the Commission and they are elected by a majority of the GA, which also has the power to suspend membership by a two-thirds vote. In order to address the non-selectivity issue, the Council has created the universal periodic review to monitor human rights compliance in all countries on a rotating schedule. The Council also meets three times a year instead of once a year and can call special sessions to address emergency situations. The members of the Council act in their capacity as representatives of their governments.

I

Independent Expert

See **Special Rapporteur**.

Indigenous People

One of the groups at risk whose importance was recognized by the Commission on Human Rights and its successor the Human Rights Council by the establishment of a thematic special procedure to address the various human rights issues related to the group. An estimated 300 million indigenous people live in the world today. While not specifically addressed in the non-discrimination provisions of the International Bill of Human Rights and the Convention on the Elimination of All Forms of Racial Discrimination, the broad prohibition of discrimination based on "race, colour, sex, language, religion, political or other opinion, national or social origin, property, birth or other status" could be construed to include indigenous people. The Convention on the Rights of the Child mentions the rights of indigenous children in three articles. Many of the UN and regional treaty bodies have also addressed the group's rights including self-determination, culture, property and religion which often come into conflict with neighboring communities. The International Labor Organization Convention 169 recognizes the collective rights of indigenous and tribal peoples.

Indiscriminate Attack

This kind of attack is prohibited against Protocol I Additional to the Geneva Conventions. Attacks that are considered indiscriminate are: (a) those that include bombardment by any method that treats as a single military objective a number that are clearly separated and distinct in localities that contain a concentration of civilians; and (b) those that may be expected to cause incidental loss or injury to civilians and damage to civilian objects which would be excessive in relation to the military advantage expected.

Information, Right to

While this right is not formally included in the core human rights treaties, it is considered to be part of the freedom of opinion and expression under both international and regional human rights treaties. Freedom to information was acknowledged by the UN General Assembly in 1946 as a fundamental human right. An attempt was made in 1948 to adopt a convention on freedom of information but due to conflicts of definitions between the Western countries and the Soviet Union, no consensus was reached on a definition. The discussion did result in the drafting of Article 19 of the Universal Declaration of Human Rights which recognizes the right to freedom of opinion and expression. Both the treaty- and charter-based human rights bodies have continued to address this right in a number of contexts, including most recently in the context of information on the Internet.

Instrument

A legal document and thus one of the words used to describe international agreements or resolutions by international bodies.

Intellectual Property, Right to

The Covenant on Economic, Social and Cultural Rights protects intellectual property by recognizing the property rights of investors and authors as well as by focusing on the public right to benefit from their inventions and works of art. In 2000, the UN Sub-Commission on the Promotion and Protection of Human Rights adopted a resolution that expressed concern that the Agreement on Trade-Related Aspects of Intellectual Property (TRIPS) did not adequately recognize human rights, in particular economic, social, and cultural rights, and indigenous and other communities' control over their own genetic and natural resources and cultural values.

Inter-American Commission of Women

Established in 1928 at the Sixth International Conference of American States after more than a month of protests by women who were not allowed to speak at the conference. The Commission has since drafted a number of treaties related to women's rights including the Convention on the Nationality of Women, the Inter-American Convention on the Granting of Civil Rights to Women and the Inter-American Convention on the Granting of Political Rights to Women. It also helped to draft and now oversees the Inter-American Convention on the Prevention, Punishment and Eradication of Violence Against Women.

Inter-American Commission on Human Rights (IACHR)

Created in 1959 by the Conference of American States, Fifth Meeting of Consultation of the Ministers of Foreign Affairs, which then approved its statute in 1960. In 1970, the entry into force of the Protocol of Buenos Aires amended the OAS Charter to elevate the status of the IACHR to recognize its role as one of the OAS institutions responsible for the promotion and protection of human rights implementing the American Declaration on the Rights and Duties of Man. When the American Convention on Human Rights came into force in 1978, the IACHR attained a role in implementing that treaty. The IACHR is headquartered in Washington, D.C. and is one of two main bodies that address human rights in the Western Hemisphere. It is composed of seven members elected in their personal capacity by the General Assembly of the OAS.

Inter-American Convention to Prevent and Punish Torture

Adopted in 1985 by the Organization of American States and entered into force in 1987. The definition of torture it contains is broader than that contained in the Convention Against Torture (CAT) in several respects. The basic definition includes acts that cause physical or mental pain or suffering, without specifying that the pain or suffering must be "grave", and no specific intent is required (Article 2). The Convention also covers a kind of torture not recognized by other treaties, namely, "methods . . . intended to obliterate the personality of the victim or to diminish his physical or mental capacities, even if they do not cause physical pain or mental anguish". The obligations of States Parties include: criminalizing and providing for "severe" penalties for torture; taking measures, including training, to prevent torture and ill-treatment; immediate investigation of any complaint of torture or information indicating that torture may have occurred; recognizing the right of victims to compensation, and making evidence obtained through torture inadmissible (Articles 6–10). It also contains provisions obliging Parties to prosecute or extradite persons accused of torture found within its territory regardless of their nationality or the place where the torture occurred (Articles 11–14). The Inter-American Court of Human Rights examines cases of alleged violations of the Convention jointly with violations of the American Convention on Human Rights, when they concern a State Party to both that recognizes the competence of the Court to examine alleged violations of the latter.

Inter-American Court of Human Rights

Established by the American Convention on Human Rights and first elected in 1979. It consists of seven part-time judges who are nominated and elected by the parties to the Convention. The court sits in San José, Costa Rica, but it may convene in any other location with the consent of the State concerned when the majority of the Court considers it desirable. The Court has contentious and advisory jurisdiction.

Inter-country Adoption (also called international adoption)

The adoption of a child who resides in one country by a person or couple living in another country. The Convention on the Rights of the Child recognizes inter-country adoption as a form of alternative care, but one that should be used only as a last resort, that is, when adoption, foster placement or suitable placement in the child's home country is not possible. The Hague Convention of 1993 on Protection of Children and Co-operation in Respect of Intercountry Adoption (in force since 1995, and in force for the United States since 2008) contains substantive, procedural and administrative requirements designed to ensure that inter-country adoption is carried out in compliance with the Convention on the Rights of the Child.

Intergovernmental Organizations (IGOs)

These are organizations whose members are governments. They include the United Nations and its specialized agencies, such as the International Labor Organization, and regional human rights bodies. These organizations play a central role in human rights protection by approving treaties and other instruments, by providing some procedures for addressing violations, and by providing expertise and support to government efforts in their specific areas.

Interim Measures

See **Provisional or Precautionary**.

Internally Displaced Persons (IDPs)

The term used to describe persons who have been forced from their homes in a variety of situations, including war, famine, floods and grave human rights abuses. It is estimated that there are 25 million people in about 50 countries who have been internally displaced for these reasons. While they have not crossed borders they often face the same problems of dislocation and suffering as refugees. IDPs often lack effective legal protection and access to international assistance, though forced population displacement may be a violation of international humanitarian law if it occurs during periods of armed conflict under Article 49 of the Fourth Geneva Convention that forbids individual or mass forcible transfers, as well as deportations of civilians from occupied territory to the territory of an occupying power. Violations of human rights are also involved in these situations, including the prohibition of forced evictions. In 1992, the UN Commission on Human Rights established a thematic procedure to address the human rights of IDPs.

International Bank for Reconstruction and Development

See **World Bank**.

International Bill of Human Rights

This is the informal name given to the basic instruments adopted by the UN for the protection of human rights: the Universal Declaration of Human Rights (UDHR) adopted by the General Assembly in 1948 and the two treaties further defining the human rights standards in the UDHR, the International Covenant on Economic, Social and Cultural Rights and the International Covenant on Civil and Political Rights. While the two sets of rights are separated into two instruments, numerous instruments refer to their interrelationship.

International Committee of the Red Cross (ICRC)

Non-governmental organization founded in 1863 to address human suffering during war. It was instrumental in preparing the drafts of the first multilateral treaty protecting victims of armed conflict – the 1864 Geneva Convention for the Amelioration of the Condition of the Wounded and Sick in Armies in the Field. The ICRC monitors compliance with the four Geneva Conventions and two Additional Protocols by visiting places of detention, making approaches to authorities, using its right of humanitarian initiative, and receiving complaints about breaches of humanitarian international law. It is thus involved in organizing exchange of visitors, reuniting families and truces to bring care for the wounded or refugees.

International Convention Against the Taking of Hostages

Treaty adopted by the UN General Assembly in 1979 and in force since 1983. It covers the seizure or detention of any person with a threat to kill, injure or continue to detain such person, in order to compel any third party to do or refrain from doing some act (Article 1). It applies only to acts having an international dimension (Article 13). The obligations of States Parties include exchanging information and coordinating activities to prevent hostage-taking; trying to obtain the release of hostages; giving their courts jurisdiction over hostage-taking based on the mere presence of an offender or accomplice (in addition to the place of the offense and nationality of the perpetrator or victim); investigating reported offenses and, if the evidence is sufficient, prosecuting or extraditing the person(s) concerned; and co-operating in the investigation and prosecution of these offenses. Fair treatment must be guaranteed and all rights recognized by national law must be respected, and extradition requests must be refused if the position of the alleged offender in the State requesting extradition or assistance would be adversely affected by his race, religion, nationality, ethnic origin or political opinion.

International Convention on the Elimination of All Forms of Racial Discrimination (CERD)

One of the core UN human rights multilateral treaties. It entered into force in 1969 and elaborates on the non-discrimination provisions of the UN Charter and the Universal Declaration of Human Rights. CERD requires that the nations that have ratified it prohibit and eliminate discrimination in all its forms and provide for special measures or affirmative action for as long as they are required to achieve equality. It prohibits discrimination in relation to a wide range of civil and political as well as economic, social and cultural rights.

International Convention on the Protection and Promotion of the Rights and Dignity of Persons with Disabilities and Optional Protocol

See **Convention on the Rights of Persons with Disabilities and Optional Protocol**.

International Convention on the Protection of All Persons from Enforced Disappearance

A treaty adopted by the General Assembly in 2006. It entered into force in 2007. It affirms that enforced disappearances are prohibited and can constitute a crime against humanity when practiced in a widespread or systemic manner. It also requires States Parties to make the offense punishable by appropriate remedies under national law.

International Convention on the Protection of Rights of All Migrant Workers and Members of Their Families

One of the core UN multilateral human rights treaties passed by the General Assembly in 1990. It entered into force in 2003 and provides for the protection of basic rights of migrant workers regardless of their status and for additional rights for those who are documented, especially those related to employment. It also includes provisions for certain categories of migrants, such as frontier workers, seasonal workers, itinerant workers, project-tied workers, specified employment workers and self-employed workers. In Part VI it provides for the promotion of sound, equitable, humane and lawful conditions in connection with international migration of workers and members of their families. This UN treaty has the lowest number of States Parties who are primarily those from sending rather than receiving countries.

International Court of Justice (ICJ)

Body created by Chapter XIV of the UN Charter which is the judicial branch of that body. The ICJ sits at the Peace Palace in The Hague, Netherlands. It consists of 15 judges elected to nine-year terms by the General Assembly and the Security Council. The Charter provides for both contentious or adversary and advisory jurisdiction. Adversary jurisdiction applies only in cases where the States Parties have referred to and accepted it and in situations where treaties provide for adjudication by the ICJ. Article 38(1) of the ICJ statute specifies the sources of law that the Court is to use. Decisions of the ICJ are only binding between the immediate parties and with respect to the specific case. Its decisions, however, are often relied upon as statements of international law. The ICJ has issued several decisions that are related to human rights issues.

International Covenant on Civil and Political Rights (ICCPR)

Multilateral treaty which is part of the International Bill of Human Rights and one of the core instruments of the UN human rights system. It was adopted by the General Assembly in 1966 and it entered into force on 23 March 1976. A large majority of the countries in the world are party to this treaty. It expands on the civil and political rights in the Universal Declaration of Human Rights, including the right to life, the prohibitions of torture, cruel, inhuman or degrading treatment or punishment as well as slavery, right to liberty and security and other protections under criminal justice systems, freedom of thought, conscience and religion, and expression, rights to privacy and family, right to freedom of association and to join trade unions, and the prohibition of discrimination. Two Optional Protocols to the Covenant have also been adopted, one to set up a communications procedure and another to abolish the death penalty.

International Covenant on Economic, Social and Cultural Rights (ICESCR)

This multilateral treaty is part of the International Bill of Human Rights and one of the core instruments of the UN human rights system. It was adopted by the General Assembly in 1966 and entered into force on 3 January 1976. A large majority of the countries in the world are party to this treaty. It expands on the economic, social and cultural rights in the Universal Declaration of Human Rights, including rights to work, form trade unions, social security, family, adequate standard of living (including food, clothing and housing), physical and mental health, education, cultural life and non-discrimination. The Covenant requires each State Party "to take steps, individually and through international assistance and co-operation, . . . to the maximum of its available resources, with a view to achieving progressively the full realization of the rights . . .". This mandate has been deemed to require that specific action be taken by the Committee overseeing its compliance. An Optional Protocol was adopted by the General Assembly in 2008 but it has yet to enter into force.

International Criminal Court (ICC)

Created pursuant to the Rome Statute for the International Criminal Court which was adopted by the UN Diplomatic Conference in 1998. The court was set up in The Hague, Netherlands in 2002 when the treaty entered into force. The ICC has jurisdiction only over individuals for crimes committed by people from States that are party to the Rome Statute and for crimes committed on the territory of a State Party. The Security Council can also refer cases to the Prosecutor acting under Chapter VII of the Charter of the United Nations. The ICC cannot pursue a case until the country involved is "unwilling or unable genuinely to carry out the investigation or prosecution" of the individual under the principle of complementarity. The ICC has jurisdiction over genocide, crimes against humanity and war crimes. It will also have jurisdiction over crimes of aggression, once the Rome Statute is amended to define that crime. The ICC Statute confirms that under international law rape, sexual slavery, enforced prostitution, forced pregnancy, enforced sterilization or other forms of sexual violence constitute crimes against humanity and war crimes. Defendants can avoid criminal responsibility if they establish that they had a legal obligation to obey the order, did not know the order was unlawful, and the order was not manifestly unlawful, which constitutes a departure from former international criminal tribunals.

International Criminal Tribunal for Rwanda (ICTR)

An ad hoc tribunal created by the Security Council in response to the armed conflict between rival Hutu, Tutsi, and Twa ethnic groups in Rwanda in 1994. The ICTR has jurisdiction over acts of genocide and crimes against humanity committed in 1994, but is limited to violations of international standards governing internal armed conflict. However, its definition of crimes against humanity does not require proof of the existence of armed conflict. The ICTR was set up in Arusha, Tanzania. By 2006, the ICTR had completed 30 cases resulting in 25 sentences. It was the first international tribunal to impose a conviction for rape as a crime against humanity in 2006 in the case of *Prosecutor v. Karemera*.

International Criminal Tribunal for the Former Yugoslavia (ICTY)

An ad hoc tribunal created by the UN Security Council in 1993 to address grave breaches of humanitarian law during the armed conflicts between rival ethnic groups of Croats, Muslims, and Serbs that started in 1991 in the former Yugoslavia. The ICTY was to apply rules of humanitarian law that had risen to the level of customary law, including the Geneva Conventions, the Convention on the Prevention and Punishment of the Crime of Genocide and the Charter of the International Military Tribunal of 5 August 1945. The ICTY meets in The Hague, Netherlands and has jurisdiction over grave breaches of the Geneva Conventions, violations of the laws or customs of war, genocide and crimes against humanity. Persons accused of planning, ordering, or committing those crimes are to be held individually responsible and will not be relieved of criminal responsibility for following superiors' orders, though that could be a mitigating factor in the determination of the punishment. The death penalty is not available under the ICTY.

International Financial Institutions

Major intergovernmental financial institutions have an impact on the promotion and protection of human rights. Those include the International Monetary Fund (IMF), the International Bank for Reconstruction and Development (World Bank), and the World Trade Organization (WTO). As international trade grows, the activities of these organizations have negative effects on people, particularly those in poor or developing countries. There have been criticisms that the efforts of these three organizations in pursuit of economic reform have resulted in making States incapable of fulfilling their human rights obligations. Included in these are privatization schemes that affect the rights to health, education, work, and an adequate standard of living. They also emphasize exports that undermine the right to adequate food. Structural adjustment programs have also been criticized for affecting decreases in the salaries of civil servants and increases in the costs of utilities, food and housing. See **International Monetary Fund; World Trade Organization**.

International Labor Organization (ILO)

One of the specialized agencies of the UN. It was originally authorized in 1919 by the Treaty of Versailles and was an agency of the League of Nations until it became the first specialized agency of the UN in 1946. It was established as a partnership between employers and employees and has a unique tripartite system which allows representatives of workers and employers to participate on an equal footing with governments in both discussions and decision making. The ILO is made up of the International Labor Conference, the Governing Body, and the International Labor Office. It employs around 2000 persons at its headquarters in Geneva and in 40 field offices around the world. The ILO has adopted labor standards in over 187 conventions and 198 recommendations. The most important are those that relate to: (a) freedom of association and the recognition of the right to collective bargaining; (b) the elimination of forced or compulsory labor; (c) the abolition of child labor; and (d) the elimination of discrimination in respect of employment and occupation.

International Labour Organization Convention of 1948 concerning Freedom of Association and Protection of the Right to Organize (ILO Convention No. 87)

One of the basic conventions of the International Labor Organization. It protects the right to freedom of association and collective bargaining and recognizes the right to strike. It protects the right to organize workers and employers and notes that the right to choose a union or employer association shall be free from interference from public authorities. Unions and employer associations cannot be dissolved or suspended by governments and are permitted to join national and international federations, confederations or associations.

International Labor Organization Forced Labor Conventions (ILO Conventions Nos. 29 and 105)

The name given collectively to two of the basic conventions of the International Labor Organization (ILO): the International Labor

Organization Forced Labor Convention of 1930 (ILO Convention No. 29) and the International Labor Convention of 1957 on the Abolition of Forced Labour (ILO No. 105). ILO Convention No. 29 calls for the abolition of forced labor, which it defines in Article 2(1) as "all work or service which is exacted from any person under the menace of any penalty and for which the said person has not offered himself voluntarily". This definition distinguishes forced labor from slavery in that it does not involve the concept of ownership. However, since it involves a similar degree of restriction of freedom, forced labor is similar to slavery with respect to its effect on the individual. While it called for States Parties to "suppress the use of forced or compulsory labour within the shortest possible time" it did not include an absolute prohibition, presumably because colonial powers often used forced labor for public works. In 1957, ILO Convention No. 105 did provide that States Parties had an obligation to suppress the use of forced labor for political purposes, for purposes of economic development, as a means for labor discipline or punishment for strike actions and for discriminatory purposes.

International Law Commission

The legal drafting body of the UN. It was created in 1947 by the General Assembly to "draft conventions on subjects which have not yet been regulated by international law or in regard to which the law has not yet been sufficiently developed in the practice of States". Thus, it assists with the progressive development of the law as well as with its codification. Its members serve in their individual capacity.

International Military Tribunal (Nuremberg)

Created by the Allied governments of the Soviet Union, United Kingdom, United States and the provisional government of the French Republic after World War II to sit in Nuremberg to address the reports of Nazi atrocities involving civilians. Its jurisdiction was over individuals responsible for crimes against peace, war crimes, and crimes against humanity under the Agreement for the Prosecution and Punishment of Major War Criminals of the European Axis (London Agreement). The Nuremberg Tribunal presided over the trial of 22 Nazi military and political leaders starting in November 1945 through October 1946. Nineteen of the accused were convicted and three were acquitted. Twelve of the convicted were sentenced to death and the remainder received sentences ranging from ten years to life.

International Military Tribunal for the Far East (Tokyo Tribunal)

Created by Special Proclamation of the Allied Supreme Commander of the Pacific on 19 January 1946 and the Charter of the International Military Tribunal for the Far East. Representatives from 11 States considered war crimes against 25 defendants. On 12 November 1948 all defendants were convicted. Seven were sentenced to death and the rest received sentences of seven and a half years to life.

International Monetary Fund (IMF)

One of the two intergovernmental financial institutions created after World War II by the Bretton Woods Agreements. Pursuant to its Articles of Agreement, the purposes of the IMF include: promotion of international monetary co-operation; facilitation of the expansion and balanced growth of trade, thereby contributing to the promotion of high levels of employment, real income, and development of productive resources of its members; and assisting with the establishment of a multilateral system of payment in order to eliminate foreign exchange restrictions which hamper the growth of world trade. Together with other human rights obligations under the UN Charter the IMF can be considered as one of the organizations that should facilitate the promotion of those rights. Critics, however, have noted that the IMF and the World Bank have been overly focused on creating wealth in developing countries without considering the unequal distribution of the benefits of economic growth and privatization schemes that can impair the rights to health, education, work and food.

International Programme on the Elimination of Child Labor (IPEC)

This program is managed by the International Labor Organization and it focuses on bonded child laborers, children working in hazardous conditions and occupations, children who are especially vulnerable such as those who are under the age of 12 and working girls. IPEC has projects to end child labor and return children to school in a number of countries.

Interpreter, Right to Free

This is one of the entitlements listed as a minimum guarantee for a fair trial under Article 14(3)(f) of the International Covenant on Civil and Political Rights. It requires the free assistance of an interpreter if the person charged with a crime cannot understand or speak the language used in court.

J

Johannesburg Declaration

See **World Summit on Sustainable Development**.

Johannesburg Plan of Implementation

See **World Summit on Sustainable Development**.

Johannesburg Principles on National Security, Freedom of Expression and Access to Information

Adopted on 1 October 1995 by a group of experts in international law, national security, and human rights convened by ARTICLE 19, the International Centre Against Censorship, in collaboration with the Centre for Applied Legal Studies of the University of the Witwatersrand, in Johannesburg, South Africa. The Principles provide that if a government uses national security as grounds for limiting freedom of expression, it bears the burden of showing the threat to national security and how the limitation on the right has the effect of reducing or removing the threat. The Johannesburg Principles were attached to the report of the Special Rapporteur on Freedom of Opinion and Expression to the Commission on Human Rights in 1996. The Commission referred to the Principles in resolutions on the topic between 1996 and 2003. Several national courts have also referred to the Principles.

Jus cogens or Peremptory Norm

This concept of international law was defined by the Vienna Convention on the Law of Treaties in 1980 as well as the Restatement of the Foreign Relations of the United States in 1987. The Vienna Convention defines a peremptory norm of international law as a "norm that is accepted and recognized by the international community of States as a whole . . . from which no derogation is permitted and which can be modified only by a subsequent norm" having the same character. A *jus cogens* or peremptory norm of general international law voids inconsistent treaty provisions. A *jus cogens* norm does not allow the persistent objection doctrine to excuse violations of customary international law. In general, the norm must be accepted by the international community of States as a whole even if over dissent by a small number of States.

Just Compensation

One of the components of the right to work under the Universal Declaration of Human Rights, which provides that "[e]veryone who works has the right to just and favorable remuneration ensuring for himself and his family an existence worthy of human dignity, and supplemented, if necessary, by other means of social protection".

Just Satisfaction

Term used to describe the remedies that injured parties are entitled to pursuant to the complaint procedure established under the [European] Convention for the Protection of Human Rights and Fundamental Freedoms. Initially the European Court of Human Rights awarded legal fees and costs pursuant to Article 41 of the Convention, but starting in 1974 the Court started to award pecuniary damages for injuries suffered by individuals whose rights were violated. Those damages include economic harm, and no pecuniary or moral damages to compensate for emotional suffering or interference with protected rights.

Juvenile

One of a protected group of people referred to as a child under international law and subject to protection under the Convention of the Rights of the Child, which defines a child as a human being below the age of 18 years of age, unless the law of the State defines majority as an earlier age. Juvenile is usually used instead of "child" when the person is involved in criminal proceedings. In that context, that treaty does not allow either the death penalty or life without parole sentences for persons under the age of 18 regardless of the age of majority in the country. Further, under the International Covenant on Civil and Political Rights, juveniles shall be separated from adults when incarcerated and the criminal justice system shall take account of their age and promote their rehabilitation.

K

Kampala Convention

See **Crime of Aggression**.

Koran

See **Quran**.

L

Labor Rights

This concept encompasses a number of rights related to employment, including the individual right to work as well as the right to freedom of association which implicates a group of workers' right to form a union. Article 23 of the Universal Declaration of Human Rights sets out the various components of the right to work, including: free choice of employment; just and favorable conditions; protection against unemployment; the right to equal pay for equal work without discrimination; the right to just compensation; and the right to form and join trade unions.

Landmines

Explosive objects usually laid underground during times of war. They can be a barrier to the return of refugees and internally displaced persons after wars are over. Because of the ongoing danger they pose well after the wars are over, there have been campaigns by non-governmental organizations to ban their use. Clearing landmines is often a prerequisite not only to the return of refugees and internally displaces persons but for humanitarian aid, reconstruction and development as well.

Language Rights

There are various aspects to the right to speak one's language. The basic principle enunciated in Article 2 of the Universal Declaration of Human Rights is that there should not be any discrimination based on a person's language. This principle is also included in the two Covenants that make up the International Bill of Human Rights. While it is not specifically included in Article 13 of the International Covenant on Economic, Social and Cultural Rights, access to education in one's language can be inferred from the mandate that "education shall be directed to the full development of the human personality and the sense of its dignity . . .". Further, Article 27 of the International Covenant on Civil and Political Rights provides that minorities are not to be denied rights to their culture, religion, "or to use their own language".

Last Resort Principle

The principle that, in the context of juvenile justice, deprivation of liberty may only be imposed "as a last resort and for the shortest appropriate period of time". This principle, recognized by the Beijing Rules (Rule 19) and the Convention on the Rights of the Child (Article 38), applies to detention before trial as well as sentencing and is also relevant to decisions regarding parole and early release, and placement in closed facilities that are not part of the correctional system (e.g. reform schools). The Beijing Rules also contain a provision that may be used to interpret this principle: "Deprivation of personal liberty shall not be imposed unless the juvenile is adjudicated of a serious act involving violence against another person or of persistence in committing other serious offences and unless there is no other appropriate response" (Rule 17(c)).

Latin American and Caribbean Group (GRULAC) (UN)

One of the informal regional groups of the United Nations made up of 33 countries from Latin America and the Caribbean, including Mexico, Central and South American countries as well as those in the Caribbean. See also **Regional Groups (UN)**.

Laws of Manu

A Hindu legal code attributed to the founder of the human race, which scholars believe dates to the fifth century BC. Although the code provided for corporal punishment and allowed torture in investigation of crimes, it also contains extensive verses on the obligation of rulers to judge fairly and impartially. They include incremental use of punishments such as using warnings and reproofs before using corporal punishment; inflicting punishment only after due consideration; and urging kings to avoid unjust punishments. The Code also indicates that the King was not above the law: "Where a common man would be fined one karshapana (coin), the king shall be fined one thousand; that is the settled rule." (Translation by George Bühler, *Sacred Books of the East*, Volume 25, Ch. VIII, Line 336 (parenthetical added by this author).)

League of Arab States

A regional organization made up of Arab States in North and Northeast Africa and the Middle East. The League established a Human Rights Commission in 1968 and adopted the Arab Charter on Human Rights in 1994.

League of Nations

Body created by the Versailles Treaty following World War I. While human rights were not explicitly mentioned in the League's Covenant, agreements administered under the League did address issues such as self-determination, minority rights, slavery, protection of life and liberty, freedom of religion, equal protection, and other civil and political rights. The League also established a mandate system for colonies and non-self-governing territories with a goal of promoting their self-determination. The main purpose of the League of Nations was to prevent resort to war, but the organization was unable to prevent the aggression by the Axis Powers and eventually many nations withdrew from it. Many of its structures were taken over by the United Nations following World War II. See also **Covenant of the League of Nations**.

League of Nations Slavery, Servitude, Forced Labour and Similar Institutions and Practices Convention of 1926 (Slavery Convention of 1926)

See **Slavery, Servitude, Forced Labour and Similar Institutions and Practices Convention (Slavery Convention of 1926)**.

Leave, Right to

This right is included in Article 13 of the Universal Declaration of Human Rights. It includes the right of a person to leave any country, including his or her own, as well as the right to return to the latter. The right to leave is also included in Article 12 of the International Covenant on Civil and Political Rights. The Human Rights Committee has elaborated on that right in a General Comment and includes the right to obtain necessary travel documents. The right to leave was first mentioned in the Magna Carta of 1215 and the concept was included in the Peace of Westphalia of

1648 and the French Constitution of 1791. This right has been accepted by most nations.

Liberty and Security of Person, Right to

The rights of liberty and security of person are included in Article 3 of the Universal Declaration of Human Rights. However, they are listed as separate rights and elaborated on in Article 9 of the International Covenant on Civil and Political Rights. The latter includes the following protections: the prohibition against arbitrary arrest or detention; the right to be informed of the reason of the arrest and promptly informed of any charges; the right to be brought promptly before a judicial officer and entitlement to a trial within a reasonable time; the right for anyone deprived of liberty or detained to go before a court to determine the lawfulness of the detention; and the right for anyone subject to unlawful arrest or detention to seek compensation. Article 10 further provides that "persons deprived of their liberty shall be treated with humanity and with respect for the inherent dignity of the human person". Further, accused persons should be segregated from convicted persons and juvenile persons shall be separated from adults and treated in accordance with their age and legal status. Finally, the goal of the penitentiary system should be the reform and social rehabilitation of convicted persons.

Life, Right to

The right to life, liberty and security of person is included in Article 3 of the Universal Declaration of Human Rights and is further elaborated in Article 6 of the International Covenant on Civil and Political Rights. The latter includes the following protections: (1) that the right should be protected by law and it cannot be arbitrarily deprived; (2) in countries that have not abolished the death penalty, the sentence can only be imposed for only the most serious crimes and pursuant to a judgment issued by a competent court; (3) if the deprivation of life is considered genocide, no derogation from the Convention on the Prevention and Punishment of the Crime of Genocide is allowed; (4) anyone sentenced to death has the right to seek pardon or commutation of the sentence; (5) the sentence of death cannot be imposed for crimes committed by someone under 18 years of age at the time of the crime; and (6) these provisions are not to be used to prevent the abolition of the death penalty. The Human Rights Committee has further defined this right to include obligations to prevent loss of life in situations such as war as well as positive obligations to reduce infant mortality and increase life expectancy, as well as to prevent arbitrary killings and prevent disappearances.

Limburg Principles on the Implementation of the International Covenant on Economic, Social and Cultural Rights

These principles resulted from a meeting of legal scholars in 1986 where one of the first attempts was made to define the obligations of States' under the International Covenant on Economic Social and Cultural Rights. See also **Maastricht Guidelines**.

London Agreement

See **Agreement for the Prosecution and Punishment of the Major War Criminals of the European Axis**.

M

Maastricht Guidelines

Guidelines that were created by a group of legal scholars in 1997 to further elaborate on the Limburg Principles that had attempted to define the obligation of States' obligations with respect to economic, social and cultural rights. The Maastricht Guidelines took into account the new instruments that had been adopted since 1986 when the Limburg Principles were developed. See also **Limburg Principles on the Implementation of the International Covenant on Economic, Social and Cultural Rights**.

Magna Carta

One of the first national documents addressing rights concepts. The Magna Carta was issued by King John of England in 1215. Its purpose was to ensure feudal rights and guarantee that the king could not encroach on the privileges of the barons, but it also guaranteed the freedom of the church and the customs of the towns. It implied the protection of the rights of subjects. It was later argued to be the basis for the guarantee of trial by jury and *habeas corpus*. It was one of the first limitations on the excessive use of royal power.

Margin of Appreciation

Concept used by the European Court of Human Rights to interpret the European Convention provisions so as to allow nations the capacity to vary their application of the treaty obligations in light of national practices.

Marry, Right to

Article 16 of the Universal Declaration of Human Rights provides that men and women have a right to marry and found a family without limitation due to race, nationality or religion. Men and women are entitled to equal rights during marriage and in the case of dissolution. Marriage shall be entered into only with the full and free consent of both spouses. It also affirms the family as the natural and fundamental group of society entitled to protection by the State. Article 23 of the International Covenant on Civil and Political Rights affirms these provisions and adds that in the case of dissolution, provision shall be made for the protection of children.

Medical and Scientific Experimentation

The International Covenant on Civil and Political Rights Article 7 includes a prohibition against medical and scientific experimentation on persons without their free consent. The UN General Assembly has also adopted the Principles of Medical Ethics relevant to the Role of Health Personnel, particularly Physicians, in the Protection of Prisoners and Detainees Against Torture and Other Cruel, Inhuman or Degrading Treatment or Punishment which also addresses the issue in the context of medical care of prisoners and detainees. The Principles provide for accountability of medical personnel engaging in violations of medical ethics.

Mexico City Declaration on Cultural Policies

This declaration was passed at the UNESCO World Conference on Cultural Policies in Mexico City in 1982. It provides that the "assertion of cultural identity . . . contributes to the liberation of peoples. Conversely, any form of domination constitutes a denial or an impairment of that identity."

Migrant Workers

One of the groups at risk deemed to be in need of protection. The International Convention on the Protection of the Rights of All Migrant Workers and Members of Their Families defines a migrant worker as a "person who is to be engaged, is engaged or has been engaged in a remunerated activity in a State of which he or she is not a national". Migrant workers are deemed to have a broad range of rights regardless of whether they are documented or in a regular situation or undocumented or in an irregular situation, though documented migrants are provided additional protections under the International Convention. In addition to providing for non-discrimination and protection of all the basic rights, the International Convention also provides for procedural and substantive protections in expulsion matters.

Millennium Declaration

This declaration was passed by the General Assembly in 2000 to reaffirm its commitment to Agenda 21 which was adopted by the United Nations Conference on the Environment and Development in Rio de Janeiro, Brazil in 1992. It was a comprehensive document for guiding the activities of the United Nations in the third millennium. The declaration notes the importance of management of all living species and natural resources in order to insure their protection for future generations.

Minorities

Refers to groups of individuals who are not part of the dominant population in a particular country or area. Minorities can be characterized by their race, ethnicity, religion, language, nationality or other protected status. A group may identify themselves as a minority if they possess those characteristics, want to preserve those characteristics, and want to be accepted as part of the group by the other members. The protection of minorities was the subject of early efforts at protection of human rights as was evidenced by peace treaties as early as the sixteenth century that included provisions protecting religious minorities. The treatment of minorities by one State has been the basis for both military and diplomatic humanitarian intervention by other States. Protection of minorities and prevention of discrimination was included as one of the basic tenets of the United Nations and several major human rights treaties include protection of categories of minority groups.

Mixed (International and National) Tribunals

In addition to using international tribunals to address accountability for gross violations of human rights such as war crimes, crimes against humanity, genocide and systemic criminal offenses, some countries have used mixed tribunals to prosecute those crimes. International personnel and standards are used together with the national system to prosecute those crimes. Examples of mixed tribunals include those in Sierra Leone, Cambodia, East Timor (Timor-Leste), Kosovo and Bosnia. The efficacy of those tribunals has been mixed.

Monist Approach to International Law

This approach to the application of international law at the international level allows for the direct incorporation of its treaty and customary international law obligations into national laws without requiring legislative action by governmental bodies. Most countries that follow the civil law tradition derived from Roman law follow the monist approach to national implementation of treaty obligations.

N

Nation

One of the words used to describe a country or State. Reference is often made to the nation-States that arose in the seventeenth century. While at that time international law rejected the notion of human rights and favored State sovereignty, eventually nations became the primary entities primarily responsible for human rights promotion and protection.

National Human Rights Institutions (NHRIs)

One of the groups of bodies that play a role in protecting human rights at the national level, which include national, regional, provincial and local structures of government, as well as ombudsmen and human rights commissions. NHRIs are generally autonomous, quasi-governmental institutions tasked with advising governments regarding human rights protection, reviewing legislation, preparing human rights reports, and investigating complaints of human rights violations. In 1991, a UN sponsored meeting developed the Paris Principles which were later endorsed by the Commission on Human Rights and the General Assembly. They became the foundation for the establishment and operation of NHRIs. Subsequently, NHRIs were specifically authorized to participate at the UN human rights bodies.

Nationality, Right to

This right is covered in Article 15 of the Universal Declaration of Human Rights, which both recognizes the right and provides that no one shall be arbitrarily deprived of it or the right to change it. Various treaties address the right in the context of avoiding statelessness. For example, the International Covenant on Civil and Political Rights provides in Article 24 that every child has the right to be registered after birth and to acquire a nationality. The International Convention on the Elimination of All Forms of Race Discrimination provides that States Parties undertake to eliminate race discrimination and to guarantee equality with respect to a number of enumerated rights including that to a nationality. Treaties addressing women's and children's rights also protect the right to nationality. Two treaties exist solely for addressing statelessness: the Convention on the Reduction of Statelessness, and the Convention relating to the Status of Stateless Persons.

National or Social Origin

One of the categories of prohibited discrimination listed in Article 2 of each of the Universal Declaration of Human Rights, the International Covenant on Economic, Social and Cultural Rights and the International Covenant on Civil and Political Rights. Regional human rights treaties include similar prohibitions on discrimination on the basis of national and/or social origin. National origin generally refers to the person's place of origin, whereas social origin refers to the person's descent. Castes could be an example of the latter.

National Security

Maintaining the security of a nation is generally the primary goal of governments so public emergencies are often grounds in treaties for derogating certain human rights. Article 4 of the International Covenant on Civil and Political Rights provides the guidelines for such derogations as well as a list of rights that can never be derogated from such as the right to life, the right to be free from torture or cruel, inhuman or degrading treatment or punishment, and the prohibition of slavery. The drafters of this provision likely were considering "armed conflict" as the main public emergency that would threaten the life of the nation. However, Article 19(3) provides that the right to freedom of expression can be subject to certain restrictions, including "[f]or the protection of national security or of public ordre (*ordre public*), or of public health or morals". Regional treaties also provide for some derogation of certain rights in cases of war or other public emergencies threatening the life of a nation.

Natural Law

One of the sources used to support the existence of human rights. Unlike positive law, which is based on actions taken by States such as legislation, natural law is based on a moral imperative that individuals have certain immutable rights as human beings. The principal natural law theory assumes that there are natural laws that are higher than any positive law. The Universal Declaration of Human Rights reflects natural law thinking in Article 1 which provides that: "All human beings are born equal in dignity and in rights." One criticism of natural law is that different religious, cultural, and national traditions may believe in different precepts and thus it could be difficult to determine what the immutable rights are.

Non-citizens

Also referred to as aliens, this term refers to persons who are not citizens of the country they are in. This was one of the earliest groups to become the subject of human rights protection as States undertook to protect the rights of their citizens living in other countries. States' intervention on behalf of non-citizens in other countries was based on two principles: the right to be treated in accordance with international standards of justice and to be treated equally with nationals in the State in which they reside. All the major human rights treaties include protection of rights regardless of national origin. The International Convention on the Elimination of All Forms of Race Discrimination does allow for distinctions, exclusions, restrictions or preferences between citizens and non-citizens, though limits have been put on when the distinctions are allowed both at the international and regional level.

Non-derogable Rights

The name given to the category of rights that cannot be violated regardless of whether there is a public emergency. The International Covenant on Civil and Political Rights provides that "in time of public emergency which threatens the life of a nation and existence of which is formally proclaimed" that States Parties may take measures derogating from their obligations under the Covenant under certain circumstances. However, the Covenant goes on to provide that there are certain rights that cannot be derogated from such as the right to life, the right to be free from torture, the prohibition against slavery, imprisonment for inability to fulfill a contract violation, the prohibition against being held guilty for offenses that were not a crime at the time of commission, the right to recognition as a person before the law and the right to freedom of thought, conscience and religion.

Non-governmental Organizations (NGOs)

This refers to a broad category of usually non-profit groups who increasingly play a variety of roles in the promotion and protection of human rights. Some NGOs, such as the International Committee of the Red Cross, have played a role in convening State representatives to draft treaties or other human rights instruments. Other NGOs provide ideas and factual information to the human rights procedures of the UN, intergovernmental organizations and regional and national human rights bodies. To participate directly at many UN bodies, NGOs must be accredited by the UN Economic and Social Council.

Non-refoulement

The principle that persons should not be forcibly returned from one country to another upon a country's request, usually to face criminal charges for acts committed in the latter. International treaties have been interpreted to prohibit the return of persons where there are substantial grounds to believe that they may be in danger of being subjected to torture if they are returned.

Non-self-executing Declaration

While usually it is up to the courts to determine whether a treaty provision may be applied without implementing legislation, the United States has ratified a number of human rights treaties with a declaration stating that the treaty is not self-executing. The declaration does not affect the obligations of the United States under the treaties and some treaty bodies have questioned the validity of the declaration. Questions have also arisen as to whether the declaration applies only when the treaty provision is the basis for a private cause of action.

Non-State Actors

Refers to persons or entities acting outside the scope of State or other governmental capacity. In general, non-State actors are responsible for respecting human rights while States are responsible for respecting human rights as well as protecting and promoting human rights. Thus, States are also responsible for ensuring that non-State actors do not commit human rights violations or provide means of redress when they do. Because of the increasing role that corporations and other business enterprises play in the international arena, questions have arisen as to who is responsible for their accountability when non-State actors commit human rights violations: the location of the violation, the location of where they are based, or some international forum. In light of the problems that have arisen in this context, there are increasing calls to establish international procedures for holding non-State actors accountable when States are not able to be so.

No Power/No Action Doctrine

At the time of the drafting of the United Nations Charter, a proposal to include protection as well as promotion of human rights was defeated. Thus, when the Commission on Human Rights first met in 1947, it took the position that it did not have the power to take any enforcement action with respect to complaints of human rights violations. This became known as the no power or no action doctrine. The Commission's oversight body, the Economic and Social Council (ECOSOC), initially affirmed this position but eventually adopted a series of resolutions that authorized the Commission and its Sub-Commission to debate and address certain kinds of violations.

Norms on the Responsibilities of Transnational Corporations and Other Business Enterprises with Regard to Human Rights

Approved by the Sub-Commission on Promotion and Protection of Human Rights in 2003 to address issues of corporate accountability. The Norms recognize that States have the primary responsibility for ensuring that transnational corporations and business enterprises promote, respect and protect human rights. The Norms define transnational corporations broadly and indicate that national companies and local businesses are also responsible. They also take a broad and comprehensive approach to human rights and are augmented by a detailed Commentary that indicates how the provisions apply to companies.

Nuremberg Charter

See **Charter of the International Military Tribunal of August 8, 1945**.

O

Office of the High Commissioner for Human Rights (OHCHR)

The Office of the UN High Commissioner for Human Rights was established in 1993 by the UN General Assembly following the 1993 World Conference on Human Rights and is based in Geneva, Switzerland. See **United Nations High Commissioner for Human Rights (UNHCHR)**.

Ombudsman

Generally refers to a governmental entity that is charged with the task of receiving and investigating complaints claims against the government. These institutions are based on the nineteenth-century Swedish model in which independent officials receive complaints or act in their own motion to investigate the basis of any claim against the government when other remedies have been exhausted. Usually, the ombudsman makes non-enforceable but usually influential recommendations to the government for resolving the complaint. In a number of countries the ombudsman functions expressly have been given a human rights mandate.

Opinio Juris

This means the "opinion of the law" and is the name given to the requirement that in order to establish that a particular practice by States can be the basis for establishing customary international law it is done in accordance with the sense that the States are acting from a sense of obligation or the belief that it was required by law.

Optional Protocol to the Convention on the Rights of Persons with Disabilities

See **International Convention on the Protection and Promotion of the Rights and Dignity of Persons with Disabilities and Optional Protocol**.

Optional Protocol to the Convention on the Rights of the Child on the Involvement of Children in Armed Conflicts

One of several international human rights instruments adopted to complement the Convention on the Rights of the Child. The purpose of this treaty is to increase the protection of children under the age of 18 from direct involvement in armed hostilities and from forced recruitment into armed forces. It was adopted by the General Assembly in 2000 and entered into force in 2002. In order for a country to become a party it needs to have become party to or signed the Convention on the Rights of the Child. It is one of the few protocols that does not require that the country ratify the underlying treaty in order to become party to it.

Optional Protocol to the International Covenant on Civil and Political Rights

The first of two instruments that were added to the International Covenant on Civil and Political Rights (ICCPR) and is open for ratification to States Parties to the ICCPR. It entered into force in 1976. This Optional Protocol establishes a complaint procedure for individuals claiming to be victims of violations of any of the rights set forth in the ICCPR by States that have ratified the ICCPR. The Optional Protocol sets forth the requirements for the complaints, including exhaustion of domestic remedies and that they are not being considered by other international bodies, as well as the procedures for consideration of the complaints.

Optional Protocol to the International Covenant on Economic, Social and Cultural Rights

An instrument creating a complaint procedure for violations of the International Covenant on Economic, Social and Cultural Rights (ICESCR). It is open for ratification to States Parties to the ICESCR. The Optional Protocol sets forth the requirements for the complaints, including exhaustion of domestic remedies and that they are not being considered by other international bodies, as well as the procedures for consideration of the complaints.

Organization for Security and Cooperation in Europe (OSCE)

This regional organization grew out of the Conference on Security and Cooperation in Europe (CSCE) which was established in 1973. It is made up of 55 European, Central Asian, and North American States and was originally created as a means for addressing Cold War concerns by entering into a non-binding agreement called the Helsinki Accords. Through this process, a unique linkage between security and human rights concerns was developed. A follow-up process resulted in documents protecting human rights such as trade union freedoms, religious freedoms, free flow of information, protection against terrorism and family unification. The CSCE changed its name to OSCE in 1994, which reflected the development of permanent structures and personnel. Its work is divided into four areas: election observation; democratization assistance; monitoring/early warning; and Roma and Sinti issues.

Organization of African Unity (OAU)

A regional intergovernmental organization made up of African States that was created in 1963. It was replaced by its successor organization, the African Union, in 2002.

Organization of American States (OAS)

The regional intergovernmental organization made up of States in the Americas or Western Hemisphere created pursuant to the Charter of the OAS when it entered into force in 1951. Its main human rights bodies include the OAS General Assembly, the Inter-American Commission on Human Rights, and the Inter-American Court of Human Rights.

Organization of American States General Assembly

The main legislative body of the Organization of American States (OAS). The OAS General Assembly provides the ultimate oversight of the human rights obligations under the Charter of the OAS, the American Declaration of the Rights and Duties of Man and the American Convention on Human Rights, in addition to the other OAS human rights instruments.

Organization of the Islamic Conference (OIC)

An organization made up of Muslim governments. It adopted the Cairo Declaration on Human Rights in 1990. It is one of the sub-regional bodies that participates at the UN. See also **Cairo Declaration on Human Rights**.

Other Status

One of the prohibited enumerated grounds of discrimination in the Universal Declaration of Human Rights, the two international covenants and numerous other human rights treaties. The treaty body created under each treaty is responsible for reviewing compliance by State Parties with respect to all the prohibited grounds of discrimination but few have actually defined what it covers, though one interpretation could be that it meant to prohibit any arbitrary discrimination. In general, not every distinction of treatment between groups of persons will constitute discrimination if the distinction serves a legitimate objective and is proportional to achieving the objective. The Human Rights Committee in General Comment 18 did address what non-discrimination means and includes "other status" in all the prohibited grounds for discrimination but did not specifically define the term. The General Comment does note that not all grounds for discrimination are listed and asks that State Parties comment on the omission of other grounds of differentiation. In paragraph 13, the Committee observed "that not every differentiation of treatment will constitute discrimination, if the criteria for such differentiation are reasonable and objective and if the aim is to achieve a purpose which is legitimate under the Covenant".

P

Pacific Charter on Human Rights

In 1989 the Law Association for Asia and the Pacific, an organization comprising members from Micronesia, Polynesia, Melanesia, Australia and New Zealand, adopted this Proposed Charter. The Charter covers economic, social and cultural rights, including the right to development and rights of peoples, including indigenous peoples. It also proposed the creation of a Commission to assist with programs to promote the rights and educate people.

Paris Principles on National Human Rights Institutions

See **Principles relating to the Status of National Institutions (Paris Principles)**.

Participation in Public Affairs, Right to

Article 21 of the Universal Declaration of Human Rights provides for public participation in government and voting rights. This right is also protected by the general requirement in Article 29 that any limitation on human rights must be for the purpose of securing respect for the rights and freedoms of others, meeting the "requirements of morality, public order and the general welfare in a democratic society". Article 25 of the International Covenant on Civil and Political Rights further provides for the protection of public participation and voting rights. This right does not include the promotion any particular system of government as long as the political system provides for public participation and free and fair elections. The Human Rights Committee has also recognized in a General Comment on minority rights that regardless of the political system, a government must adopt "measures to ensure the effective participation of members of minority communities in decisions which affect them".

Party

Refers to a country that has ratified or adhered to a treaty. The government is more generally referred to as a State Party in most international instruments.

Peace

Article 1 of the United Nations Charter provides that the preservation of peace and the protection of human rights are the two principal objectives of the organization. Article 2 provides that international disputes should be settled by peaceful means and that the use of force should only be used pursuant to the "Purposes of the United Nations". Chapter VII of the UN Charter provides that the Security Council is to determine when there has been a breach of the peace and decide when the use of force is appropriate. Article 41 identifies non-military measures the Security Council may take to address threats to peace and Article 42 authorizes the Security Council to use military forces to secure international peace and security when non-military measures fail. The UN Charter, human rights treaties and other international and regional instruments emphasize the relationship between peace and human rights.

Peaceful Assembly and Association

See **Freedom of Peaceful Assembly and Association**.

Peremptory Norm

See *Jus cogens*.

Permanent Court of International Justice (PCIJ)

This tribunal was authorized in the Covenant of the League of Nations. It held its first session in 1922 and was dissolved in 1946 when it was replaced by the International Court of Justice. The PCIJ was the first permanent international tribunal with general jurisdiction. Its jurisprudence clarified and developed a number of concepts of international law. Between 1922 and 1940 the PCIJ dealt with 29 contentious cases between States and issued 27 advisory opinions.

Persistent Objection Doctrine

A concept that relates to the application of customary international law. Once it is established, customary international law binds States whether or not they have accepted it, unless they have persistently objected to the development of the norm. In order for the persistent objection doctrine to apply, the State has to have objected from the inception of the doctrine and consistently as it developed. The doctrine does not apply if a norm reaches the level of a *jus cogens* or peremptory norm of international law.

Political or Other Opinion

One of the prohibited enumerated grounds of discrimination in the Universal Declaration of Human Rights (UDHR), the two international covenants and numerous other human rights treaties. The treaty body created under each treaty is responsible for reviewing compliance by State Parties with respect to all the prohibited grounds of discrimination but few have actually defined what it covers. In addition, Articles 19 of the UDHR and the International Covenant on Civil and Political Rights provide for the right to freedom of opinion and expression. See **Freedom of Opinion and Expression**.

Positive Law

One of the sources of law used to support the existence of human rights. Positive law is based on actions taken by States, such as legislation. Positivists of the nineteenth century tried to describe law in morally neutral terms, but in the context of authority and coercion. Later theorists tried to argue that positive law should be put in the context of those who accept the legal system. Multilateral instruments are considered laws under the positivist approach because they reflect the agreement of the States that drafted and ratified them.

Precautionary Measures

See **Provisional or Precautionary**.

Presumption of Innocence, Right to

Article 11 of the Universal Declaration of Human Rights provides that everyone "charged with a penal offense the right to be presumed innocent until proved guilty according to law in a public trial at which he has had all the guarantees necessary for his defence". Article 14(2) of the International Covenant on Civil and Political Rights reaffirms this right as one of the components of the right to a fair and public hearing.

Princeton Principles on Universal Jurisdiction

See **Universal Jurisdiction**.

Principles on National Security and Right to Information

See **Johannesburg Principles on National Security, Freedom of Expression and Access to Information**.

Principles relating to the Status of National Institutions (Paris Principles)

Adopted by a meeting of National Human Rights Institutions (NHRIs) sponsored by the UN in 1991. It sets out a detailed set of principles on the status of NHRIs, which was subsequently endorsed by the Commission on Human Rights and the General Assembly. The Paris Principles provide that NHRIs should be given a broad mandate, legitimized by legislation or under the constitution. Tasks described in the Paris Principles include submission of recommendations or reports, harmonization of national legislation with human rights instruments, encouragement of ratification of human rights instruments, contribution to State reports submitted to treaty and other UN bodies, and assistance with the development of human rights education programs. The NHRIs are to be as autonomous from the government as possible, represent various interests in society, and be given adequate resources and power to investigate human rights issues.

Privacy, Right to

Article 12 of the Universal Declaration of Human Rights provides for the protection of the right to privacy. It states that privacy, family, home or correspondence cannot be subjected to arbitrary interference and that a person's honor and reputation cannot be subjected to attacks. The right to privacy is also protected by Article 17 of the International Covenant on Civil and Political Rights. The earliest known definitions of "privacy" is the "right to be left alone", but the Human Rights Committee has interpreted this to cover a number of situations, including the right to change one's surname, to guarantee confidentiality of correspondence and telephone communications, to prohibit various forms of surveillance and to ensure that personal and body searches are carried out in a manner that is consistent with the dignity of the person being searched.

Private Actor

Refers to non-State persons or entities, which include businesses and corporations. Nation States are the principal actors responsible for respecting, protecting and fulfilling human rights. Those obligations include adopting measures to ensure that private actors also respect human rights and to provide effective remedies for victims of violations. Article 2(3) of the International Covenant on Civil and Political Rights was one of the first treaties to set forth this obligation though it does so by requiring that any person whose rights are violated is provided with a remedy, "notwithstanding that the violation has been committed by persons acting in an official capacity". This presumes that violations by non-State actors are also covered. The Guiding Principles on human rights and business further delineate the human rights obligations for businesses.

Prohibition

Some human rights are framed as acts that are prohibited, such as the prohibition against slavery in Article 7 of the Universal Declaration of Human Rights and Article 8 of the International Covenant on Civil and Political Rights. Both provide that slavery shall be prohibited, which includes a prohibition of slavery by the government as well as an obligation to prohibit slavery. Other articles do not make use of the word "prohibited" but imply that individuals shall not be subjected to a particular act, such as torture or arbitrary arrest, detention or exile.

Propaganda for War

Article 20 of the International Covenant on Civil and Political Rights provides that propaganda for war shall be prohibited by law. Thus, this is one of the limitations that is permitted on the right to freedom of expression.

Property, Right to

Article 17 of the Universal Declaration of Human Rights (UDHR) provides for the right to own property alone or with others and for protection against arbitrary deprivation. However, a compromise between developing and developed countries during the drafting of the two International Covenants that implement the UDHR resulted in no mention of the right in either treaty. Both International Covenants do provide that property cannot be the basis for discrimination and include protections of resources and means of subsistence for peoples under the principle of self-determination. The International Covenant on Economic, Social and Cultural Rights also recognizes the property rights of inventors and authors and mentions the public right to benefit from scientific progress in Article 15. The two Committees overseeing implementation of the two International Covenants have addressed protection of property rights in various contexts, such as the right to housing and women's right to own property. The Convention on the Elimination of All Forms of Racial Discrimination forbids discrimination in relation to the right to own property and the Convention on the Elimination of All Forms of Discrimination Against Women provides for equality for women regarding ownership and management of property. Several other treaties, such as those related to refugees and stateless persons, also provide for the right to property.

Protect

The responsibility to protect (R2P) is part of the framework of the responsibility to respect, protect and fulfill. This particular responsibility was developed as an initiative in 2005 by the UN General Assembly and focused on preventing genocide, war crimes, crimes against humanity and ethnic cleansing. Rights are often framed in terms of requiring the protection of States Parties in human rights treaties. See also **Responsibility to Respect, Protect, and Fulfill**.

Protocol

One of the names given to amendments or instruments adding provisions to treaties. In general, to sign on to a protocol to a treaty requires that the State already be a State Party to the treaty, but a protocol can specifically allow for membership in other situations. For example, the Optional

Protocol to the Convention on the Rights of the Child on the Involvement of Children in Armed Conflicts specifically provides in Article 9 that it is open for signature by any State that is a party to the Convention on the Rights of the Child or has signed it.

Protocol I Additional to the Geneva Conventions of 12 August 1949, and relating to the Protection of Victims of International Armed Conflicts

Identifies wars of liberation or self-determination as a second category of international conflict. The most important contribution of Additional Protocol I is the affirmation that Parties to a conflict do not have unlimited rights to choose methods of warfare. It prohibits the use of weapons that cause superfluous injury or unnecessary suffering as well as those that will cause "widespread, long-term and severe damage to the natural environment". It also affirms the need for Parties in conflicts to distinguish between civilians and combatants so that they direct their operations only against military objectives. It prohibits attacks on civilians, civilian objects, "historic monuments, works of art or places of worship which constitute the cultural or spiritual heritage of peoples" as well as indiscriminate attacks.

Protocol II Additional to the Geneva Conventions of 12 August 1949, and relating to the Protection of Victims of Non-International Armed Conflicts

Addresses the category of non-international armed conflict under the Geneva Conventions. While it narrowly defines what is "armed conflict not of an international character" it expands on the humanitarian protections available in such conflicts. It specifies the criteria for using the factors that have been used to interpret Common Article 3 for determining when non-international armed conflict takes place in the territory of a High Contracting Party between its armed forces and dissident or other organized armed groups in its territory.

Protocol of Amendment to the Charter of the Organization of American States (Protocol of Buenos Aires)

An amendment to the Organization of American States (OAS) Charter which had been signed in 1948. The Protocol was adopted in 1967 and entered into force in 1970. The Protocol of Buenos Aires created the General Assembly of the OAS as the ultimate organ of the organization. It also elevated the status of the existing Inter-American Commission on Human Rights to that of an organ of the OAS and called for the adoption of an American Convention on Human Rights.

Protocol of Buenos Aires

See **Protocol of Amendment to the Charter of the Organization of American States**.

Protocol relating to the Status of Refugees

An international instrument supplementing the Convention relating to the Status of Refugees of 28 July 1951. The Protocol extended the definition of refugee to cover any person who meets the definition under the Convention, irrespective of the dateline of 1 January 1951.

Protocol to Prevent, Suppress and Punish Trafficking in Persons, especially Women and Children, Supplementing the United Nations Convention Against Transnational Organized Crime

An instrument adopted by the UN General Assembly in 2000 as part of the effort to address trafficking of women and children. It defines trafficking in persons in Article 3 as "recruitment, transportation, transfer, harbouring or receipt of persons, by means of the threat or use of force or other forms of coercion, of abduction, of fraud, of deception, or the abuse of power or of a position of vulnerability or of the giving or receiving of payments or benefits to achieve the consent of a person having control over another person, for the purpose of exploitation".

Protocol to the African Charter for the establishment of the African Court on Human and Peoples' Rights

This protocol to the African Charter on Human and Peoples' Rights was adopted in 1998 and entered into force in 2004. It established the African Court on Human and Peoples' Rights.

Protocol to the African Charter on Human and Peoples' Rights on the Rights of Women in Africa

This protocol to the African Charter on Human and Peoples' Rights was signed in 2003 and entered into force in 2005. It covers a broad range of rights for women, and includes an explicit reference to sustainable development in Article 19.

Provisional or Precautionary

These are requests to States from treaty bodies that they take action to protect alleged victims of human rights violations until a decision is made on the merits of their case. Provisional measures are provided under the Statute of the International Court of Justice and the Regulations of the Inter-American Commission on Human Rights (IACHR). The latter provide that the IACHR can request precautionary measures or ask the Inter-American Court of Human Rights to take protective action on an urgent basis in cases pending before the bodies. The purpose of the precautionary measures is to prevent irreparable mental or physical harm to individuals and they are taken without prejudice to future decisions on the merits. Other treaty bodies and the European Court of Human Rights have also issued provisional measures often called "Interim Measures" in individual petitions. Questions have arisen as to whether failure to comply with provisional measures is a violation of the treaty involved. It is clear that this is the case when the provisional measures are provided for in the treaty, but some treaty bodies have determined that it is a violation even when the treaty does not provide for them.

Public Emergency

One of the grounds permitting derogations from certain rights. For example, Article 4 of the International Covenant on Civil and Political Rights (ICCPR) provides for derogations for States Parties from their obligations under that treaty when a "public emergency which threatens the life of the nation and the existence of which is officially proclaimed ...". However, the derogation is only allowed to the "extent strictly required by the exigencies of the situation, provided that such measures are not inconsistent with" other obligations under international law and are not discriminatory. Further, the ICCPR also provides in Article 4(2) that States Parties may not derogate from certain rights even in a public emergency and Article 4(3) sets out notification requirements to other States Parties. The Human Rights Committee has further elaborated on the meaning of the various requirements including the definition of public emergency, the need for an official proclamation, the necessity and non-discrimination requirements, compliance with other international obligations, rights that cannot be derogated from and international notification. The European Court of Human Rights and the human rights bodies of the Organization of American States have also further defined these requirements.

Q

Quotas

A special measure for addressing discrimination primarily in relation to education, employment and public office. Generally, quotas require that members of groups that have been discriminated against with respect to those rights receive a certain number of positions or slots in relation to those rights. Several treaties provide that special measures do not constitute discrimination if they are being used to address legal or structural discrimination. Quotas can be controversial, but have been very useful in increasing the number of women in elected positions in a number of countries.

Quran

One of the holy books of Islam, which serves as the core of the Islamic faith as well as the main source of *shari'a*, or Islamic law. Along with the *hadith*, another source of Islamic law, it provides for fundamental principles guaranteeing individual and group rights. The protections include affirmation of human dignity; equality of humankind; the protection of minorities; freedom of conscience; the collective obligation to provide for the public welfare; the application of justice; the sanctity of life; the rights to property, privacy, education; and the duty to provide for future generations.

R

Rape

A crime involving non-consensual sexual acts committed by private actors and thus subject to jurisdiction of national criminal systems. Under human rights treaties, States Parties have the obligation to prosecute this crime. However, as this crime has also been committed during armed conflict, there has been a trend to hold private actors directly responsible under international law. The Statute of the International Tribunal for the Former Yugoslavia of 1993 was the first time rape was included as a crime within the jurisdiction of an international court. The Statute of the International Court of Justice includes rape, sexual slavery, enforced prostitution, forced pregnancy, enforced sterilization, or any other form of sexual violence of comparable gravity as crimes against humanity and war crimes, which can be prosecuted under the statute under the principle of complementarity when national systems are unwilling or unable to prosecute those crimes committed under its jurisdiction.

Ratification

One of the ways a country can become a party to a treaty. It is one of four such procedures mentioned in the Vienna Convention on the Law of Treaties whereby a State establishes at the international level that it consents to be bound by a treaty. Generally, the process for ratification is defined under the national law of each country though the Vienna Convention does provide definitions and international standards for the ratification process.

Recognition Before the Law, Right to

Article 6 of the Universal Declaration of Human Rights provides that everyone "has the right to recognition everywhere as a person before the law". This implicates a number of protections including those to security of person and criminal justice.

Refoulement

The forcible return of a person from one country to another upon a country's request usually to face criminal charges for acts committed in the latter. International treaties have been interpreted to prohibit the return of persons where there are substantial grounds to believe that they may be in danger of being subjected to torture if they are returned. See also **Extradition; Non-refoulement**.

Refugees

A group of persons entitled to protections under international law. Issues of refugee rights were the subject of the earliest efforts to identity and protect human rights. The Convention relating to the Status of Refugees defines a refugee as a person who "owing to the well-founded fear of being persecuted for reasons of race, religion, nationality, membership of a particular social group or political opinion, is outside the country of his nationality and is unable, or owing to such fear, is unwilling to avail himself of the protection of that country; or who, not having a nationality and being outside the country of his former habitual residence ... is unable or, owing to such fear, is unwilling to return to it". Refugees are entitled to certain protections including the rights to non-refoulement and non-discrimination.

Regional Groups (UN)

The United Nations was originally informally divided into geopolitical regional groups for purposes of membership in General Assembly committees. This system has expanded to include other purposes such as elections to UN-related positions, coordination on substantive policy and fronts for negotiating and voting. Working Groups of the Human Rights Council, for example, are made up of one representative of each of the five regional groups. The five groups are: the African Group with 54 Member States, the Asia-Pacific Group with 53 Member States, the Eastern European Group with 23 Member States, the Latin American and Caribbean Group (GRULAC) with 33 Member States, and the Western European and Others Group (WEOG) with 28 Member States and an observer.

Regional Human Rights Systems

State-based systems outside of the United Nations created to address human rights based on the major geographical regions of the world: Africa (under the African Union), the Americas (under the Organization of American States) and Europe (under the Council of Europe). Asian and Middle Eastern governments have not yet created human rights and norm-setting instruments or implementation procedures, though there are some sub-regional instruments, such as the Arab Charter on Human Rights and the Pacific Charter on Human Rights.

Rehabilitation of Offenders

The importance of social rehabilitation in the treatment of prisoners was first recognised by the 1955 Standard Minimum Rules for the Treatment of Prisoners (Rules 24, 61–64, 67, 75, 80). The International Covenant on Civil and Political Rights took this a step further, providing that the "reformation and social rehabilitation" of offenders shall be the "essential aim" of prison systems for adults (Article 10.3) and juveniles (Article 10.4). This principle is reaffirmed and developed by the Havana Rules, which indicate that juvenile prisoners "should be guaranteed the benefit of meaningful activities and programmes which would serve to promote and sustain their health and self-respect, to foster their sense of responsibility and encourage those attitudes and skills that will assist them in developing their potential as members of society". (Rule 12; see also Rule 3 and Article 40 of the Convention on the Rights of the Child.)

Religion, Freedom of

Article 18 of the Universal Declaration on Human Rights provides for the right to freedom of thought, conscience and religion. The right includes freedom to change religion, to express or practice alone or with others in public or private, and to manifest it in teaching, practice, worship, or observance. The freedom to change one's religion is controversial and that aspect was not included in the International Covenant on Civil and Political Rights. The Human Rights Committee (HRC) has interpreted the right as absolute but has limitations on the right to manifest it. Also, the HRC has interpreted the right to include the right not to profess any religion or belief as well to protect theistic, nontheistic and atheistic beliefs. Its General Comment 22 also notes that the right to have or adopt a religion or belief includes the freedom to choose or to replace one's religion or belief with another. It has also been interpreted to include the right to conscientious objection to military service. Religion is also protected in many anti-discrimination provisions of numerous international and regional treaties.

Remedy, Right to

Refers to the relief individuals are provided when there is a finding that their human rights have been violated. Article 8 of the Universal Declaration of Human Rights provides that everyone has a right to an effective remedy. Remedies in treaties are usually provided under individual complaint procedures and can range from pecuniary relief to orders calling for the cessation of the violations. Pecuniary relief can include reimbursement for costs and attorneys' fees as well as compensation for injuries suffered as a result of the violations. Specific orders to the government that it take actions to address the effects of the violations, such as resettlement assistance, clean-up of land and rivers damaged by non-state actors are remedies that have been provided for under some regional bodies such as the African Commission. Governments are also responsible for ensuring that there are national remedies available for addressing human rights violations.

Reservations

The Vienna Convention on the Law of Treaties defines this term as "a unilateral statement, however phrased or named, made by a State, when signing, ratifying, accepting, approving, or acceding to a treaty, whereby it purports to exclude or to modify the legal effect of certain provisions of the treaty in their application to that State". The Vienna Convention goes on to provide in Article 19 that reservations are not allowed if they are prohibited by the treaty, the treaty does not provide for that type of reservation, or they are incompatible with the object and purpose of the treaty. Articles 20–22 address various processes related to the acceptance and objection to reservations, the legal effects of reservations and objections to them, the withdrawal of reservations and objections, and the procedures for making reservations.

Respect

See **Responsibility to Respect, Protect and Fulfill**.

Responsibility to Respect, Protect, and Fulfill

This framework regarding the obligations of States with respect to human rights has developed from a 1983 report prepared by Asbjørn Eide, a member of the Sub-Commission on the Promotion and Protection of Human Rights, on the right to adequate food. It originally referred to four layers of State obligations that were later revised to the responsibility to respect, protect and fulfill. In general, the obligation to respect involves not taking measures that prevents access to rights; the obligation to protect requires that the State take measures so that private actors do not deprive individuals of access to rights; and the obligation to fulfill entails the requirement that the State take affirmative measures to ensure access to the rights. This framework has been used in a number of contexts including by the Special Representative of the Secretary General on Transnational Corporations and other Business Enterprises with Regard to Human Rights in carrying out his mandate and drafting the Guiding Principles on Business and Human Rights.

Rest and Leisure, Right to

Article 24 of the Universal Declaration of Human Rights provides that everyone "has the right to rest and leisure, including reasonable limitations of working hours and periodic holidays with pay". This right is reaffirmed in Article 7(d) of the International Covenant on Economic, Social and Cultural Rights.

Restorative Justice

Criminal justice systems have various aims, including deterrence, punishment or retribution and the prevention of reoffending by the rehabilitation or socialization of offenders. Restorative justice refers to procedures and measures that aim to repair the damage that crime has caused to individual victims or the community, and to give victims a greater role in the response to crimes. Restorative procedures, such as victim-offender mediation (VOM) and family group conferencing, require recognition of guilt by the offender and voluntary participation by the victim. Restorative measures include compensation of the victim, apologies and community service. The UN Economic and Social Council approved Basic Principles on the use of Restorative Justice in Criminal Matters in 2000.

Retroactive Punishment

Article 11(2) of the Universal Declaration on Human Rights and Article 15 of the International Covenant on Civil and Political Rights (ICCPR) prohibit holding someone guilty of any criminal offense for an act or omission which did not constitute a criminal offense at the time it was committed. It also prohibits imposition of a heavier penalty than one that was applicable at the time of the commission of the crime. However, under the ICCPR, the offender should benefit from changes in the law made after the commission of the crime that provide for a lighter penalty.

Rights

These are the entitlements or freedoms that persons or groups of persons have. The human rights treaties refer to them as rights, freedoms, or rights to freedoms. Rights involve more individually based rights while freedoms refer to concepts that include connotations to collective rights. However, the distinction is not always clear and the concepts are not treated uniformly by all treaties and instruments. Some rights are put in negative terms such as "no one shall be subjected to torture" or "no one shall be arbitrarily deprived of his property". Others are put in positive terms, such as "everyone has the right to an adequate standard of living". Some rights are recognized in the context of the State having an obligation to "undertake to ensure" a particular right such as the right of everyone to form trade unions, or propaganda for war shall be prohibited by law. Rights are also referred to in the context of positive rights, those covered in treaties or other instruments, and natural rights, those founded in an underlying moral imperative. See also **Freedoms**.

Rights of Athenian Citizens

One of the ancient codes that is said to be the basis for human rights concepts. Under Athenian law certain males were given certain citizenship rights, including the right to vote.

Right to a Defense

One component of the right to a fair and public hearing before an independent and impartial tribunal, in the determination of rights and obligations regarding criminal charges as set forth in Article 10 of the Universal Declaration on Human Rights. Article 14 of the International Covenant on Civil and Political Rights further lists the rights of individuals facing criminal charges including the right to be informed promptly of the charges, to have adequate time to prepare a defense, to consult with counsel and be appointed one if he or she cannot afford one, to defend oneself in person or through counsel, to examine witnesses, to have the assistance of an interpreter and the right not to testify against oneself or to confess guilt. The regional treaties include similar provisions.

Right to Counsel

One of the components to the right of a defense. Individuals charged with a crime are entitled to consult with counsel and to be appointed one if they cannot afford one themselves. Individuals also have the right to defend themselves before the court in person or through counsel.

Rio Declaration on Environment and Development (UN Conference on Environment and Development)

This declaration was adopted at the UN Conference on Environment and Development in 1992 in Rio de Janeiro, Brazil and was intended to build upon the Stockholm Declaration adopted in 1972. It made more explicit the international community's commitment to sustainable development by providing that human beings are the central concern of such development, that the right to development must be equitably fulfilled for present and future generations, and that environmental protection must be an integral part of the development process. See also **Agenda 21**; **Development, Right to**; **Declaration of the United Nations Conference on the Human Environment**.

Riyadh Guidelines

See **United Nations Guidelines for the Prevention of Juvenile Delinquency**.

Rome Declaration on World Food Security

International proclamation adopted at the World Food Summit, organized in 1996 in Rome by the United Nations Food and Agriculture Organization (FAO). The FAO called the Summit in response to widespread under-nutrition and growing concern about the capacity of agriculture to meet future food needs. The Declaration renewed the global commitment to the fight against hunger and reaffirmed the right of everyone to have access to safe and nutritious food. It also affirmed that food should not be used as an instrument for political and economic pressure. Heads of State and Government recognized the importance of international co-operation to achieve food security, and committed to make international efforts supplementing and reinforcing national action. In particular, they committed to attain the following goals: create the best political, social, and economic conditions for the eradication of poverty; pursue participatory and sustainable development policies; ensure that overall trade policies are fostering food security; prevent and be prepared for natural disasters and man-made emergencies; and promote optimal allocation of investments to foster human resources, sustainable food, agriculture, fisheries and forestry systems and rural development in all areas. The World Food Summit Plan of Action further defined those commitments in several detailed objectives and recommendations.

Rome Statute of the International Criminal Court

Adopted on 17 July 1998 by the UN Diplomatic Conference in Rome for the creation of the International Criminal Court. It entered into force in 2002. It provides jurisdiction for the Court for the following crimes: genocide, crimes against humanity, war crimes and crimes against aggression. It includes definitions for the first three crimes but provides that the latter crime cannot be the basis for jurisdiction until it is defined. The treaty provides for exercise of jurisdiction when a State Party or the Security Council refers a case to the Prosecutor or when the Prosecutor initiates a case under Article 15. The Rome Statute addresses admissibility issues as well as the responsibility of commanders and other superiors for acts committed under their command, authority, and control. See also **International Criminal Court**.

S

Safeguards Guaranteeing Protection of the Rights of Those Facing the Death Penalty

Adopted by the UN Economic and Social Council in 1984 and provides for protection of the rights of persons sentenced to death. They provide that the penalty should only be used for the most serious crimes committed with intent and with lethal or extremely serious consequences. Further, the penalty should not be used on offenders younger than 18 at the time of the commission of the crime. Other protections include the requirement that there be a final judgment, access to appeal and right to seek pardon or commutation and that it inflict the minimum possible suffering.

Sanctions

Measures that can be used by the UN Security Council in order to maintain or restore international peace and security. Article 41 of the UN Charter sets out the non-military measures that the Security Council may take to address threats to the peace, including "complete or partial interruption of economic relations and of rail, sea, air, postal, telegraphic, radio, and other means of communication, and the severance of diplomatic relations".

Sanitation, Right to

See **Water, Right to**.

Sankey Declaration

See **French Declaration of the Rights of Man and of the Citizen**.

Second Optional Protocol to the International Covenant on Civil and Political Rights, Aiming at Abolition of the Death Penalty

This is the second of two instruments that were added to the International Covenant on Civil and Political Rights (ICCPR) and is open for ratification to States Parties to the ICCPR. It entered into force in 1991. State Parties agree to take measures to abolish the death penalty within their jurisdictions. It does not allow for reservations for the protocol, except those made at the time of ratification or accession that provides for "application of the death penalty in time of war pursuant to a conviction for a most serious crime of a military nature committed during wartime".

Second World Conference on Human Rights

See **World Conference on Human Rights**.

Secretary General, UN

The name of the head of the Secretariat of the United Nations, one of the main bodies of the United Nations. Pursuant to the Charter of the United Nations, the Secretary General is appointed by the General Assembly upon recommendation of the Security Council for five-year terms. There are no limits to the terms, but thus far Secretary Generals have served only two terms. Article 98 of the Charter also indicates that the Secretary General is the Chief Administrative Officer of the United Nations and as such is responsible for overseeing all its organs including the Security Council, General Assembly, the Economic and Social Council and all their subsidiary bodies. Thus, the Secretary General plays a broad role in addressing human rights issues both by ensuring that the various bodies carry out their roles and by using their good offices in addressing and negotiating problems and violations related to human rights.

Security Council, UN

One of the main organs created under the United Nations Charter. Pursuant to Chapter V of the Charter its membership consists of five permanent members and ten non-permanent members elected for two-year terms by the General Assembly. Article 24 of the Charter confers upon the Security Council "the primary responsibility for the maintenance of international peace and security". Chapter VI of the Charter sets forth the terms and methods for the pacific settlement of disputes and Chapter VII provides for the actions the Security Council may take with respect to threats to the peace, breaches of the peace and acts of aggression. Thus, the

Security Council may authorize troops to protect human rights and take other military action for humanitarian intervention. The International Court of Justice has held that the use of force must be necessary and proportional to the threat.

Self-defense

The use of force is authorized by Article 51 of the UN Charter when necessary for self-defense which provides that there is a "right of individual or collective self-defense if an armed attack occurs against a Member of the United Nations . . .". The use of self-defense must be necessary and proportionate and directed against an imminent attack. The concept of self-defense also applies when individuals are charged with certain crimes.

Self-determination

The UN Charter Articles 1 and 55 call for the respect for the principle of self-determination of peoples but does not define it. Self-determination and decolonization were important issues at the UN during the drafting of the International Covenant on Economic, Social and Cultural Rights and the International Covenant on Civil and Political Rights and thus the right to self-determination appears in Article 1 of both. Both articles refer to the right in the context of the right of peoples to determine their political status and pursue their economic, social and cultural development and the right of peoples to freely dispose of their natural wealth and resources and to have their own means of subsistence. States Parties agree to promote the realization of the right to self-determination and to respect the right. To claim self-determination, a people should have significant ties of racial, linguistic, religious, cultural, economic and/or historical nature as well as a common economic base within a certain geographic area. While it is sometimes difficult to distinguish between peoples and minorities, only the former are entitled to the right to self-determination.

Self-executing Treaties

This doctrine relates to the application of treaties at the national judicial level. The concept generally provides that treaty provisions may be applied directly by national courts if they are clear enough so that implementing legislation is not necessary. Some countries require that the treaties be implemented by legislation regardless of whether they are clear enough.

Self-incrimination, Right Against

This is one of the entitlements to a minimum guarantee for a fair trial. Article 14(3)(g) provides that persons charged with a crime cannot be compelled to testify against themselves or to confess to guilt.

Servitude or Servile Status

This term refers to one of the components of slavery that is prohibited by numerous treaties and other international instruments.

Sex

This term refers to the gender of a person and is one of the prohibited enumerated grounds of discrimination in Article 2 of each of the Universal Declaration of Human Rights (UDHR), the two international covenants and numerous other international and regional human rights treaties. While some treaties specifically call for the prohibition of discrimination against women, the Convention on the Elimination of all Forms of Discrimination Against Women specifically embodies the principle of equality between men and women while prohibiting discrimination on the basis of sex.

Sexual Orientation

Pursuant to the Yogyarkarta Principles, this term refers to each person's capacity for emotional, affectional, and sexual attraction to, and intimate and sexual relations with, individuals of a different gender (heterosexual), same gender (homosexual or gay) or more than one gender (bisexual). While not listed as one of the prohibited categories of discrimination, it could be included in the category of "other status" in Article 2 of each of the Universal Declaration of Human Rights, the International Covenant on Economic, Social and Cultural Rights, and the International Covenant on Civil and Political Rights. Generally, at issue under law is whether homosexuals are entitled to protection from arbitrary discrimination in the exercise of their rights. The European Court of Human Rights has found that Article 8 of the [European] Convention for the Protection of Human Rights and Fundamental Freedoms protects the right to privacy of gay members of the armed forces. The United States Supreme Court has also decided that the United States Constitution's privacy provisions protect the right of heterosexual adults to engage in intimate, consensual conduct. Increasingly, national courts and legislatures have extended protection from discrimination to homosexuals, though international standards have developed more slowly. The Committee on Economic, Social and Cultural rights has issued General Comments on the rights to water, work and health that address the prohibition of discrimination on the basis of sexual orientation. The Committee on the Elimination of Discrimination Against Women has criticized States for discrimination on the basis of sexual orientation.

Signatory

The term used for a State that has signed a treaty. Signing a treaty is usually the first step towards ratifying or acceding to a treaty. Generally, a signatory is not obligated to comply with the provisions of the treaty, though there is a general obligation not to take steps that would violate the object and purpose of the treaty.

Single European Act (SEA)

This act was the first amendment to the original three foundational treaties of the European Union (EU). It was adopted in 1986 and established the free internal market in Europe and mentioned human rights. The Preamble mentions the promotion of democracy, the European Convention for the Protection of Human Rights and Fundamental Freedoms, and the European Social Charter. See also **European Union**.

Slavery

This practice is prohibited under Article 4 of the Universal Declaration of Human Rights and numerous other international instruments. Slavery has existed since ancient times but became the subject of an abolitionist movement in the early nineteenth century to stop the Atlantic slave trade and to free slaves in colonies of European countries and in the United States. The 1815 Declaration Relative to the Universal Abolition of the Slave Trade was the first of a number of instruments that include the prohibition of slavery. The first definition of slavery was adopted in the Slavery Convention of 1926 and was expanded upon in the Supplementary Convention on the Abolition of Slavery, the Slave Trade and Institutional Practices Similar to Slavery of 1956. Those combined definitions continue to be the basis for the prohibition of this practice in subsequent treaties. The practice has also been accepted as a crime against humanity. Despite the numerous efforts to abolish the practice, various forms of slavery remain.

Slavery, Servitude, Forced Labour and Similar Institutions and Practices Convention of 1926 (Slavery Convention of 1926)

This treaty was passed by the League of Nations in 1926 as part of its efforts to end slavery after World War I. It included the first definition of slavery in an international instrument: "the status or condition of a person over whom any or all the powers attaching the right of ownership are exercised". It also included definitions of slave trade and forced labor. While the Slavery Convention outlawed slavery and similar practices, it did not include a procedure for reviewing those practices in States Parties or a body that could evaluate allegations of violations. The League of Nations was able to encourage the abolition of slavery in several countries.

Slave Trade

One of the practices prohibited by Article 4 of the Universal Declaration of Human Rights. This was one of the terms originally defined by the Slavery Convention of 1926. The slave trade was defined as "all acts involved in the capture, acquisition, or disposal of a person with the intent to reduce him to slavery; all acts of disposal by sale or exchange of a slave acquired with a view to being sold or exchanged, and in general, every act of trade or transport in slaves". All these acts were prohibited by the treaty.

Social Rights

While the International Covenant on Economic, Social and Cultural Rights includes the group of social rights in its title, it does not define them. This grouping may encompass the right to a family, the right to education and the right to health.

Social Security

This right is provided by Article 22 of the Universal Declaration of Human Rights and Article 9 of the International Covenant on Economic, Social and Cultural Rights. Article 22 of the UDHR provides that it is entitled to realization through both national effort and international co-operation and is part of the rights that are indispensable for the dignity and development of personality of each person. The International Convention on the Elimination of All Forms of Racial Discrimination and the Convention on the Elimination of All Forms of Discrimination Against Women also provide for the right to social security as do some of the regional human rights treaties.

Soft Law

The body of law made up of non-treaty instruments such as declarations and resolutions of international bodies and decisions of international courts and tribunals. While not as authoritative as hard law, soft law can be used to establish customary international law and norms.

Sovereign Immunity

A theory of law that foreign sovereigns are entitled to immunity from suit. Under the restrictive interpretation of this concept, immunity is recognized for a State's public acts (*acta jure imperii*) but not its private acts (*acta jure gestionis*).

Specialized Agencies, UN

The name given to the various agencies of the United Nations that focus on specific topics that are also known as intergovernmental organizations.

They include: the International Labor Organization (ILO), the United Nations Children's Fund (UNICEF), the United Nations Educational, Scientific and Cultural Organization (UNESCO), the Food and Agricultural Organization (FAO), and the World Health Organization (WHO).

Special Measures

The name given to the obligation that States Parties have under a number of treaties to undertake action to meet the requirements of the treaty in question. For example, the International Convention on the Elimination of All Forms of Racial Discrimination requires that States Parties undertake special measures in order to reach the goals of attaining equality in the rights covered by the treaty. Treaties generally provide that special measures that are undertaken for this purpose do not constitute discrimination. Special measures are also referred to as affirmative action. See **Affirmative Action**.

Special Procedures

These are procedures created by the Commission on Human Rights and its replacement body the Human Rights Council to address human rights violations in specific countries through the appointment of a Special Rapporteur or thematic violations through the appointment of a Special Rapporteur, special representative, independent expert or Working Group. Generally, the mandate holders are given authority to investigate human rights issues related to a specific country or human right. They can conduct country visits if a country permits it and can respond to complaints by individuals. They prepare reports on their country visits as well as topics related to their mandates. See also **Special Rapporteur/ Representative/Independent Expert**; **Thematic Procedures**; **Working Group**.

Special Proclamation, Establishment of the International Tribunal for the Far East

A proclamation signed by General Douglas MacArthur, as Supreme Commander for the Allied Powers, on 14 January 1946 calling for the establishment of the International Tribunal for the Far East after World War II. Article 2 of the Proclamation provides: "The Constitution, jurisdiction and functions of this Tribunal are those set forth in the Charter of the International Military Tribunal for the Far East, approved by me this day." The Tribunal was made up of representatives of 11 States who considered war crime charges against 25 defendants in May of 1946. See also **Charter of the International Military Tribunal for the Far East**; **International Military Tribunal for the Far East (Tokyo Tribunal)**.

Special Rapporteur/Representative/Independent Expert

Titles given to the mandate holders of special procedures set up by the UN Commission on Human Rights and its replacement body the UN Human Rights Council. The resolutions have authorized country rapporteurs as well as thematic mandates relating to a broad spectrum of both civil and political and economic, social and cultural rights. Special Rapporteurs are usually the highest ranking procedures in that they have more resources available to them. The other two types of mandates are usually created to address broad topics, as is the case with the Special Representative of the Secretary General on human rights and transnational corporations and other business enterprises and the Independent Expert on minority issues. These thematic procedures analyze the human rights issues and problems related to violations and enforcement. They receive information from individuals and non-governmental organizations and try to address the specific cases. They generally visit two countries a year to address the rights falling within their mandates. While the special procedures report to the Human Rights Council, some also report to other bodies such as the General Assembly and the Security Council.

State Actors

Refers to persons and entities acting on behalf of governments. These actors are the ones primarily entrusted with the duty to respect, protect, and fulfill human rights obligations. They have the responsibility to carry out the State's obligations to ensure that non-State actors do not violate human rights and provide remedies for those whose rights are violated.

Stateless Person

Refers to persons who for various reasons may not have a nationality. The right to a nationality is recognized by many international instruments, although most of them do not clearly define the corresponding obligation of States regarding nationality. The reason for this is that there are two different systems for recognizing nationality, one based on place of birth (*jus soli*) and the other based on the nationality of one's parents (*jus sanguinis*). Article 15 of the Universal Declaration of Human Rights protects the right of everyone to a nationality and provides that persons may not be arbitrarily deprived of that right. It also recognizes the right to change one's nationality. Article 24 of the International Covenant on Civil and Political Rights and Article 7 of the Convention on the Rights of the Child provide that every child has the right to acquire a nationality, and Article 8 recognizes that nationality is part of the child's right to an identity, a concept not recognized by earlier human rights treaties. Article 7 of the Convention on the Rights of the Child also recognizes the link between mandatory birth registration and the right to acquire a nationality. Article 9 of the Convention on the Elimination of all forms of Discrimination Against Women provides that women may not be made stateless because of marriage. Article 34 of the Convention on the Status of Refugees and Article 32 of the Convention on the Status of Stateless persons obliges States Parties to facilitate the assimilation and naturalization of refugees and stateless persons, respectively. (Naturalization means giving nationality to someone who has not had that particular nationality since birth.) The Convention on the Reduction of Statelessness is the only international treaty that clearly defines the obligations of States to recognize nationality. Despite these mandates persons may end up in a stateless legal state as a result of armed conflict or disasters. Stateless persons are subject to protection under the mandate of the UN High Commissioner for Refugees, which estimates that there are 12 million stateless persons in the world. See also **Convention on the Reduction of Statelessness**; **Convention Relating to the Status of Stateless Persons**.

State of Emergency

Describes a situation declared by a government that allows for derogation of some human rights. In order to qualify as a state of emergency, the situation must involve a public emergency that threatens the life of the nation. Various instruments and international decisions have defined this to mean a threat to the whole population and the whole or part of the territory. Article 4 of the International Covenant on Civil and Political Rights (ICCPR) requires that the public emergency must be officially proclaimed. Derogations of rights under states of emergency must be required by the exigencies of the situation and cannot be discriminatory. Some instruments require that a State comply with its international obligations. Derogations are not allowed to certain rights, including the right to life, the prohibition of torture or cruel, inhuman or degrading treatment or punishment, the prohibition of slavery or involuntary servitude, and the prohibition of retroactive criminal law.

State Party

The name given to countries that ratify or become party to a treaty.

State Sovereignty

The concept that States have supreme authority or rule that cannot be impinged upon by the rights of individuals arose during the seventeenth century with the rise of nation States. Under this theory, efforts outside of the State to address human rights violations would violate the theory of sovereignty. During the eighteenth and nineteenth centuries, protection of certain individual rights began to arise first in the context of treatment of aliens abroad and religious minorities, as well as in efforts to abolish the slave trade and protect workers' rights. Theories of natural law that supported the concept that individuals are autonomous in nature also resulted in additional limits on sovereignty of the State.

Statute of Limitations

Refers in general to rules requiring that claims be brought before courts or tribunals within a certain time period. The Convention on the Non-Applicability of Statutory Limitations to War Crimes and Crimes Against Humanity of 1968 established that there was no statutory period of limitations for claims brought regarding war crimes or crimes against humanity. However, some treaties setting up procedures for filing petitions for human rights violations generally require they be brought in a timely manner, often within six months of notification by a domestic court or within a reasonable time of the occurrence as is required by Article 46(1)(b) of the American Convention on Human Rights and Protocol 11 to the [European] Convention for the Protection of Human Rights and Fundamental Freedoms.

Stockholm Declaration of the United Nations Conference on the Human Environment

See **Declaration of the United Nations Conference on the Human Environment**.

Sub-Commission on Promotion and Protection of Human Rights (formerly Sub-Commission on Prevention of Discrimination and Protection of Minorities)

This body was established in 1946. It reported to the UN Commission on Human Rights and was made up of 26 individual experts, nominated by their countries and voted on by the Commission. Throughout its existence, the Sub-Commission proved to be innovative in advancing human rights. It drafted a number of international instruments including those protecting disappeared persons, indigenous peoples, ethnic, religious and linguistic minorities as well as addressed topics such as corporate accountability. It also prepared groundbreaking studies on a number of topics such as the right to adequate housing, the right to food, the rights of non-citizens, the right to a fair trial and states of emergency. The Human Rights Council which replaced the Commission replaced the Sub-Commission with an 18-member Advisory Committee.

Summary Execution and Extrajudicial Killings

See **Arbitrary Killing or Execution**.

Supplementary Convention on the Abolition of Slavery, the Slave Trade, and Institutions and Practices Similar to Slavery

This treaty expanded the definition of slavery found in the Slavery Convention of 1926 in order to abolish practices identified as "servile status", which included debt bondage, serfdom, practices related to selling women into marriage and practices related to selling children for their labor.

Sustainable Development, Right to

This right involves the concept that the needs of present populations should be met without compromising the ability of future generations to meet their needs. None of the human rights treaties include a reference to either the right to development or sustainable development, but Article 55 of the UN Charter does commit the United Nations to the promotion of "conditions of economic and social progress and development". The right to sustainable development includes all rights with a focus on the right to a healthy development. It has been addressed in a number of environmental conferences including those held in Stockholm, Rio de Janeiro, and Johannesburg. See also **Development, Right to**; **Commission on Sustainable Development**.

T

Ten Commandments

One of the early religious codes that form the basis for the ideas behind human rights principles. As the summary of divine law given by God to Moses they were the basis for the ethical systems in Judaism, Christianity and Islam. The commandments include duties towards God, one's neighbors and society.

Terrorism

Despite a number of treaties authorizing the use of force to combat various aspects of terrorism such as the hijacking of airplanes, there is no internationally accepted definition of terrorism. After the 11 September 2001 attacks on the United States, several countries initiated a "war on terror" to justify the use of force against it, but questions have been raised as to whether terrorism qualifies as an international armed conflict or a non-international armed conflict under international humanitarian law (the four Geneva Conventions and two Additional Protocols). If it does not, then new rules must be developed to address under what circumstances the use of force is justified so that human rights are protected by State and non-state actors. Several international and regional treaties have attempted to define terrorism but some efforts have been criticized for being imprecise and not meeting the requirements of legality under either international human rights or humanitarian law. In 2003, UN Secretary General Kofi Annan initiated a High-Level Panel on Threats, Challenges and Change that offered the following for a definition of terrorism: (1) recognition that State use of force against civilians is regulated by the Geneva Conventions and can constitute a war crime; (2) a restatement that acts under the 12 anti-terrorism conventions are terrorism and are a crime under international law and are prohibited by the Geneva Conventions; (3) a reference to the 1999 International Convention for the Suppression of the Financing of Terrorism and Security Council resolution 1566 (2004); and (4) a description of terrorism as "any action, in addition to actions already specified by the existing conventions on aspects of terrorism, the Geneva Conventions and Security Council resolution 1566 (2004), that is intended to cause death or serious bodily harm to civilians or non-combatants, when the purpose of such an act, by its nature or context, is to intimidate a population, or to compel a Government or an international organization to do or to abstain from doing any act". These efforts are an indication of an emerging definition of terrorism under international law.

Terrorism Conventions

A dozen conventions on terrorism have been adopted by the United Nations: the 1963 Convention on Offences and Certain Other Acts Committed On Board Aircraft, the 1970 Convention for the Suppression of Unlawful Seizure of Aircraft, the 1971 Convention for the Suppression of Unlawful Acts Against the Safety of Civil Aviation, the 1973 Convention on the Prevention and Punishment of Crimes Against Internationally Protected Persons, including Diplomatic Agents, the 1979 International Convention Against the Taking of Hostages and the 1979 Convention on the Physical Protection of Nuclear Material, the 1988 Convention for the Suppression of Unlawful Acts Against the Safety of Maritime Navigation, the 1988 Protocol to the Convention for the Suppression of Unlawful Acts Against the Safety of Fixed Platforms Located on the Continental Shelf, the 1988 Protocol for the Suppression of Unlawful Acts of Violence at Airports Serving International Civil Aviation, the 1991 Convention on the Marking of Plastic Explosives for Purposes of Detection, the 1997 International Convention for the Suppression of Terrorist Bombings and the 1999 International Convention for the Suppression of Financing of Terrorism. Many of these treaties, in particular those two most recent, contain provisions concerning human rights. In 1996 the UN General Assembly established an Ad Hoc Committee that prepared the treaties adopted in 1997 and 1999, and continues to work on the preparation of a comprehensive treaty on international terrorism. The Council of Europe (CoE), the Organization of American States (OAS), the League of Arab States, the Organization of the Islamic Conference (OIC), the Organization of African Unity (now the African Union), the South Asian Association for Regional Cooperation (SAARC) and the Commonwealth of Independent States (CIS) also have all adopted treaties against terrorism.

Thematic Procedures

These procedures were set up by the Commission on Human Rights to address individual violations of human rights based on specific themes. The thematic rapporteurs and Working Groups have the ability to respond quickly to information of violations of human rights and have been successful in preventing or stopping them. The Commission created 26 thematic procedures. The earliest mandates were focused on civil and political rights, but eventually special procedures on economic, social and cultural rights were also established. The thematic procedures now report to the Human Rights Council which has created additional mandates.

Tokyo Tribunal

See **International Military Tribunal for the Far East**.

Torah

The first five books of the Jewish bible. It includes statements of law and ethics, as well as concepts of fairness, equality and human dignity. It is sometimes referred to as biblical law or commandments, and includes the Ten Commandments, one of the early religious codes that form the basis for the ideas behind human rights principles. See also **Bible**; **Golden Rule**; **Ten Commandments**.

Torture

Along with cruel, inhuman and degrading treatment, torture is prohibited by Article 5 of the Universal Declaration of Human Rights and Article 7 of the International Covenant on Civil and Political Rights. The Geneva Conventions of 1949 also prohibit torture during armed conflict. The Convention Against Torture and Other Cruel, Inhuman or Degrading Treatment or Punishment, which entered into force in 1987, defines torture in Article 1 as "any act by which severe pain or suffering, whether physical or mental, is intentionally inflicted on a person for such purposes as obtaining from him or a third person information or a confession, punishing him for an act he or a third person has committed or is suspected of having committed, or intimidating or coercing him or a third person, or for any reason based on discrimination of any kind, when such pain or suffering is inflicted by or at the instigation of or with the consent or acquiescence of a public official or other person acting in an official capacity. It does not include pain or suffering arising only from, inherent in or incidental to lawful sanctions."

Trade-Related Aspects of Intellectual Property

See **Agreement on Trade-Related Aspects of Intellectual Property Rights (TRIPS)**.

Trade Unions, Right to Join and Form

The right to join and form unions is one of the core aspects of the right to work. Article 23(4) of the Universal Declaration of Human Rights provides that everyone has the right to form and to join trade unions. The importance of this right is recognized in both International Covenants. Article 8 of the International Covenant on Economic, Social and Cultural Rights provides that States Parties have the obligation to ensure this right both at the national and international level and also provides for protection of the right to strike. Article 22 includes the right to form and join trade unions as part of the right to freedom of association with others. Restrictions of the right are only allowed when necessary for national security, public safety, public order, the protection of public health or morals, or the protection of the rights and freedoms of others. International Labour Organization instruments protect various aspects of this right as do numerous regional instruments.

Trafficking in Children and Other Persons

This is a human rights violation committed by private actors which involves transporting and selling children and other persons for exploitation for sexual, labor and other purposes. Article 6 of the Convention Against All Forms of Discrimination Against Women requires that States Parties suppress all forms of trafficking in women and Article 35 of the Convention on the Rights of the Child requires that States Parties take "national, bilateral, and multilateral measures to prevent the abduction of, the sale of or traffic in children for any purpose or in any form".

Treaties of Westphalia

Series of two peace treaties signed on 24 October 1648 in Germany and ending the Thirty Years' War. The treaties, jointly known as the "Peace of Westphalia", were each negotiated in a different seat of an Imperial prince-bishop in the land of Westphalia. The Treaty of Osnabrück was concluded between Emperor Ferdinand III and Queen Christina of

Sweden and their respective allies. The Treaty of Münster was adopted by Emperor Ferdinand III and the King of France, Louis XIV and their respective allies. The Treaties redesigned national boundaries within Europe, restored the Religious Peace of 1555 and extended religious toleration. They are also considered to have originated the modern concept of sovereign statehood and the international system of States. The foundation of this system is the sovereign character of the nation State in its territory and the exclusion of external actors from domestic affairs. These early rules of international law have been modified over time, however. The ratification of multiple international human rights instruments, binding on States Parties, has progressively eroded the long-standing principle against interference in the internal affairs of nation States.

Treaty

This is one of the names given to bilateral or multilateral agreements between nations that are intended to having binding legal effect between those who have formally agreed to them. Treaties are one of the main sources of international law. Bilateral treaties are agreements between two countries whereas multilateral treaties are between more than two countries. Nations that make treaties enforceable automatically in their national law are considered to take a monist approach to international law while those that require national legislation to enforce it directly are considered to take a dualist approach, though the latter countries are nonetheless consider the treaties binding between the governments.

Treaty-based Procedures

Treaties often provide for enforcement procedures. The main human rights treaties set up committees to enforce the treaties by reviewing reports prepared by the States Parties regarding their compliance with the treaties. These are called the treaty-based procedures, which in contrast with the UN Charter based procedures require ratification by countries before they can be used. The human rights treaty based procedures range from 2–4 years on how often States Parties must submit reports and very often the reports are not filed in a timely manner. The committees that oversee the treaties issue reports making recommendations to countries on how to meet better meet the obligations under the treaties. If the country has ratified optional protocols that provide for individuals to file petitions under the treaties, the committees also make decisions on the petitions.

Treaty Establishing the European Economic Community

See **Treaty on the Functioning of the European Union**.

Treaty of Maastricht

See **Treaty on European Union**.

Treaty on European Union

This international instrument was adopted by the members of the European Union in 1992 to mark a new stage in the process of European integration. Entering into force in 1993, the Treaty on European Union (TEU) is one of the main treaties of the European Union. The TEU confirms the members' attachment to the principles of liberty, democracy, respect for human rights and fundamental freedoms, and establishes that the Union's aim is to promote peace, its values and the well-being of its peoples. As amended by the Treaty of Lisbon of 2007, it provides for the accession of the Union to the Convention on the Protection of Human Rights and Fundamental Freedoms of 1950, and provides that the Union recognizes the rights, freedoms and principles set out in the Charter of Fundamental Rights of the European Union of 2000.

Treaty on the Functioning of the European Union (Treaty Establishing the European Economic Community)

This international instrument was adopted in 1957 as the Treaty establishing the European Economic Community, to lay the foundations of a union among the peoples of Europe. The Treaty entered into force in 1958. It was amended multiple times and renamed "Treaty on the Functioning of the European Union" (TFEU) in 2007 by the Treaty of Lisbon. Along with the Treaty on European Union, the TFEU is one of two main treaties on which the European Union is based. As amended by the Treaty of Lisbon, the TFEU provides for the accession of the Union itself to the Convention on the Protection of Human Rights and Fundamental Freedoms of 1950, and expresses the members' attachment to the fundamental social rights set out in the European Social Charter of 1961 and in the Community Charter of the Fundamental Social Rights of Workers of 1989. The TFEU also contains provisions addressing specific human rights issues, such as trafficking in human beings and sexual exploitation of women and children, the protection of human health, or access to justice.

Trusteeship Council

See **United Nations Trusteeship Council**.

Truth and Reconciliation Commissions

These bodies, also known as Truth Commissions, have been established since 1973 by presidential decree, legislative decision, non-governmental organizations and the United Nations to facilitate the process of reconciliation after periods of violence and grave human rights abuses. The main objectives of the Commissions have been to give individuals suffering from such abuses an opportunity to communicate their experiences to persons in authority and to receive collective acknowledgment of responsibility. The Commissions are generally temporary in duration and cover a specific period of time. Their mandates require the ability to access sensitive files and subpoena political figures as well as protection for commission members in order to be effective. They also necessitate a proper definition of the Truth Commission's scope, relevant time periods, areas of the country and types of acts that will be investigated.

Twelve Tables (Law of the Twelve Tables)

The ancient law that became the foundation for Roman law. Because they were the result of the struggles between the patricians and the plebeians, the Twelve Tables established procedural protections for Roman citizens in relation to the various classes. They were primarily definitions of private rights and procedures. The right to a speedy trial and the right of both parties to call witnesses were recognized, and the death penalty was applicable for false testimony and for corrupt judges. Provisions on criminal law banned laws directed against specific individuals and prohibited the execution of criminals who had not been convicted and the use of deadly force in the capture of criminals during daylight, unless the criminal offered armed resistance.

U

United Nations

This organization was created in 1945 following the end of World War II. Its main goals include maintaining international peace and security as well as protection of human rights. All countries of the world are members of this organization, which now number 193. The chief executive is the Secretary General and its main bodies include the Security Council, the General Assembly and the International Court of Justice. The General Assembly oversees various bodies that address human rights such as the Economic and Social Council and since 2006 the Human Rights Council (which replaced the Commission of Human Rights, created in 1945 to develop, promote, and oversee human rights). The international human rights treaty bodies, though set up by separate treaties, are overseen by the United Nations. The United Nations is based in New York, United States while the human rights work is based in Geneva, Switzerland. The International Court of Justice is based at The Hague, Netherlands where other tribunals also sit. Some of the specialized agencies have offices in other countries and there are United Nations field offices throughout the world fulfilling various aspects of its mandates.

United Nations Charter

See **Charter of the United Nations**.

United Nations Children's Fund (UNICEF)

The United Nations Fund for Children (formerly UN International Children's Emergency Fund) was established in 1946. UNICEF headquarters is located in New York. It has regional offices in Panama City (for Latin America and the Caribbean), Geneva (for the CEE-CIS region), Kathmandu (for South Asia), Bangkok (for East Asia and the Pacific), Amman (for the Middle East and North Africa), Dakar (for West and Central Africa) and Nairobi (for Eastern and Southern Africa) and field operations in some 150 countries. National Committees for UNICEF carry out fund-raising, public education and advocacy in another 36 countries. UNICEF activities cover education, especially for girls; child, adolescent and maternal health, emergency assistance in natural and man-made disasters and "child protection". Child protection includes a wide variety of activities and programs concerning the rights of children, in areas such as birth registration, adoption and alternative care, juvenile justice, and the abolition of violence against children, child marriage, child labor and trafficking of children. The budget and activities of UNICEF are approved by the Executive Board, which meets annually. UNICEF publishes the State of the World's Children annually.

United Nations Conference on Environment and Development

See **Rio Declaration**.

United Nations Conference on the Human Environment

See **Declaration of the United Nations Conference on the Human Environment (Stockholm Declaration)**.

United Nations Department of Economic and Social Affairs (UN DESA)

The mission of UN DESA is to promote development for all. It works within the framework of the UN Development Agenda on a broad range of issues, including poverty reduction, climate change, and sustainable development. It provides support to intergovernmental bodies within the UN on development issues and engages with a variety of stakeholders, including non-governmental organizations, the private sector, and academic institutions.

United Nations Educational, Scientific, and Cultural Organization (UNESCO)

A specialized agency of the United Nations which promotes rights to education and culture, based in Paris, France. It seeks to improve the quality of education, including educational innovation. It has also promoted numerous instruments defining and protecting the right to culture by promoting: that each culture has dignity and value which must be protected and preserved; that all people have the right and duty to develop their culture; and that all cultures form part of the common heritage belonging to all mankind. These efforts culminated with the adoption of the Universal Declaration on Cultural Diversity in 2001 which sets out the various aspects of that right.

United Nations Guidelines for the Prevention of Juvenile Delinquency

International standards known as the Riyadh Guidelines, adopted in 1990 by resolution of the United Nations General Assembly to prevent juvenile delinquency pursuant to a child-centered orientation. The Guidelines were developed by the Eighth United Nations Congress on the Prevention of Crime and the Treatment of Offenders. They complement the 1985 Standard Minimum Rules for the Administration of Juvenile Justice, known as the Beijing Rules. The Riyadh Guidelines recommend adopting preventive policies facilitating the socialization and integration of young persons through their family, the education system, the community and mass media. The Guidelines also recommend funding social services and ensuring that such resources reach and actually benefit young persons. Finally, they encourage the enactment of specific laws and procedures to promote and protect the rights and well-being of all young persons. The Riyadh Guidelines constitute a pro-active and comprehensive approach to juvenile delinquency.

United Nations High Commissioner for Human Rights (UNHCHR)

The UNHCHR's purpose is to coordinate and oversee human rights efforts at the UN and it is accountable to the UN Secretary General. The functions of the UNHCHR include: promotion of the universal enjoyment of all human rights as well as international co-operation on human rights; promotion of universal ratification of international standards; support of human rights organizations, including the UN Human Rights Council and treaty monitoring bodies; responding to serious violations of human rights; prevention of human rights violations; promotion of national human rights structures; education, advisory services, and technical assistance; and human rights field activities and operations.

United Nations High Commissioner for Refugees (UNHCR)

The Office of the UN High Commissioner for Refugees, also informally called the UN refugee agency, was established in 1950 to provide assistance to persons displaced by the Second World War and refugees from Eastern Europe. Its headquarters is located in Geneva, Switzerland and it has field offices and operations in some 126 countries. UNHCR's core mandate is defined by its Statute, the 1951 Convention on the Status of Refugees and the 1967 Protocol, which made the Convention applicable to refugees fleeing persecution in continents other than Europe. UNHCR provides material, legal and social assistance to refugees, asylum seekers and returnees. Asylum seekers are persons who have fled their country and seek refugee status, but whose claim has not been decided; returnees are refugees and asylum seekers who have returned to their country of origin, usually as the result of a change of government or the end of a conflict. During the last two decades the mandate of UNHCR has gradually been expanded to include internally displaced persons, in particular those who have fled persecution but remain within the territory of their own country. (Only in exceptional circumstances does it provide assistance to persons displaced by major natural disasters.) In 2011 it provided some form of assistance to nearly 34 million persons, including more than 10.5 million refugees and more than 14 million internally displaced persons. The Department of International Protection protects the rights of refugees through technical assistance, training, advocacy and legal assistance. The program and budget of UNHCR are approved by its Executive Committee, which meets annually. UNHCR received the Nobel Prize in 1954 and 1981.

United Nations International Children's Emergency Fund

See **United Nations Children's Fund (UNICEF)**.

United Nations International Commission of Inquiry on East Timor

In 1999 the UN Commission on Human Rights created this Commission of Inquiry to investigate breaches of humanitarian law in East Timor after January 1999 when residents there voted for independence from Indonesia. After the vote, pro-Indonesian militias had been involved in property destruction and human rights abuses. The Commission of Inquiry was made up of five distinguished individuals from Costa Rica,

Germany, India, Nigeria and Papua New Guinea. The Commission issued a report in 2000 with findings of major human rights and humanitarian law violations and recommended that the UN set up a tribunal to try to sentence the people responsible for the violations. The tribunal was not created because investigations and some prosecutions were carried out by the UN Transitional Administration in East Timor (UNTAET) and the Indonesian government.

United Nations Mission Interim Administration in Kosovo (UNMIK)

Established by the UN Security Council in June 1999. A month later the UN Secretary General asked UNMIK to re-establish a multi-ethnic judiciary in Kosovo. At first only local judges were used but after unrest in 2000, UNMIK appointed international judges and prosecutors to serve in the Kosovo judicial system. The judges could hear any cases brought before the courts and were not limited to addressing violations of human rights or humanitarian law. The international judges were perceived to be more impartial and less subject to pressure in dealing with cases involving different ethnic groups.

United Nations Office for Drugs and Crime (UNODC)

A UN office based in Vienna, Austria that is responsible for programs concerning international crime, in particular trafficking in drugs and persons, and terrorism. It also contributes to the development of international standards concerning crime prevention, law enforcement, corrections and the administration of justice, and technical assistance in these areas. It coordinates the UN Congresses on Crime Prevention and Criminal Justice (formerly Congresses on Prevention of Crime and Treatment of Offenders) that take place every five years, most recently in Salvador (Brazil) in 2010. It has coordinated the drafting of many human rights instruments, from the Standard Minimum Rules on the Treatment of Prisoners, adopted at the first Congress in 1955, to the UN Rules for the Treatment of Women Prisoners and Non-custodial Measures for Women Offenders (the Bangkok Rules), adopted by the UN Economic and Social Council in 2010. The work-plan and budget of the UNODC is approved by the UN Commission on Crime Prevention and Criminal Justice. UNODC coordinates the UN Crime Prevention and Criminal Justice Network, which includes the UN Interregional Crime and Justice

Research Institute (UNICRI) in Rome, and regional institutes in Helsinki (HEUNI), Kampala (UNAFRI), San José (ILANUD), Riyadh (NAUSS) and Tokyo (UNAFEI).

United Nations Rules for the Protection of Juveniles Deprived of their Liberty

International standards adopted by resolution of the United Nations General Assembly in 1990 to address the conditions and circumstances under which persons under the age of 18 are being deprived of their liberty. The Rules were developed by the Eighth United Nations Congress on the Prevention of Crime and the Treatment of Offenders. They complement the 1985 Standard Minimum Rules for the Administration of Juvenile Justice, known as the Beijing Rules. The Rules for the Protection of Juveniles Deprived of their Liberty are applicable to juveniles in penal institutions as well as children deprived of liberty on the basis of their welfare and health. They affirm that juvenile justice systems should uphold the rights and safety of juveniles and use imprisonment as a last resort. The Rules address specific issues faced by juveniles under arrest or awaiting trial, provide guidelines for the management of juvenile facilities and affirm certain human rights of juveniles in detention, such as the right to recreation, the right to practice a religion and the right to receive adequate medical care. They also address the rights of the detainee's family and stress that all juveniles should benefit from arrangements designed to assist them in returning to society.

United Nations Standard Minimum Rules for the Administration of Juvenile Justice (Beijing Rules)

International standards known as the Beijing Rules, adopted in 1985 by resolution of the United Nations General Assembly as a guide to amend existing national legislation, policies and practices. The Beijing Rules constitute the first international legal document to comprehensively detail norms for the administration of juvenile justice, drafted as a direct response to a call made by the Sixth United Nations Congress on the Prevention of Crime and the Treatment of Offenders, held in 1980. The Rules recognize that the young, owing to their early stage of human development, require particular care, assistance and legal protection. They provide guidance to States for the protection of children's rights in the administration of justice and for the respect for their needs in the development of separate and specialized systems of juvenile justice. The Rules address many aspects of the administration of juvenile justice, including investigation, prosecution, adjudication, disposition or sentencing and juvenile institutions. Although the Beijing Rules predate the Convention on the Rights of the Child of 1989, several of their fundamental principles have been incorporated into the Convention and they are expressly referred to in its Preamble.

United Nations Standard Minimum Rules for the Treatment of Prisoners

This is considered to be one of the prominent non-treaty human rights instruments. This document was adopted by the First UN Congress on Prevention of Crime and the Treatment of Offenders in 1955 and approved by the UN Economic and Social Council in 1955 and 1977. The instrument covers a broad range of protections for accused persons and prisoners, including food, clothing, hygiene, medical treatment and exercise. They focus on the reintegration and rehabilitation of the prisoner. They provide for the separation of convicted and untried persons as well as adults from children.

United Nations Transitional Administration in East Timor (UNTAET)

This body was set up by the UN in East Timor after an Australian led UN force went there in 1998 to end the violence that resulted after residents of East Timor voted for independence from Indonesia. The purpose of UNTAET was to re-establish the rule of law and set up institutions for its maintenance. It set up a commission to recommend candidates for judicial and prosecutorial offices as well as a court system. One appeal court was given jurisdiction to hear "serious crimes" including war crimes, crimes against humanity, murder, sexual offenses and torture. Since that court was only authorized to hear cases that took place from January–October 1999, the first Serious Crimes Panel was established in 2000. It applied the law of East Timor and used definitions of war crimes and crimes against humanity that were the same as those for the Rome Statute for the International Criminal Court. The Serious Crimes panel faced problems with issues related to whether the violations took place during war and the fact that many of the perpetrators were no longer in East Timor (or Timor-Leste as it was called when it became a nation in 2002). As a result, trials eventually took place under a Commission appointed by the government of Indonesia.

United Nations Trusteeship Council

This body was established in 1945 at the time of the founding of the United Nations, when approximately 750 million people were living under colonial rule and had not achieved their right to self-determination. Under the Trusteeship Council and its Special Committee on Decolonization, more than 80 former colonies gained independence from countries such as Belgium, England, France, the Netherlands, Portugal and Spain. While most of its work was accomplished by 1994 and it suspended its operations at that time, the Trusteeship Council continues to exist since it was created under the Charter of the United Nations.

United Nations Voluntary Fund for Victims of Torture

Fund established in 1981 by the UN General Assembly. Its purpose is to provide support to rehabilitation efforts and legal advocacy for victims of torture around the world.

Universal Declaration of Human Rights (UDHR)

The document drafted by the Commission on Human Rights and adopted by the General Assembly in 1948 that provided the authoritative definition of the human rights obligations under Articles 1, 55 and 56 of the UN Charter. It articulated the rights that had been at risk during the 1940s, such as: the rights to life, liberty and security of person; freedom of expression, peaceful assembly, association, religious belief and movement; and protections from slavery, arbitrary arrest, imprisonment without fair trial and invasion of privacy. However, the UDHR also included provisions for economic, social and cultural rights. The interrelationship of both sets of rights has subsequently been affirmed by the UN General Assembly and numerous other bodies. The UDHR set forth the core principles of international human rights law many of which are now considered to constitute customary international law. While the UDHR was limited by broad exclusions and did not include monitoring or enforcement provisions, it was the basis for subsequent treaties which further defined human rights and provided for enforcement mechanisms.

Universal Declaration on Bioethics and Human Rights

This international human rights proclamation adopted in 2005 by resolution of the General Conference of UNESCO provides guidance to States, individuals, communities, institutions and corporations with regard to ethical issues related to medicine, life sciences and associated technologies as applied to human beings. By enshrining bioethics in international human rights, the Declaration recognizes the interrelation between ethics and human rights in the specific field of bioethics. The Declaration establishes a series of principles to guarantee human dignity, human rights and fundamental freedoms. Those principles include consent to medical intervention, respect for human vulnerability and personal integrity, non-discrimination, promotion of health, sharing of benefits resulting from scientific research and protection of future generations. Together with the Declaration, the General Conference of UNESCO adopted a resolution which calls upon Member States to make every effort to give effect to the principles set out in the Declaration.

Universal Declaration on Cultural Diversity

Declaration adopted by UNESCO in 2005. It was derived from a number of earlier attempts to define and protect cultural rights. The Declaration affirms language rights, education and training that respect cultural identity, and the right to participate in cultural life and conduct cultural practices. It confirms the interrelated nature of cultural diversity and other human rights especially those associated with equal access to information and of expression, including multilingualism, equal access to art and to scientific and technological knowledge, including digital form, among those means that guarantee cultural diversity.

Universal Declaration on the Human Genome and Human Rights

International proclamation adopted by resolution of the General Conference of UNESCO in 1997 and endorsed by the General Assembly in 1998, with a view to promoting scientific and technical progress in the fields of biology and genetics in a manner respectful of fundamental rights. The Declaration aims at providing principles to inform policy-making at national, regional and international levels to ensure that human rights and human dignity are fully respected in the application of scientific and technological advances, particularly those which relate to the human genome. It recognizes the risks posed to fundamental values of human dignity and human rights if science is applied inappropriately, and therefore prohibits all forms of discrimination based on genetic characteristics as well as "practices which are contrary to human dignity, such as reproductive cloning of human beings". The Declaration provides other ethical safeguards such as prior-informed consent, confidentiality of data, reparation, protection of public health, and use of research for strictly peaceful purposes. It also includes principles such as benefit-sharing, freedom of research, and international co-operation. The Declaration has been used as a basis for further proclamations: the International Declaration on Human Genetic Data, the Universal Declaration on Bioethics and Human Rights and the United Nations Declaration on Human Cloning.

Universal Jurisdiction

The idea that persons accused of certain crimes may be prosecuted by any State, regardless of where the offense took place and the nationality of the perpetrator and victim(s). Customary international law recognizes universal jurisdiction for piracy. The Princeton Principles, drafted by a group of international experts in 2001, proposed that universal jurisdiction should also be recognized for slavery, genocide, torture, war crimes, crimes against peace and crimes against humanity. Strictly speaking, universal jurisdiction does not exist unless an offense may be prosecuted in every State. The term is frequently used in a broader sense, to refer to the gradual construction of worldwide jurisdiction through treaties, such as the Convention Against Torture, that recognize the jurisdiction of all States Parties over certain grave offenses, regardless of where they occur and the nationality of the perpetrator(s) and victim(s). Universal jurisdiction is an important tool against impunity that is most often recognized, in the second, broader sense, for crimes against humanity, especially grave violations of human rights and international terrorism.

Universal Periodic Review (UN)

This was a new mechanism established by the UN Human Rights Council after it replaced the Commission on Human Rights in 2006 pursuant to General Assembly Resolution 60/251, which called for a procedure based on universality of coverage and equal treatment of all countries. This mechanism reviews the human rights performance of all countries in the world every four years regardless of which treaties they have ratified. The purpose for creating this mechanism was to avoid the perception that political considerations were the reason why only certain countries had been the subject of review under the procedures of the Commission on Human Rights. The Universal Periodic Review, or UPR as it is commonly known, set up a process of constructive engagement based on the language in the General Assembly resolution which provided that it should be a "cooperative mechanism" that involves an "interactive dialogue" with the "full involvement of the country concerned". The guiding principles behind the UPR are universality, impartiality, objectivity, and non-selectivity. It has been referred to as a capacity building mechanism that will help States enhance their human rights commitments.

V

Vienna Convention on Consular Relations

A multilateral treaty that was concluded in 1963 and entered into force in 1967. It provides under Article 36 that non-citizens have a right to be notified of their right to communicate with consular officers of their country when detained. In a case filed by Mexico against the United States, the International Court of Justice (ICJ) ruled in 2004 that failure to provide this notice at the time of the arrest of the 52 Mexican citizens then on death row required that the United States provide a mechanism for review and reconsideration of the death sentences. The ICJ also recommended that States add a Vienna Convention notice similar to that required by the United States Supreme Court in *Miranda v. Arizona* at the time of the arrest of non-citizens.

Vienna Convention on Diplomatic Relations

A multilateral treaty concluded in 1961 which entered into force in 1964. It includes protections for the rights of diplomats in countries other than their own. In 2005, the ICJ ruled that the armed forces of the Democratic Republic of the Congo violated this treaty when they attacked the diplomatic property of Uganda.

Vienna Convention on the Law of Treaties

A multilateral treaty concluded in 1969 which entered into force in 1980. It provides for standards for interpreting treaties. It includes the following: definitions of terms relevant to international law; the capacity of States to conclude treaties, means of adoption, expressing consent and ratification of treaties; procedures for making, accepting and objecting to reservations as well as the legal effects of reservations; application and general rules of interpretation of treaties; and the invalidity, termination and suspension of the operation of treaties. While not all countries have ratified this treaty, many of its provisions are considered to be customary law for interpreting treaties.

Vienna Declaration and Programme of Action

See **World Conference on Human Rights**.

Violence Against Children

The Convention on the Rights of the Child contains several provisions concerning the right of children to protection from violence. Article 38 prohibits torture and other cruel, inhuman or degrading treatment or punishment; Article 34 obliges States to protect children from sexual abuse; Article 28 provides that disciplinary methods used in schools must respect the dignity of children; Article 24 calls for the abolition of harmful traditional practices; and Article 19 obliges the State to protect children from "all forms of physical or mental violence, injury or abuse, neglect or negligent treatment, maltreatment or exploitation, including sexual abuse, while in the care of parents" or other carers. In 2003 the Secretary General appointed a Special Representative who coordinated preparation of the 2006 World Report on Violence Against Children. The report embraces the broad definition contained in Article 19 of the Convention and applies it more broadly, urging a comprehensive global effort to banish "all forms of violence against children, in all settings". A second Special Representative of the Secretary General on Violence Against Children was appointed in 2009 to continue efforts to advocate for and support implementation of the recommendations contained in the 2006 Report. She reports annually to the Security Council and General Assembly.

Violence Against Women

All the major treaties prohibiting torture and other cruel, inhuman and degrading treatment or punishment apply equally to men and women and thus violence against women is prohibited. Nonetheless, women are often subject to practices that can constitute violence against them. This was recognized by the Commission on Human Rights which established a Special Rapporteur for addressing violence against women in 1994. This mandate has been continued by the Human Rights Council that replaced the Commission. The Special Rapporteur has investigated reports of violence against women and has prepared reports further elaborating on what constitutes violence against women. The UN Commission on the Status of Women also addresses this topic on a regular basis.

Vote, Right to

Article 21 of the Universal Declaration of Human Rights refers to the right of everyone to take part in government directly or through freely chosen representatives and that the basis of government shall be the will of the people "expressed in periodic and genuine elections which shall be by universal and equal suffrage and shall be held by secret ballot or by equivalent free voting procedures". While this provision does not guarantee a democracy, it does provide for public participation in government and voting rights for "every citizen", recognizing that this is one right where non-citizens can be treated differently. Like all rights, limitations are only allowed under Article 29 "as determined by law solely for the purpose of securing due recognition and respect for the rights and freedoms of others and of meeting the just requirements of morality, public order and the general welfare in a democratic society". Article 25 of the International Covenant on Civil and Political Rights further codifies the principles of public participation and voting. The Human Rights Committee that oversees compliance with that treaty has confirmed in a general comment that Article 25 lies at the core of democratic government and is consistent with the right to self-determination. It has confirmed in decisions that Article 25 does not guarantee the right to direct participation, but regardless of the system of government must provide for the participation of minority groups.

W

War Crimes

Crimes defined by international humanitarian law, or the law of war, the branch of international law that governs the conduct of armed conflict (and occupation). The Rome Statute of the International Criminal Court contains a long list of war crimes, divided into four categories: grave breaches of the 1949 Geneva Conventions; other serious violations of the "laws and customs" applicable to international armed conflicts; serious violations of Common Article 3 of the Geneva Conventions committed against non-combatants during non-international armed conflicts; and other serious violations of the laws and customs applicable in non-international armed conflicts (Article 8). Acts against the person that constitute war crimes regardless of the nature of the conflict in which they occur include: murder, mutilation, torture and cruel, humiliating and degrading treatment; rape or any other form of sexual violence; hostage-taking; execution without a sentence imposed by a regularly court affording all indispensable guarantees of due process; attacks against the civilian population or individual civilians not taking direct part in hostilities; displacement of the civilian population without compelling reasons; conscripting or enlisting children under the age of 15 years; and killing or wounding through treachery (for example, improper use of a flag of truce, an enemy flag or uniform, the Red Cross or Crescent, UN flag or emblems). The legal standards concerning international armed conflicts are more comprehensive, especially with regard to the methods of combat and treatment of prisoners of war. Acts recognized as war crimes in international conflicts include: killing or wounding a combatant who has surrendered; the use of poisonous gas, poisoned weapons, "dum-dum" bullets or any weapon, material or methods of warfare likely to cause superfluous injury or unnecessary suffering or which are inherently indiscriminate; launching an attack knowing that it will cause loss of life or injury to civilians, damage to civilian objects or widespread, long-term and severe damage to the natural environment clearly excessive in relation to the military advantage anticipated; and compelling a prisoner of war to serve in enemy forces or depriving him or her of the rights of fair and regular trial. Other acts that constitute war crimes whether they occur in an international or non-international conflict include pillage and extensive, unlawfully and wanton destruction or appropriation of property unjustified by military necessity; attacks against hospitals, ambulances, medical personnel marked by the Red Cross or Red Crescent; attacks against personnel, installations, material, units or vehicles involved in humanitarian assistance or peacekeeping missions; and attacks against buildings dedicated to religion, education, art, science or charitable purposes, historic monuments, hospitals and places where the sick and wounded are collected, provided they are being used for military purposes.

Water, Right to

While water is clearly a human need, this right was not specifically included in the Universal Declaration of Human Rights or the Covenant on Economic, Social and Cultural Rights. The Committee on Economic, Social and Cultural Rights issued General Comment 15 in 2002 to address the right to water. The General Comment notes that water is needed to realize a number of other rights such as those to food, health and work, and to enjoy certain cultural practices. Several international and regional human rights treaties do refer to the right to water, including the Convention on the Elimination of all Forms of Discrimination Against Women, the Convention on the Rights of the Child, the Geneva Conventions for the protection of victims of armed conflict, and the African Charter on the Rights and Welfare of the Child. Resolutions of various UN bodies have also addressed the right to water. In 2010 the General Assembly passed a resolution that recognized the rights to water and sanitation.

Western European and Others Group (WEOG)

One of the five regional groups at the United Nations. This group consists of the Western European countries, Australia, Canada and New Zealand for a total of 28 States. The United States of America participates on some matters with this group as does Israel. See also **Regional Groups (UN)**.

Westphalia, Treaties of

See **Treaties of Westphalia**.

Women

One of the groups of persons protected by anti-discrimination language in the Universal Declaration of Human Rights, which specifically prohibits discrimination on the basis of sex. The same non-discrimination language was included in the two Covenants as well as other treaties protecting specific rights. In 1981 the Convention on the Elimination of all Forms of Discrimination Against Women entered into force. This treaty provides for broad protection against discrimination against women as well as affirmative obligations for governments to take steps to ensure equality for women in all rights. It also adds new obligations such as the taking of measures to suppress all forms of trafficking in women and exploitation of prostitution of women. It is one of the most widely ratified human rights treaties with only a handful of countries that have yet to become party to it.

Working Group (UN)

The name given to one of the thematic mandates created by the Commission on Human Rights and its replacement body the Human Rights Council. The Working Groups were created to cover thematic issues deemed to be of great importance since they usually have five members instead of the single person responsible for the mandates covered by Special Rapporteurs and independent experts. The five members represent the five groups of the UN: African, Asia-Pacific, Latin American and Caribbean (GRULAC), Eastern European and Western European and Others (WEOG). Like other special procedures, Working Groups can investigate violations, make country visits and prepare reports on topics related to the mandate.

Working Group on Arbitrary Detention (UN)

This special procedure was established in 1991 as one of the thematic procedures of the Commission on Human Rights. It now reports to the Human Rights Council. Since arbitrary detention was not defined by the major treaties, the Working Group has provided a detailed body of standards for defining what constitutes arbitrary detention. It also has investigated a number of complaints from people claiming that they were subject to arbitrary detention.

Working Group on Enforced or Involuntary Disappearances (UN)

This thematic procedure was established in 1982 by the Commission on Human Rights and it now reports to the Human Rights Council. The mandate of this Working Group is to investigate claims of persons who have allegedly disappeared due to governmental action. Like other special procedures it can do so by raising cases with the government and visiting countries if invited by governments. Like other thematic procedures, this Working Group can also prepare general reports and develop standards regarding the violation of rights implicated in the disappearances of individuals. In 1986, the Working Group improved the effectiveness in reporting these violations by using graphs to demonstrate recent disappearances in certain countries.

Working Group on Human Rights and Transnational Corporations (UN)

The most recent thematic procedure established by the Human Rights Council in June 2011. Its mandate is to promote the Guiding Principles on human rights and business developed by the Special Representative of the Secretary General on business and human rights.

Working Group on Indigenous Populations (UN)

Working Group established by the Sub-Commission on Promotion and Protection of Human Rights in 1982. It worked on the Declaration on the Rights of Indigenous Peoples from 1985 to 1993 when the document was submitted to the Sub-Commission which then submitted it to the Commission on Human Rights in 1994. After the Human Rights Council replaced the Commission the mandate of this Working Group was reviewed as some countries argued that it duplicated the work of the United Nations Permanent Forum on Indigenous Issues (UNPFII). Indigenous peoples and non-governmental organizations were successful in arguing that UNPFII was not a human rights body and that the Working Group was the only body within the UN addressing standard setting for indigenous persons, and while the Working Group was disbanded, it was replaced by the Expert Mechanism on the Rights of Indigenous Peoples.

Working Group on People of African Descent (UN)

Working Group established by the Commission on Human Rights in 2002 following the recommendation made at the World Conference Against

Racism, Racial Discrimination, Xenophobia, and Related Intolerance held in Durban, South Africa in 2001. Since 2006 it has reported to the Human Rights Council and continues to address complaints regarding discrimination and issues related to the topics in its mandate.

Work-related Rights

Article 23 of the Universal Declaration of Human Rights provides for the right to work, to free choice of employment, to just and favorable conditions of work and to protection against unemployment. It also provides for the right to equal pay for equal work, as well as just and favorable remuneration, including supplementation if necessary by social protection. It further provides for the right to form and join trade unions. These rights are further elaborated in the two International Covenants and numerous instruments of the International Labor Organization. The International Covenant on Economic, Social and Cultural Rights (ICESCR) recognizes the right to work in Article 6 where it also lists the steps that a State Party should take to achieve the full realization of this right. In Article 7, the IESCR recognizes the right to just and favorable conditions of work, which includes equal pay for equal work, provision for a decent living, safe and healthy working conditions, equal opportunity for promotion, and rest, leisure and reasonable limitation of working hours with pay for holidays. Article 8 of the IESCR recognizes the right to form and join trade unions. The International Covenant on Civil and Political Rights (ICCPR) prohibits slavery, servitude and forced or compulsory labor. Article 22 recognizes the right to freedom of association with others including the right to form and join trade unions. Besides noting that restrictions of this right can only be those that are necessary in the interest of national security or public safety, public order, or protection of public health or morals or the rights and protection of the rights and freedoms of others, it acknowledges the rights in the International Labour Organization Convention of 1948 concerning Freedom of Association and Protection of the Right to Organize (ILO Convention No. 87).

World Bank (International Bank for Reconstruction and Development)

Along with the International Monetary Fund (IMF), this is one of the two intergovernmental financial institutions created after World War II by the Bretton Woods Agreements. Pursuant to its Articles of Agreement, the purposes of the World Bank include: to assist in the development of its members; to promote private investment; to promote balanced growth of international trade and maintain equilibrium in balances of payments; and to conduct its operations with due regard to the effect of international investment on business conditions in members' territories. It shares common goals of furthering international trade and economic development with the IMF and the World Trade Organization (WTO). While the founding documents of these three bodies do not explicitly mention human rights, the call for "development" or "balanced growth" could be read to include human rights in light of the fact that the UN Charter has been ratified by all nations that are States Parties to these organizations. Despite this, the World Bank, IMF and WTO have been criticized for promoting policies that have made it difficult for States Parties to fulfill their human rights obligations.

World Conference Against Racism, Racial Discrimination, Xenophobia, and Related Intolerance

This conference was held in Durban, South Africa in 2001. It was attended by nearly 19,000 people and delegates from 146 countries took the floor during the plenary session of the conference and representatives from 125 non-governmental organizations (NGOs) also spoke. The conference was initially sidetracked by the walk-out by the United States delegation due to various proposals that were marred by anti-Semitism. However, the outcome document, the Durban Declaration and Programme of Action of the World Conference Against Racism recognizes concern about anti-Semitism and Islamophobia in various parts of the world and called upon States, United Nations bodies and specialized agencies, international and regional organizations, youth and civil society to take an active part in the process for ending the "scourges of racism, racial discrimination, xenophobia, and related intolerance". The Conference also discussed reparations for slavery and the transatlantic slave trade. See also **Durban Declaration and Programme of Action of the World Conference Against Racism**.

World Conference on Human Rights

The first World Conference on Human Rights was held in Teheran, Iran in 1968 to celebrate the twentieth anniversary of the Universal Declaration of Human Rights (UDHR). The outcome document of the World Conference proclaimed the importance of the UDHR and reaffirmed that it constitutes an obligation for the members of the international community. The Second World Conference Human Rights was held in Vienna, Austria in 1993. Seven thousand persons representing 171 countries and more than 800 non-governmental organizations attended. Its outcome document is called the Vienna Declaration and Programme of Action of the World Conference on Human Rights, which called for a "commitment to women's equality and the human rights of women". It also recommended the establishment of the UN High Commissioner for Human Rights which the General Assembly implemented that same year. Another important issue that was discussed was whether rights should be limited in their cultural context which was resolved with the declaration that: "All human rights are universal, indivisible and interdependent."

World Conferences

Large-scale conferences held by the United Nations on human rights issues which have become a way for strengthening and developing international human rights law. The concluding documents from these conferences are not binding on countries, but they have played an important role in framing the relevant UN human rights laws and programs. The first World Conference on Human Rights was held in Teheran, Iran in 1968 to celebrate the twentieth anniversary of the Universal Declaration of Human Rights. The Second World Conference was held in Vienna, Austria in 1993. Since then there have been nine world conferences on human rights topics: UN Conference on Environment and Development (UNCED, Earth Summit) (Rio de Janeiro, 1992); the International Conference on Population Development (Cairo, 1994); the World Conference on Women (Beijing, 1995); the World Summit on Social Development (Copenhagen, 1995); the World Food Summit (Rome, 1996); Habitat II (Istanbul, 1996); the World Conference Against Racism, Racial Discrimination, Xenophobia, and Related Intolerance (Durban, 2001); the World Summit on Sustainable Development (Johannesburg, 2002); and the Small Arms Review Conference (New York, 2006). Follow-up conferences to assess progress on some of the issues discussed in these conferences have taken place every five or ten years. Outcome documents from those conferences also help to further define standards and encourage progress on various issues.

World Conferences on Women

The UN Commission on the Status of Women (CSW) has organized the following World Conferences on Women: Mexico (1975); Copenhagen (1980); Nairobi (1985); and Beijing (1995). The outcome documents from the 1995 conference are called the Beijing Declaration and Platform for Action. The first review in 2000, called Beijing+5, was held as a Special Session of the General Assembly with the CSW acting as the Ad-Hoc Preparatory Committee. Since then, the CSW has held a review conference at its annual session every five years. The CSW adopts resolutions and agreed conclusions at these review sessions that continue to identify gaps in protection of women's rights and call for increased implementation of the 12 critical areas of concern identified in the Beijing Platform for Action. See also **Beijing Declaration and Platform for Action**.

World Declaration on Education for All

International human rights proclamation adopted in 1990 by the United Nations World Conference on Education for All, convened jointly by UNICEF, UNDP, UNESCO and the World Bank. The World Declaration on Education for All, along with the Framework for Action to Meet Basic Learning Needs, are products of a wide process of consultation conducted in 1989 and 1990 under the auspices of an inter-agency commission. Earlier drafts of the documents were discussed at nine regional and three international consultations by experts and representatives from governments, inter-governmental and non-governmental organizations, development agencies and research institutes. The elected rapporteurs of the consultations met as a Working Group to advise the inter-agency commission regarding the two texts for submission to the World Conference. As adopted, the Declaration aims at promoting basic education of children, youths and adults. It reaffirms that education is a fundamental right, and provides several recommendations, including the broadening of the concept of basic education, the strengthening of partnerships between educational authorities, the development of supportive social, cultural, and economic policies, the mobilization of financial and human resources and the strengthening of international solidarity.

World Federation of Trade Unions

International labor organization founded in Paris on 3 October 1945 by the World Trade Union Congress, to combat war and fascism and to advocate for the rights of workers. The Federation was initially oriented toward the Soviet Union, and despite attempts to reconcile the differences between communist and noncommunist factions within the organization, the intensification of the Cold War finally led to a split. The non-communist elements withdrew and in 1949 formed the International Confederation of Free Trade Unions. Today, the World Federation of Trade Unions is headquartered in Athens, Greece, although its largest affiliates are found in Asia, Latin America and Africa. It holds consultative status with several UN agencies. Its current priorities include following principles of class struggle and militant orientation, insuring the independence of trade union organizations from monopolies and transnational corporations and guaranteeing trade union liberties.

World Food Conference

International conference held in 1974 in Rome under the auspices of the United Nations Food and Agriculture Organization. The Conference was entrusted by the General Assembly with developing means whereby the international community could take specific action to resolve the world food problem within the broader context of development and international economic co-operation. It adopted the Universal Declaration on the Eradication of Hunger and Malnutrition, which proclaimed that "every man, woman and child has the inalienable right to be free from hunger and malnutrition in order to develop their physical and mental faculties". The Conference also recommended the establishment of a World Food Council.

World Food Summit

International conference held in 1996 in Rome under the auspices of the United Nations Food and Agriculture Organization, which called the Summit in response to widespread under-nutrition and growing concern about the capacity of agriculture to meet future food needs. The Summit let to the adoption of the Rome Declaration on World Food Security and the World Food Summit Plan of Action. Countries renewed their commitment to eradicate hunger worldwide. They also agreed to work to reverse the decline in funding for agriculture, to improve governance of global food issues in partnership with relevant stakeholders, and to proactively face the challenges of climate change to food security. In 2002, the FAO held another international conference entitled "World Food Summit: five years later", to examine the progress made since 1996 in eradicating hunger and to consider ways to accelerate these efforts.

World Health Organization (WHO)

The United Nations agency responsible for providing leadership on global health matters, shaping the health research agenda, setting norms and standards in the area of public health, articulating policy options, providing technical support to countries and monitoring and assessing health trends. The organization was established on 7 April 1948, when its constitution came into force. It is headquartered in Geneva, Switzerland. Since its creation, it has been credited for playing a leading role in the eradication of smallpox. Its current priorities include: combating communicable diseases, in particular, HIV/AIDS, malaria and tuberculosis; promoting access to drinking water and sanitation; improving maternal and child health; eradicating polio; and developing partnerships for development. WHO publishes the World Health Report, which focuses on a specific subject every year.

World Summit for Social Development

International conference held in 1995 in Copenhagen, Denmark, to recognize the significance of social development and human well-being, and largely attended by world leaders. Governments reached a consensus on the need to put people at the center of development. The Summit pledged to make the eradication of poverty, the goal of full employment and the fostering of social integration overriding objectives of development. At the conclusion of the Summit, the delegates agreed on the adoption of the Copenhagen Declaration on Social Development, and the Programme of Action of the World Summit for Social Development. In 2000, they reconvened in Geneva to review what has been achieved in five years, and to commit to new initiatives.

World Summit on Sustainable Development

International conference held in 2002 in Johannesburg, South Africa, to focus the world's attention and direct action toward improving people's lives while conserving natural resources in a world with ever-increasing demands for food, water, shelter, sanitation, energy, health services and economic security. Ten years after the Conference on Environment and Development held in Rio, the international community reviewed the progress made since 1992. Unlike its predecessor, the Johannesburg Summit was primarily concerned with implementation rather than with setting new goals, although a number of new targets were agreed upon, for example on sanitation. The Summit issued the Johannesburg Declaration which includes a series of commitments in five priority areas: health, water, energy, agriculture and biodiversity, and establishes the Plan of Implementation of the World Summit on Sustainable Development.

World Trade Organization (WTO)

International organization aiming at liberalizing international commerce and providing a multilateral forum for governments to negotiate trade agreements and settle international trade disputes. Since 1948, the General Agreement on Tariffs and Trade had provided the rules for the current WTO system, but the organization was itself created in 1995. Headquartered in Geneva, Switzerland, the organization oversees the implementation of the agreements negotiated under its auspices, and which increasingly include human rights provisions. These safeguards range from privacy rights to political participation, due process, access to information, cultural rights, indigenous rights and access to affordable medicines, among others. However, in the face of recurring accusations denouncing the ill-effects of free trade on human rights, the organization has had to defend its role and its reputation in this regard.

X

Xenophobia

This word comes from two Greek words: "xenos", meaning foreigner or stranger, and "phobos", meaning fear. Dictionary definitions include an unreasonable fear or hatred of foreigners or strangers, or an unreasonable fear or hatred of the unfamiliar, especially other races. Xenophobia is often aimed at immigrants, but it can also be directed at groups within society that have been present for centuries. While the prohibition against xenophobia was not included in early documents prohibiting discrimination, including the Universal Declaration of Human Rights, norms that prohibit discrimination on the ground of national origin or nationality, such as Universal Declaration of Human Rights, Article 2; International Covenant on Civil and Political Rights, Article 2.1; International Covenant on Economic Social and Cultural Rights, Article 2.2; and the International Convention on the Elimination of all Forms of Racial Discrimination, Article 1, define discrimination on grounds of national origin as a form of racial discrimination. When the UN Commission on Human Rights created the special procedure to address racism in 1993, it named it the Special Rapporteur on contemporary forms of racism, racial discrimination, xenophobia and related intolerance. One of the specific mandates of the Special Rapporteur is to focus on the phenomena of xenophobia. The Commission began to define the various contexts in which xenophobia arises and called for governments to prohibit and prevent it. In 1999 the term was also included in the first world conference on the topic: the World Conference Against Racism, Racial Discrimination, Xenophobia, and Related Intolerance which was held in 2001, and has been included in numerous other documents addressing discrimination since.

Y

Yogyakarta Principles on the Application of International Human Rights Law in relation to Sexual Orientation and Gender Identity

Principles adopted at a conference organized by two non-governmental organizations (NGOs) at Gadja Mada University in Java, Indonesia in 2006. They are named after the province in Indonesia. They were signed by 29 human rights experts from around the world, including Mary Robinson, the former UN High Commissioner for Human Rights. The document is not a treaty but the Yogyakarta Principles are intended to act as interpretive guides for treaties. They were drafted in response to violations of a broad spectrum of human rights around the world on the basis of perceived or actual sexual orientation or gender identity. The completed Yogyakarta Principles were launched by the two NGOs in Geneva, Switzerland following a session of the UN Human Rights Council in March 2007. The document was presented at an event at the UN General Assembly in New York in November 2007 by a number of countries. In July 2010, the General Assembly Third Committee voted against adopting the Principles. The document includes 29 principles which cover a wide spectrum of human rights including those of redress and accountability. It also includes 16 recommendations addressed to a number of players in the human rights arena, including: national human rights institutions, professional bodies, funders, NGOs, UN agencies, treaty bodies, and Special Procedures.

APPENDIX

Emboldened documents are defined in the dictionary.
Citations and URLs are provided wherever possible.

1. **A Declaration of the Rights of Man**
   Description: Declaration prepared under the chairmanship of Lord Sankey, and originally drafted by H.G. Wells, in the United Kingdom. It became known as the "Sankey Declaration". It identified 11 fundamental human rights: the right to life, the protection of minors, the duty to the community, the right to knowledge, freedom of thought and worship, the right to work, the right to personal property, freedom of movement, personal liberty, freedom from violence, and the right of law-making.
   Date: Drafted in 1940.
   URL: http://www.voting.ukscientists.com/sankey.html (last visited 13 December 2012).

2. Abolition of Forced Labour Convention: See Convention Concerning the Abolition of Forced Labour.

3. Additional Protocol to the American Convention on Human Rights in the Area of Economic, Social and Cultural Rights
   Description: International human rights instrument ratified by members of the Organization of American States for the purpose of incorporating other rights and freedoms into the protective system of the American Convention on Human Rights. The Protocol recognizes the right to work in just conditions, trade union rights, the right to social security, health, food, education and the benefits of culture. It also provides for the protection of families, children, the elderly, and the handicapped.
   Date: Adopted 17 November 1988 (entered into force 16 November 1999).
   Citation: O.A.S.T.S. A-52.
   URL: http://www.oas.org/juridico/english/treaties/a-52.html (last visited 13 December 2012).

4. **African Charter on Human and Peoples' Rights**
   Description: International human rights convention ratified by almost all African countries and designed to promote and protect human and peoples' rights and freedoms in Africa. The Charter

178 *Dictionary of international human rights law*

recognizes civil and political rights, as well as economic, social, and cultural rights.
Date: Adopted 27 June 1981 (entered into force 21 October 1986).
Citation: 1520 U.N.T.S. 217, UN Doc 26363.
URL: http://treaties.un.org/doc/Publication/UNTS/Volume%2015 20/volume-1520-I-26363-English.pdf (last visited 13 December 2012).
See also: **Protocol to the African Charter on Human and Peoples' Rights on the Establishment of the African Court on Human and Peoples' Rights; Protocol to the African Charter on Human and Peoples' Rights on the Rights of Women in Africa.**

5. **African Charter on the Rights and Welfare of the Child**
   Description: International human rights instrument ratified by members of the Organization of African Unity. The Charter recognizes the need to take appropriate measures to promote and protect the rights, freedoms and welfare of the African Child, and calls for the creation of a Committee of Experts to enforce the convention.
   Date: Adopted 1 July 1990 (entered into force 29 November 1999).
   Citation: OAU Doc. CAB/LEG/24.9/49.
   URL: http://www.achpr.org/files/instruments/child/achpr_instr_cha rterchild_eng.pdf (last visited 13 December 2012).

6. **African Union Convention for the Protection and Assistance of Internally Displaced Persons in Africa**
   Description: International human rights instrument adopted by Member States of the African Union as a legal framework to prevent and eliminate root causes of internal displacement. The Convention would aim to strengthen regional and national measures to protect and assist internally displaced persons in Africa, as well as to provide for durable solutions.
   Date: Adopted 23 October 2009 (not entered into force).
   URL: http://www.au.int/en/sites/default/files/AFRICAN_UNION_ CONVENTION_FOR_THE_PROTECTION_AND_ASSISTAN CE_OF_INTERNALLY_DISPLACED_PERSONS_IN_AFRICA _%28KAMPALA_CONVENTION%29.pdf (last visited 13 December 2012).

7. **African Union Convention on Preventing and Combating Corruption**
   Description: International instrument adopted by Member States of the African Union to fight corruption. The Convention obligates State Parties to respect democratic principles and institutions,

popular participation, the rule of law and good governance, as well as human and peoples' rights in accordance with the African Charter on Human and Peoples Rights and other relevant human rights instruments. Subject to domestic law, any person alleged to have committed acts of corruption shall receive a fair trial in accordance with the guarantees contained in those instruments.
Date: Adopted 11 July 2003 (entered into force 5 August 2006).
URL: http://www.au.int/en/sites/default/files/AFRICAN_UNION_CONVENTION_PREVENTING_COMBATING_CORRUPTION.pdf (last visited 13 December 2012).

8. African Youth Charter
Description: International human rights instrument adopted by Member States of the African Union as a legal framework for governments to develop supportive policies and programs for persons between the ages 15 and 35 years. The Charter recognizes several basic freedoms and fundamental rights, emphasizes youth participation, and provides for obligations of the States with respect to the right to education, employment, health and leisure, among other rights.
Date: Adopted 2 July 2006 (entered into force 8 August 2009).
URL: http://www.africa-union.org/root/ua/conferences/mai/hrst/charter%20english.pdf (last visited 13 December 2012).

9. **Agenda 21**
Description: International plan of action for sustainable development, adopted by the United Nations Conference on Environment and Development. Agenda 21 reflects a global consensus and political commitment on development and environment co-operation. It identifies "programme areas", described in terms of the basis for action, objectives, activities and means of implementation to be carried out by various actors in respect of the principles contained in the Rio Declaration on Environment and Development.
Date: Adopted 14 June 1992.
Citation: UN Doc. A/CONF.151/26/Rev.1 (Vol. I) at 9.
URL: http://www.un-documents.net/agenda21.htm (last visited 13 December 2012).

10. Agreement for the Prosecution and Punishment of the Major War Criminals of the European Axis
Description: International agreement by which the Governments of the United States of America, the United Kingdom and the Union of Soviet Socialist Republics, and the provisional Government of

the French Republic agreed to establish an International Military Tribunal for the purpose of trying major war criminals of the European Axis after World War II.
Date: Adopted 8 August 1945.
Citation: 82 U.N.T.S. 279, UN Doc. 251.
URL: http://treaties.un.org/doc/Publication/UNTS/Volume%2082/v82.pdf (last visited 13 December 2012).

11. **American Convention on Human Rights**
    Description: International human rights instrument adopted by members of the Organization of American States and affirming their intention to consolidate a system of personal liberty and social justice based on respect for essential human rights. The Convention recognizes civil and political rights, as well as economic, social, and cultural rights, and provides for the creation of organs competent with respect to human rights matters.
    Date: Adopted 22 November 1969 (entered into force 18 July 1978).
    Citation: 1144 U.N.T.S. 143, UN Doc. 17955.
    URL: http://www.oas.org/juridico/english/treaties/b-32.html (last visited 13 December 2012).
    See also Additional Protocol to the American Convention on Human Rights in the Area of Economic, Social and Cultural Rights.

12. **American Declaration of the Rights and Duties of Man**
    Description: The world's first international human rights instrument of a general nature, adopted in 1948 by nations of the Americas and recognizing civil, political, economic, social and cultural rights.
    Date: Adopted 2 May 1948.
    Citation: OEA/Ser.L.V/II.82 doc.6 rev.1 at 17.
    URL: http://www.cidh.oas.org/Basicos/English/Basic2.American%20Declaration.htm (last visited 13 December 2012).

13. **American Declaration on the Rights of Indigenous Peoples**
    Description: Draft international human rights instrument drawn up by the Organization of American States, which would recognize the rights of indigenous peoples and the necessity to preserve the indigenous cultures of the Americas. The Declaration would address individual human rights, collective rights, cultural identity, organizational and political rights, as well as social, economic and property rights of indigenous peoples.
    Date: Last draft adopted 20 January 2011 (not entered into force).
    URL: http://www.oas.org/consejo/cajp/Indigenous%20documents.asp#Record (last visited 13 December 2012).

14. An Act Declaring the Rights and Liberties of the Subject and Settling the Succession of the Crown
    Description: One of the early documents addressing individual rights, also known as the English Bill of Rights of 1689. Following the revolution of 1688 in England, the English Parliament adopted the Declaration to protect citizens from violations by the monarchy. The Act stated the rights of the subject and the liberties of Parliament.
    Date: Adopted December 1689.
    URL: http://avalon.law.yale.edu/17th_century/england.asp (last visited 13 December 2012).

15. **Arab Charter on Human Rights**
    Description: International human rights instrument adopted by the Council of the League of Arab States, protecting civil, cultural, economic, political and social rights. Among other purposes, the Charter seeks to place human rights at the centre of the key national concerns of Arab States, and to entrench the principle that all human rights are universal, indivisible, interdependent and interrelated.
    Date: Adopted 22 May 2004 (entered into force 15 March 2008).
    Citation: Reprinted *in* 12 Int'l Hum. Rts. Rep. 893 (2005).
    URL: http://www1.umn.edu/humanrts/instree/loas2005.html?msource=UNWDEC19001&tr=y&auid=3337655 (last visited 13 December 2012).

16. **Arab Convention on the Suppression of Terrorism**
    Description: International instrument adopted by the Council of the League of Arab States to promote mutual co-operation in the suppression of terrorist offenses. The Arab States affirm their commitment to the humanitarian heritage of an Arab Nation that rejects violence and terrorism and advocates the protection of human rights, while asserting the right of peoples to combat foreign occupation and aggression in order to secure self-determination.
    Date: Adopted 22 April 1998.
    URL: http://www.unhcr.org/refworld/docid/3de5e4984.html (last visited 10 December 2012) [unofficial translation from Arabic by the UN English translation service 29 May 2000].

17. Banjul Charter: See **African Charter on Human and Peoples' Rights**.

18. Bangkok Principles on the Status and Treatment of Refugees
    Description: International standards adopted by resolution of the Asian-African Legal Consultative Organization, an

intergovernmental organization established to serve as an advisory body to its Member States in the field of international law. The Principles define the term "refugee", and provide certain norms on the issue of asylum, non-refoulement, minimum standard of treatment, expulsion and deportation, right of return, voluntary repatriation, international co-operation and the right to compensation, among other topics.
Date: Adopted 31 December 1966; Revised 24 June 2001.
URL: http://www.unhcr.org/refworld/publisher,AALCO,,,3de5f2d52,0.html (last visited 13 December 2012).

19. **Basic Principles for the Treatment of Prisoners**
    Description: International standards adopted by resolution of the United Nations General Assembly, setting forth conditions for the acceptable detention of all prisoners. Except for those limitations necessitated by the fact of incarceration, all prisoners shall retain the human rights and fundamental freedoms set out in the Universal Declaration of Human Rights of 10 December 1948.
    Date: Adopted 14 December 1990.
    Citation: UN Doc. A/RES/45/111.
    URL: http://www.un.org/documents/ga/res/45/a45r111.htm (last visited 13 December 2012).

20. **Basic Principles on the Independence of the Judiciary**
    Description: International standards adopted by the Seventh United Nations Congress on the Prevention of Crime and the Treatment of Offenders and endorsed by the General Assembly to assist Member States in securing and promoting the independence of the judiciary. The Principles set forth certain duties, freedoms, required qualifications and personal immunity of judges.
    Date: Adopted 26 August–6 September 1985; Endorsed by General Assembly resolutions 40/32 of 29 November 1985 and 40/146 of 13 December 1985.
    Citation: UN Doc. A/CONF.121/22/REV.1 at 59.
    URL: http://www2.ohchr.org/english/law/indjudiciary.htm (last visited 13 December 2012).

21. **Basic Principles on the Role of Lawyers**
    Description: International standards adopted by the Eighth United Nations Congress on the Prevention of Crime and the Treatment of Offenders to assist Member States in promoting and ensuring the proper role of lawyers, especially in criminal justice matters. The Principles set forth guidelines about the access to legal

services, and the duties, freedoms and required qualifications of lawyers.
Date: Adopted 27 August–7 September 1990.
Citation: UN Doc. A/CONF.144/28/Rev.1 at 118.
URL: http://www2.ohchr.org/english/law/lawyers.htm (last visited 13 December, 2012).

22. Basic Principles on the Use of Force and Firearms by Law Enforcement Officials
Description: International standards adopted by the Eighth United Nations Congress on the Prevention of Crime and the Treatment of Offenders, in order to ensure the proper use of force and firearms by law enforcement officials. The Principles set forth guidelines for the administration of justice, the protection of the right to life, liberty and security of the person, and affirm the importance of law enforcement officials' qualifications and training.
Date: Adopted Aug. 27-Sept.7, 1990.
Citation: UN Doc. A/CONF.144/28/Rev.1 at 112.
URL: http://www2.ohchr.org/english/law/firearms.htm (last visited 13 December 2012).

23. Beijing Declaration
Description: International proclamation adopted by the Fourth World Conference on Women, to advance the goals of equality, development and peace for all women. The Declaration reaffirms the signatories' attachment to equal rights and inherent human dignity of both women and men, and makes a commitment to enhance further the advancement and empowerment of women.
Date: Adopted 15 September 1995.
Citation: UN Doc. A/CONF.177/20.
URL: http://www.un-documents.net/beijingd.htm (last visited 12 April 2012).
See also Beijing Platform for Action.

24. Beijing Platform for Action
Description: Agenda for women's empowerment deriving from the Beijing Declaration, adopted by the Fourth World Conference on Women and aiming at removing all the obstacles to women's active participation in all spheres of public and private life. The Platform for Action identifies critical areas of concern, such as violence against women or education and training of women, and proposes strategic objectives and concrete actions for each area.
Date: Adopted 15 September 1995.

Citation: UN Doc. A/CONF.177/20.
URL: http://www.un-documents.net/beijingp.htm (last visited 13 December 2012).

25. Beijing Rules: See United Nations Standard Minimum Rules for the Administration of Juvenile Justice.

26. **Body of Principles for the Protection of All Persons Under Any Form of Detention or Imprisonment**
Description: International standards adopted by resolution of the United Nations General Assembly, providing for the protection of the fundamental rights of persons held in any type of detention, whether they are deprived of liberty as a result of conviction for an offense or not.
Date: Adopted 9 December 1988.
Citation: UN Doc. A/RES/43/173.
URL: http://www.un.org/documents/ga/res/43/a43r173.htm (last visited 13 December 2012).

27. **Cairo Declaration on Human Rights in Islam**
Description: Declaration issued by the Organization of the Islamic Conference to serve as a general guidance for Muslim countries in the field of human rights. The Declaration affirms the right to a dignified life in accordance with the Islamic *shari'a*.
Date: Adopted 31 July–5 August 1990.
Citation: UN Doc. A/CONF.157/PC/62/Add.18.
URL: http://www.oic-oci.org/english/article/human.htm (last visited 13 December 2012).

28. Cartagena Declaration on Refugees
Description: Declaration adopted by the Colloquium on the International Protection of Refugees in Central America, Mexico and Panama, to promote the application of the 1951 Convention relating to the Status of Refugees and its 1967 Protocol. The Declaration reiterates commitments to ensure that any repatriation is voluntary and to reinforce programs for protection of and assistance to refugees in countries of asylum, with a view to safeguarding their human rights and insuring their self-sufficiency and integration into the host society.
Date: Adopted 22 November 1984.
URL: http://www.unhcr.org/45dc19084.html (last visited 13 December 2012).

29. Charter of the Fundamental Rights of the European Union
    Description: Approved by the European Council, the European Parliament and the European Commission, and proclaimed by the Presidents of all three bodies on behalf of their institutions, the Charter sets out in a single text, for the first time in the European Union's history, the whole range of civil, political, economic and social rights of European citizens and all persons resident in the Union. The Charter became legally binding with the ratification of the Treaty of Lisbon on 1 December 2009.
    Date: Adopted 7 December 2000.
    Citation: OJ C 83 of 30.3.2010.
    URL: http://www.europarl.europa.eu/charter/pdf/text_en.pdf (last visited 13 December 2012).

30. Charter of the International Military Tribunal for the Far East
    Description: Instrument approved by the Supreme Commander for the Allied Powers and establishing the International Military Tribunal for the Far East. The Charter set forth the constitution, jurisdiction and functions of the Tribunal, created for the trial of the major Far Eastern war criminals in Tokyo, after World War II.
    Date: Adopted 19 January 1946.
    Citation: T.I.A.S. 1589.
    URL: http://www.macalester.edu/~tam/HIST194%20War%20Crimes/documents/Nuremberg/Charter%20of%20the%20International%20Military%20Tribunal%20Far%20East.htm (last visited 13 December 2012).

31. **Charter of the International Military Tribunal of 8 August 1945**
    Description: Instrument adopted pursuant to the Agreement for the Prosecution and Punishment of the Major War Criminals of the European Axis by the Governments of the United States of America, the United Kingdom, the Union of Soviet Socialist Republics and the provisional Government of the French Republic. The Charter set forth the constitution, jurisdiction and functions of the International Military Tribunal, established for the trial of the major war criminals of the European Axis in Nuremberg, after World War II.
    Date: Adopted 8 August 1945.
    Citation: In Agreement for the Prosecution and Punishment of the Major War Criminals of the European Axis, 82 U.N.T.S. 279, UN Doc. 251.
    URL: http://www.un-documents.net/imtchart.htm (last visited 13 December 2012).

32. Charter of the Organization of American States
    Description: Pan-American treaty creating the Organization of American States as a regional body to pursue peace, justice, solidarity, collaboration, sovereignty, territorial integrity, and independence of the Western Hemisphere.
    Date: Adopted 30 April 1948 (entered into force 13 December 1951).
    Citation: 119 U.N.T.S. 3, UN Doc. 1609.
    URL: http://www.oas.org/dil/treaties_A-41_Charter_of_the_Organization_of_American_States.htm (last visited 13 December 2012).
    See also **Protocol of Amendment to the Charter of the Organization of American States**.

33. **Charter of the United Nations**
    Description: Foundational treaty of the United Nations, which includes the Statute of the International Court of Justice.
    Date: Adopted 26 June 1945 (entered into force 24 October 1945).
    Citation: 1 U.N.T.S. XVI, T.I.A.S. 993.
    URL: http://www.un-documents.net/charter.htm (last visited 13 December 2012).

34. Chemical Weapons Convention: See Convention on the Prohibition of the Development, Production, Stockpiling and Use of Chemical Weapons and on their Destruction.

35. Civil Law Convention Against Corruption
    Description: International instrument adopted by Member States of the Council of Europe to strengthen international co-operation in the fight against corruption. The Convention takes a comprehensive approach to the fight against corruption as a threat to the rule of law, democracy and human rights, fairness and social justice, economic development and the proper and fair functioning of market economies.
    Date: Adopted 4 November 1999 (entered into 1 November 2003).
    Citation: E.T.S. 174.
    URL: http://conventions.coe.int/Treaty/en/Treaties/html/174.htm (last visited 13 December 2012).

36. Community Charter of the Fundamental Social Rights of Workers
    Description: International instrument adopted by Member States of the European Union, and establishing major principles of European labor law. The Charter sets forth fundamental social rights of workers such as freedom of movement, fair remuneration, improved working conditions, social protection, freedom of

association and collective bargaining, training, equal treatment between genders and safety in the workplace.
Date: Adopted by declaration 9 December 1989.
URL: http://www.aedh.eu/plugins/fckeditor/userfiles/file/Convent ions%20internationales/Community_Charter_of_the_Fundamental _Social_Rights_of_Workers.pdf (last visited 13 December 2012).

37. **Code of Conduct for Law Enforcement Officials**
Description: International standards adopted by resolution of the United Nations General Assembly. The Code of Conduct provides principles to be observed by all officers of the law who exercise police powers, to protect human dignity and the basic human rights of all persons, especially during arrest and detention.
Date: Adopted 17 December 1979.
Citation: UN Doc. A/RES/34/169.
URL: http://www2.ohchr.org/english/law/codeofconduct.htm (last visited 13 December 2012).

38. **Constitutive Act of the African Union**
Description: Pan-African treaty creating the African Union, successor of the Organization of African Unity. The Act set forth the objectives, organs, and procedures of the Union.
Date: Adopted 11 July 2000 (entered into force 26 May 2001).
Citation: 2158 U.N.T.S. 3, UN Doc. 37733.
URL: http://www.africa-union.org/root/au/aboutau/constitutive_ act_en.htm (last visited 13 December 2012).

39. **Control Council Law No. 10**
Description: Law enacted by the body governing the military occupation of Germany after World War II, in order to establish a legal basis for the prosecution of war criminals. The Law defined crimes against peace, war crimes and crimes against humanity.
Date: Adopted 20 December 1945.
Citation: 3 Official Gazette Control Council for Germany 50–55 (1946).
URL: http://www1.umn.edu/humanrts/instree/Sccno10.htm (last visited 13 December 2012).

40. Convention Against Discrimination in Education
Description: International human rights instrument adopted by the General Conference of the United Nations Educational, Scientific and Cultural Organization. The Convention proscribes any form of discrimination in education and intends to promote equality of opportunity and treatment in education.

Date: Adopted 14 December 1960 (entered into force 22 May 1962).
Citation: 429 U.N.T.S. 93, UN Doc. 6193.
URL: http://www.un-documents.net/cde.htm (last visited 13 December 2012).

41. **Convention Against Torture and Other Cruel, Inhuman or Degrading Treatment or Punishment**
    Description: International human rights instrument adopted by resolution of the General Assembly of the United Nations to make more effective the struggle against torture and other cruel, inhuman or degrading treatment or punishment throughout the world. The Convention defines torture, obligates State Parties to take measures for its implementation, provides jurisdictional rules, and establishes a Committee against Torture.
    Date: Adopted 10 December 1984 (entered into force 26 June 1987).
    Citation: 1465 U.N.T.S. 85, UN Doc. A/RES/39/46.
    URL: http://www.un-documents.net/a39r46.htm (last visited 13 December 2012).

42. Convention concerning Forced or Compulsory Labour, as Modified
    Description: International human rights instrument adopted by the General Conference of the International Labor Organization, and modified by the Final Articles Revision Convention. The Convention obligates the contracting States to suppress within the shortest possible period all work or service which is exacted from any person under the menace of any penalty and for which said person has not offered himself or herself voluntarily.
    Date: Adopted 28 June 1930 (entered into force 1 May 1932); Modified 9 October 1946 (entered into force 28 May 1947).
    Citation: 39 U.NT.S. 55; C29.
    URL: http://www.ilo.org/ilolex/cgi-lex/convde.pl?C029 (last visited 13 December 2012).

43. **Convention concerning Indigenous and Tribal Peoples in Independent Countries**
    Description: International human rights instrument adopted by the General Conference of the International Labor Organization. The Convention aims to protect the aspirations of indigenous and tribal peoples to exercise control over their own institutions, ways of life and economic development and to maintain and develop their identities, languages and religions, within the framework of the States in which they live.
    Date: Adopted 27 June 1989 (entered into force 5 September1991).

Citation: 1650 U.N.T.S. 383, C169.
URL: http://www.un-documents.net/c169.htm (last visited 13 December 2012).

44. Convention concerning the Abolition of Forced Labour
Description: International human rights instrument adopted by the General Conference of the International Labor Organization. The Convention obligates the contracting States to suppress and not to make use of any form of forced or compulsory labor as a means of political coercion, education or punishment for holding political views, as a method of mobilizing for purposes of economic development, as a means of labor discipline, as a punishment for having participated in strikes, or as a means of racial, social, national or religious discrimination.
Date: Adopted 25 June 1957 (entered into force 17 January 1959).
Citation: 320 U.N.T.S. 291; C105.
URL: http://www.ilo.org/dyn/normlex/en/f?p=1000:12100:0::NO::P12100_INSTRUMENT_ID:312250 (last visited 13 December 2012).

45. Convention concerning the Prohibition and Immediate Action for the Elimination of the Worst Forms of Child Labour
Description: International human rights instrument adopted by the General Conference of the International Labor Organization to prohibit and eliminate all forms of slavery or practices similar to slavery of children, as well as the use, procuring or offering of a child for prostitution, pornographic performances, other illicit activities, and all work which, by its nature or the circumstances in which it is carried out, is likely to harm the health, safety or morals of children. The Convention obligates State Parties to take appropriate measures and organizes international co-operation
Date: Adopted 6 June 1999 (entered into force 19 November 2000).
Citation: 2133 U.N.T.S 161; C182.
URL: http://www.ilo.org/ilolex/cgi-lex/convde.pl?C182 (last visited 13 December 2012).

46. **Convention concerning the Protection of World Cultural and Natural Heritage**
Description: International instrument adopted by the General Conference of the United Nations Educational, Scientific and Cultural Organization. The Convention aims to establish a permanent system of collective protection of the cultural and natural heritage of outstanding universal value. The Convention defines

cultural and natural heritage, organizes its national and international protection, and establishes a World Heritage Committee and a World Heritage Fund.
Date: Adopted 16 November 1972 (entered into force 17 December 1975).
Citation: 1037 U.N.T.S. 151, UN Doc. No. 15511.
URL: http://www.un-documents.net/cpwcnh.htm (last visited 13 December 2012).

47. **Convention for the Protection of Cultural Property in the Event of Armed Conflict**
Description: International instrument adopted in the wake of massive destruction of cultural heritage during World War II. It is the first treaty with a worldwide vocation focusing exclusively on the protection of cultural heritage in armed conflicts. The Convention intends to protect both immovable and movable cultural property through the adoption of peacetime safeguarding measures, the granting of special protected status to a limited number of refuges to shelter cultural property in the event of a conflict and other provisions.
Date: Adopted 14 May 1954 (entered into force 7 August 1956).
Citation: 249 U.N.T.S. 240, UN Doc. 3511.
URL: http://www.un-documents.net/cpcpeac.htm (last visited 13 December 2012).

48. **Convention for the Protection of Human Rights and Fundamental Freedoms**: See [European] Convention for the Protection of Human Rights and Fundamental Freedoms.

49. **Convention for the Suppression of the Traffic in Persons and of the Exploitation of the Prostitution of Others**
Description: International human rights instrument adopted by resolution of the General Assembly of the United Nations to protect the dignity and worth of the human person. The Convention consolidates several prior international instruments and requires State Parties to punish anyone who procures another for purposes of prostitution, or who exploits the prostitution of another, even with the consent of that person.
Date: Adopted 2 December 1949 (entered into force 25 July 1951).
Citation: 96 U.N.T.S. 271, UN Doc. A/RES/4/317.
URL: http://www.un-documents.net/a4r317.htm (last visited 13 December 2012).

50. Convention for the Suppression of Unlawful Acts Against the Safety of Civil Aviation
    Description: International instrument adopted for the purpose of deterring unlawful acts against the safety of civil aviation. The Convention obligates contracting parties to take preventive measures and to punish offenders by severe penalties, and it organizes extradition. The Convention will be superseded by the Convention on the Suppression of Unlawful Acts Relating to International Civil Aviation of 10 September 2010, if it enters into force.
    Date: Adopted 23 September 1971 (entered into force 26 January 1973).
    Citation: 974 U.N.T.S. 177, UN Doc. 14118.
    URL: http://treaties.un.org/doc/Publication/UNTS/Volume%2097 4/volume-974-I-14118-English.pdf (last visited 13 December 2012).
    See also **Protocol for the Suppression of Unlawful Acts of Violence at Airports Serving International Civil Aviation**.

51. **Convention for the Suppression of Unlawful Acts Against the Safety of Maritime Navigation**
    Description: International instrument adopted to protect the right to life, liberty, and security, and the dignity of persons threatened by unlawful acts against ships, including the seizure of ships by force, acts of violence against persons on board ships and the placing of devices on board a ship to destroy or damage it. The Convention obligates contracting governments to extradite or prosecute persons committing such acts. Any person taken into custody pursuant to the Convention shall be guaranteed fair treatment, including the enjoyment of all the rights and guarantees of the States in which that person is present.
    Date: Adopted 10 March 1988 (entered into force 1 March 1992).
    Citation: 1678 U.N.T.S. 201, UN Doc. No. 29004.
    URL: http://treaties.un.org/doc/db/Terrorism/Conv8-english.pdf (last visited 5 February 2012).
    See also **Protocol for the Suppression of Unlawful Acts Against the Safety of Fixed Platforms Located on the Continental Shelf**.

52. **Convention for the Suppression of Unlawful Seizure of Aircraft**
    Description: International instrument obligating contracting States to make unlawful acts of seizure or exercise of control of aircraft an offense punishable by severe penalties. The Convention aims at protecting the safety of persons and property, by deterring such acts.

192 *Dictionary of international human rights law*

    Date: Adopted 16 December 1970 (entered into force 14 October 1971).
    Citation: 860 U.N.T.S. 105, UN Doc. 12325.
    URL: http://treaties.un.org/doc/db/Terrorism/Conv2-english.pdf (last visited 13 December 2012).

53. **Convention Governing the Specific Aspects of Refugee Problems in Africa**
    Description: International instrument adopted by members of the Organization of African Unity. The Convention recommends measures to solve the problem of refugees in Africa, and affirms the necessity of a close and continuous collaboration between States, the Organization of African Unity and the Office of the United Nations High Commissioner for Refugees.
    Date: Adopted 10 September 1969 (entered into force 20 June 1974).
    Citation: 1001 U.N.T.S. 45, UN Doc. 14621.
    URL: http://www.africa-union.org/Official_documents/Treaties_%20Conventions_%20Protocols/Refugee_Convention.pdf (last visited 13 December 2012).

54. Convention of Belem do Para: See **Inter-American Convention on the Prevention, Punishment and Eradication of Violence Against Women**.

55. Convention on Cluster Munitions
    Description: International arm control instrument adopted to put an end to the suffering and casualties caused by cluster munitions, a type of conventional munitions designed to disperse or release explosive submunitions which remnants often kill or maim civilians. The Convention obligates States Parties to provide adequate age- and gender-sensitive assistance to victims of cluster munitions, including medical care, rehabilitation and psychological support, as well as to provide for their social and economic inclusion.
    Date: Adopted 30 May 2008 (entered into force 1 August 2010).
    Citation: CCM/77, UN Doc. 47713.
    URL: http://www.clusterconvention.org/files/2011/01/Convention-ENG.pdf (last visited 13 December 2012).

56. **Convention on Human Rights and Biomedicine**
    Description: International human rights instrument adopted by Member States of the Council of Europe, Member States of the European Community, and other States, to protect the dignity and identity of all human beings and guarantee respect for their integrity

and other rights and fundamental freedoms with regard to the application of biology and medicine.
Date: Adopted 4 April 1997 (entered into force 1 December 1999).
Citation: E.T.S. 164.
URL: http://conventions.coe.int/Treaty/en/Treaties/html/164.htm (last visited 13 December 2012).

57. Convention on Jurisdiction, Applicable Law, Recognition, Enforcement and Co-operation in Respect of Parental Responsibility and Measures for the Protection of Children
Description: International instrument adopted by the Hague Conference on Private International Law to improve the protection of children at risk in cross-frontier situations. The Convention covers a wide range of civil measures of protection such as orders concerning parental responsibility and contact, public measures of protection and care, matters of representation and the protection of children's property. It also requires that States designate a central authority to discharge the duties which are imposed by the Convention and provides uniform rules for determining which country's authorities are competent to take measures of protection.
Date: Adopted 19 October 1996 (entered into force 1 January 2002).
Citation: HCCH Convention No 35.
URL: http://www.hcch.net/upload/conventions/txt34en.pdf (last visited Mar. 17, 2012).

58. Convention on Offences and Certain Other Acts Committed On Board Aircraft
Description: International instrument applicable to offenses against penal law and to acts which may or do jeopardize the safety of civil aircrafts or of persons or property therein or which jeopardize good order and discipline on board. The Convention provides jurisdictional rules, recognizes certain powers and immunities of aircraft commanders and imposes obligations on States.
Date: Adopted 14 September 1963 (entered into force 4 December 1969).
Citation: 404 U.N.T.S. 219, UN Doc. 10106.
URL: treaties.un.org/doc/db/Terrorism/Conv1-english.pdf (last visited 13 December 2012).

59. Convention on the Civil Aspects of International Child Abduction
Description: International instrument adopted by the Hague Conference on Private International Law to protect children internationally from the harmful effects of their wrongful removal or

retention and to establish rapid procedures to ensure their prompt return to the State of their habitual residence. The Convention seeks to combat parental child abduction by providing a system of co-operation between central authorities designated by each State to discharge the duties which are imposed by the Convention.
Date: Adopted 25 October 1980 (entered into force 1 December 1983).
Citation: HCCH Convention No 28.
URL: http://www.hcch.net/upload/conventions/txt28en.pdf (last visited 13 December 2012).

60. **Convention on the Elimination of All Forms of Discrimination Against Women**
    Description: International human rights instrument adopted by the United Nations General Assembly to eliminate discrimination against women in all its forms and manifestations. The Convention defines what constitutes discrimination against women and establishes a series of measures for States to undertake in order to end such discrimination.
    Date: Adopted 18 December 1979 (entered into force 3 September 1981).
    Citation: 1249 U.N.T.S. 13, UN Doc. A/34/46.
    URL: http://www.un-documents.net/cedaw.htm (last visited 13 December 2012).

61. Convention on the Marking of Plastic Explosives for Purpose of Detection
    Description: International instrument adopted to contribute to the prevention of terrorist acts aimed at destroying aircrafts and other targets. The Convention mandates the marking of plastic explosives, which have been used for such acts, for the purpose of facilitating their detection. Contracting States are obligated to take measures to prohibit and prevent the manufacture of unmarked explosives on their territory.
    Date: Adopted 1 March 1991 (entered into force 21 June 1998).
    Citation: 2122 U.N.T.S. 359, UN Doc. 36984.
    URL: http://treaties.un.org/doc/db/Terrorism/Conv10-english.pdf (last visited 13 December 2012).

62. **Convention on the Means of Prohibiting and Preventing the Illicit Import, Export and Transfer of Ownership of Cultural Property**
    Description: International instrument adopted by the General Conference of the United Nations Educational, Scientific and

Cultural Organization to protect cultural heritage. The States Parties recognized that the illicit import, export and transfer of ownership of cultural property impoverishes the cultural heritage of countries, affirmed that international co-operation is necessary to protect cultural property and resolved to oppose such practices through national legislation.
Date: Adopted 14 November 1970 (entered into force 24 April 1972).
Citation: 823 U.N.T.S. 231, UN Doc. 11806.
URL: http://www.un-documents.net/cppiiecp.htm (last visited 13 December 2012).

63. **Convention on the Nationality of Married Women**
    Description: International human rights instrument protecting the rights of women with regard to the loss or acquisition of nationality as a result of marriage, its dissolution or the change of nationality by the husband during marriage.
    Date: Adopted 20 February 1957 (entered into force 11 August 1958).
    Citation: 309 U.N.T.S. 65, UN Doc. 4468.
    URL: http://treaties.un.org/doc/Publication/UNTS/Volume%2030 9/v309.pdf (last visited 13 December 2012).

64. Convention on the Nationality of Women: See **[Inter-American] Convention on the Nationality of Women**.

65. **Convention on the Non-Applicability of Statutory Limitations to War Crimes and Crimes Against Humanity**
    Description: International human rights instrument adopted by resolution of the United Nations General Assembly to affirm the international law principle that no period of statutory limitation shall apply to war crimes and crimes against humanity, irrespective of the date of their commission.
    Date: Adopted 26 November 1968 (entered into force 11 November 1970).
    Citation: 754 U.N.T.S. 73, UN Doc. A/RES/2391.
    URL: http://treaties.un.org/doc/Publication/UNTS/Volume%2075 4/volume-754-I-10823-English.pdf (last visited 13 December 2012).

66. **Convention on the Physical Protection of Nuclear Material**
    Description: International instrument adopted to avert the potential dangers posed by the unlawful taking and use of nuclear material. The Convention obligates State Parties to meet defined standards of physical protection for international shipments of nuclear material

196   *Dictionary of international human rights law*

for peaceful purposes, defines punishable offenses, establishes penalties, and provides that any person regarding whom proceedings are being carried out in connection with the Convention shall be guaranteed fair treatment.
Date: Adopted 3 March 1980 (entered into force 8 February 1987).
Citation: 1456 U.N.T.S. 124, UN Doc. INFCIRC/274.
URL: http://treaties.un.org/doc/Publication/UNTS/Volume%201456/volume-1456-I-24631-English.pdf (last visited 13 December 2012).

67. **Convention on the Prevention and Punishment of Crimes Against Internationally Protected Persons, including Diplomatic Agents**
    Description: International instrument adopted by resolution of the United Nations General Assembly. The Convention provides for the prevention and punishment of crimes against diplomatic agents and other internationally protected persons, and states that any person regarding whom proceedings are being carried out in connection with the Convention shall be guaranteed fair treatment.
    Date: Adopted 14 December 1973 (entered into force 20 February 1977).
    Citation: 1035 U.N.T.S. 167, UN Doc. A/RES/3166.
    URL: http://untreaty.un.org/ilc/texts/instruments/english/conventions/9_4_1973.pdf (last visited 13 December 2012).

68. **Convention on the Prevention and Punishment of the Crime of Genocide**
    Description: International human rights instrument adopted by resolution of the United Nations General Assembly. The Convention defines genocide and provides for international co-operation to liberate mankind from it, whether it is committed in time of peace or in time of war, by constitutionally responsible rulers, public officials and private individuals alike.
    Date: Adopted 9 December 1948 (entered into force 12 January 1951).
    Citation: 78 U.N.T.S. 277, UN Doc. 1021.
    URL: http://www.un-documents.net/cppcg.htm (last visited 13 December 2012).

69. Convention on the Prohibition of the Use, Stockpiling, Production and Transfer of Anti-Personnel Mines and on their Destruction
    Description: International arms control instrument known as the "Ottawa Convention", adopted to put an end to the suffering and casualties caused by anti-personnel mines, that kill or maim many

people, mostly civilians and especially children. The Convention obligates States Parties to refrain from using anti-personnel mines and to provide assistance for the care, rehabilitation, and social and economic reintegration of mine victims and for mine awareness programs.
Date: Adopted 18 September 1997 (entered into force 1 March 1999).
Citation: 2056 U.N.T.S. 211, UN Doc. 35597.
URL: http://www.un-documents.net/mbt.htm (last visited 13 December 2012).

70. Convention on the Prohibition of the Development, Production, Stockpiling and Use of Chemical Weapons and on their Destruction
Description: International arms control instrument known as the "Chemical Weapons Convention", adopted to achieve chemical disarmament by prohibiting the development, production, acquisition, stockpiling, retention, transfer or use of chemical weapons by States Parties. The Convention established the Organization for the Prohibition of Chemical Weapons, mandated to conduct compliance verifications and promote international co-operation.
Date: Adopted 3 September 1992 (entered into force 29 April 1997).
Citation: 1974 U.N.T.S. 45, UN Doc. 33757.
URL: http://www.opcw.org/chemical-weapons-convention/articles/ (last visited 13 December 2012).

71. Convention on the Protection of Children and Co-operation in Respect of Intercountry Adoption
Description: International instrument adopted by the Hague Conference on Private International Law to establish safeguards ensuring that adoptions involving a country of origin and a receiving country take place in the best interest of the child and with respect for the child's fundamental rights. By setting out procedures and prohibiting improper financial gain, the Convention seeks to provide security, predictability and transparency for all parties to the adoption. It also establishes a system of co-operation between central authorities designated by States to discharge the duties which are imposed by the Convention.
Date: Adopted 29 May 1993 (entered into force 1 May 1995).
Citation: HCCH Convention No 33.
URL: http://www.hcch.net/upload/conventions/txt33en.pdf (last visited 13 December 2012).

198 *Dictionary of international human rights law*

72. Convention on the Reduction of Statelessness
    Description: International human rights instrument adopted by the United Nations Conference on the Elimination or Reduction of Future Statelessness, in order to reduce such condition. The Convention obligates contracting States to grant under certain conditions their nationality to persons who would otherwise be stateless, and establishes rules for the deprivation of nationality.
    Date: Adopted 30 August 1961 (entered into force 13 December 1975).
    Citation: 989 U.N.T.S. 175, UN Doc. A/RES/896.
    URL: http://untreaty.un.org/ilc/texts/instruments/english/conventions/6_1_1961.pdf (last visited 13 December 2012).

73. **Convention on the Rights of Persons with Disabilities**
    Description: International human rights instrument adopted by resolution of the United Nations General Assembly to promote and protect the human rights, fundamental freedoms and dignity of persons with disabilities. The Convention defines persons with disabilities and mandates that contracting States ensure the full realization of all human rights for these persons.
    Date: Adopted 13 December 2006 (entered into force 3 May 2008).
    Citation: 2515 U.N.T.S. 3, UN Doc. A/RES/61/106.
    URL: http://www.un-documents.net/a61r106.htm (last visited 13 December 2012).

74. **Convention on the Rights of the Child**
    Description: International human rights instrument adopted by resolution of the United Nations General Assembly, setting forth the civil, cultural, economic, political and social rights of all individuals under the age of 18. The Convention establishes a Committee on the Rights of the Child to receive reports submitted by States about the measures they have adopted to give effect to the Convention.
    Date: Adopted 20 November 1989 (entered into force 2 September 1990).
    Citation: 1577 U.N.T.S. 3, UN Doc. A/RES/44/25.
    URL: http://www.un-documents.net/crc.htm (last visited 13 December 2012).
    See also Optional Protocol to the Convention on the Rights of the Child on a communications procedure; **Optional Protocol to the Convention on the Rights of the Child on the Involvement of Children in Armed Conflicts**; Optional Protocol to the Convention on the Rights of the Child on the Sale of Children, Child Prostitution and Child Pornography.

Appendix 199

75. **Convention relating to the Status of Refugees**
    Description: International human rights instrument adopted by the United Nations Conference of Plenipotentiaries on the Status of Refugees and Stateless Persons, defining who is a refugee, codifying the rights of refugees at the international level, and providing for the co-operation of States with the United Nations High Commissioner for Refugees.
    Date: Adopted 28 July 1951 (entered into force 22 April 1954).
    Citation: 189 U.N.T.S. 137, UN Doc. A/RES/429(V).
    URL: http://www.un-documents.net/crsr.htm (last visited 13 December 2012).
    See also **Protocol relating to the Status of Refugees**.

76. **Convention relating to the Status of Stateless Persons**
    Description: International human rights instrument adopted by a Conference of Plenipotentiaries convened by a resolution of the United Nations Economic and Social Council to regulate and improve the status of stateless persons. The Convention guarantees the fundamental rights and freedoms, as well as some economic and social rights of persons who are not considered as a national by any State.
    Date: Adopted 28 September 1954 (entered into force 6 June 1960).
    Citation: 360 U.N.T.S. 117, UN Doc. 5158.
    URL: http://www2.ohchr.org/english/law/Stateless.htm (last visited 13 December 2012).

77. Convention on the Suppression of Unlawful Acts Relating to International Civil Aviation
    Description: International instrument adopted at the International Conference on Air Law, and prevailing over the Convention for the Suppression of Unlawful Acts Against the Safety of Civil Aviation of 23 September 1971 and the Protocol for the Suppression of Unlawful Acts of Violence at Airports Serving International Civil Aviation of 24 February 1988. The Convention includes a provision stating that any person taken into custody pursuant to the Convention shall be guaranteed fair treatment, including the enjoyment of all rights and guarantees in conformity with international human rights law.
    Date: Adopted 10 September 2010 (not entered into force).
    Citation: ICAO Doc. 9960.
    URL: http://legacy.icao.int/DCAS2010/restr/docs/beijing_conven tion_multi.pdf (last visited 13 December 2012).

200   *Dictionary of international human rights law*

78. Copenhagen Declaration on Social Development
    Description: International proclamation adopted at the World Summit for Social Development, recognizing the significance of social development and human well-being for all. The Declaration includes an assessment of the world social situation, sets forth general principles and goals for social development and establishes a series of ten commitments to launch a global drive for social progress and development.
    Date: Adopted 14 March 1995.
    Citation: UN Doc. A/CONF.166/9.
    URL: http://www.un-documents.net/cope-dec.htm (last visited 13 December 2012).
    See also Programme of Action of the World Summit for Social Development.

79. Covenant of the League of Nations
    Description: International agreement adopted as part I of the Treaty of Versailles at the Paris Peace Conference of 1919, after World War I. The Covenant created the League of Nations in order to promote international co-operation and to achieve international peace and security.
    Date: Adopted 28 April 1919 (entered into force 10 January 1920).
    URL: http://www.unhcr.org/refworld/publisher,LON,,,3dd8b9854,0.html (last visited 13 December 2012).

80. Criminal Law Convention Against Corruption
    Description: International instrument adopted by Member States of the Council of Europe to pursue a common criminal policy aimed at the protection of society against corruption. The Convention takes a comprehensive approach to the fight against corruption as a threat to the rule of law, democracy and human rights, good governance, fairness and social justice, economic development, the stability of democratic institutions and the moral foundations of society.
    Date: Adopted 27 January 1999 (entered into force 1 July 2002).
    Citation: E.T.S. 173.
    URL: http://conventions.coe.int/Treaty/en/Treaties/html/173.htm (last visited 13 December 2012).

81. Cultural Charter for Africa
    Description: International instrument adopted by Member States of the Organization of African Unity to promote the harmonious cultural development of African States. The Charter recognizes cultural diversity, the right to education and to access culture, the need

to protect cultural heritage, and it sets forth principles to govern national cultural policies.
Date: Adopted 5 July 1976 (entered into force 19 September 1990).
URL: http://www.au.int/en/sites/default/files/CULTURAL_CHARTER_AFRICA.pdf (last visited 13 December 2012).

82. Dakar Framework for Action
Description: Collective commitment taken at the World Education Forum organized in 2000, and entitled "Education For All: Meeting Our Collective Commitments". The Framework reaffirmed the vision of the World Declaration on Education for All of 9 March 1990. It committed the signatories to attain new education goals, based on an extensive evaluation of education levels conducted throughout the world between 1990 and 2000.
Date: Adopted 28 April 2000.
Citation: UNESCO Doc. ED-2000/CONF/211/1.
URL: http://www.un-documents.net/dakarfa.htm (last visited 13 December 2012).

83. Dayton Peace Agreement: See **General Framework Agreement for Peace in Bosnia and Herzegovina**.

84. Declaration by the European Council on the Environmental Imperative
Description: International proclamation adopted by the European Council to set out guidelines for future action by the European Community to protect and enhance the environment. The heads of State and government of the Community recognized their responsibility to both European citizens and the wider world, and intended their action to be coordinated and based on the principles of sustainable development and preventative and precautionary action.
Date: Adopted 26 June 1990.
Citation: DOC/90/2, Annex II.
URL: http://europa.eu/rapid/pressReleasesAction.do?reference=DOC/90/2&format=HTML&aged=1&language=EN&guiLanguage=en (last visited 13 December 2012).

85. Declaration of Alma-Ata
Description: International human rights proclamation adopted by the International Conference on Primary Health Care to protect and promote the health of all people. The Declaration reaffirmed that health is a fundamental human right and that the attainment of the highest possible level of health is one of the most important worldwide social goals. It also set a deadline of the year 2000 for

achieving a level of health that would enable all people to lead a socially and economically productive life.
Date: Adopted 12 September 1978.
URL: http://www.un-documents.net/alma-ata.htm (last visited 13 December 2012).

86. Declaration of Basic Principles of Justice for Victims of Crime and Abuse of Power
Description: International human rights proclamation adopted by the United Nations General Assembly to secure the universal and effective recognition of, and respect for, the rights of persons who have suffered harm through acts or omissions that are in violation of national criminal laws, including laws proscribing criminal abuse of power. The Declaration recognizes the need for access to justice and fair treatment, as well as restitution, compensation and governmental assistance for such victims.
Date: Adopted 29 November 1985.
Citation: UN Doc. A/RES/40/34.
URL: http://www.un.org/documents/ga/res/40/a40r034.htm (last visited 13 December 2012).

87. Declaration of Mexico on the Equality of Women and Their Contribution to Development and Peace
Description: International human rights proclamation adopted by the World Conference of the International Women's Year. The Conference promulgated a number of principles affirming equality in rights and opportunities between women and men, and proclaimed its commitment to achieve equality, development and peace.
Date: Adopted 2 July 1975.
Citation: E/CONF.66/34.
URL: http://www.un-documents.net/mex-dec.htm (last visited 13 December 2012).

88. **Declaration of Principles on International Cultural Co-operation**
Description: International declaration proclaimed by the General Conference of the United Nations Educational, Scientific and Cultural Organization, to strengthen international co-operation and advance peace and welfare through the educational, scientific and cultural relations of the peoples of the world.
Date: Adopted 4 November 1966.
URL: http://www.un-documents.net/dpicc.htm (last visited 13 December 2012).

89. **Declaration of the Advancement of Women in the ASEAN Region**
    Description: International human rights proclamation adopted by the Association of Southeast Asian Nations, recognizing the multiple roles of women in the family, in society and in the nation. The Declaration calls for Member States to provide facilities and opportunities to enable women in the region to undertake these tasks effectively.
    Date: Adopted 1988.
    URL: http://www.asean.org/8685.htm (last visited Sept. 26, 2011).

90. Declaration of the Rights of Man and of the Citizen
    Description: Human rights declaration adopted by the National Assembly of France in 1789, proclaiming that men are born and remain free and equal in rights, and recognizing the unalienable rights to liberty, property, security and resistance to oppression.
    Date: Adopted 26 August 1789.
    URL: http://www.unhcr.org/refworld/docid/3ae6b52410.html (last visited 13 December 2012).

91. Declaration of the Rights of the Child
    Description: International proclamation adopted by resolution of the United Nations General Assembly, calling upon parents, individuals, voluntary organizations, local authorities and national governments to recognize the rights and freedoms of children and to strive for their observance. It provides that measures taken to promote these rights should be in accordance with the ten principles contained in the Declaration.
    Date: Adopted 20 November 1959.
    Citation: UN Doc. A/RES/14/1386.
    URL: http://www.un-documents.net/a14r1386.htm (last visited 13 December 2012).

92. **Declaration of the United Nations Conference on the Human Environment**
    Description: International human rights proclamation adopted by the United Nations Conference on the Human Environment. The Declaration sets forth inspirational principles to preserve and enhance the environment of all human beings, including the right to adequate conditions of life in an environment of a quality that permits a life of dignity and well-being, and the responsibility to protect and improve the environment for present and future generations.
    Date: Adopted 16 June 1972.

Citation: UN Doc. A/CONF.48/14/Rev. 1.
URL: http://www.un-documents.net/unchedec.htm (last visited 13 December 2012).

93. Declaration on Fundamental Principles and Rights at Work and Follow-up to the Declaration
Description: International human rights proclamation adopted by the International Labor Conference to promote freedom of association, the effective recognition of the right to collective bargaining, the elimination of forced or compulsory labor, the abolition of child labor and the elimination of discrimination in employment. The Declaration is supported by a follow-up procedure, pursuant to which States that have not ratified one or more of the core International Labor Organization Conventions are asked each year to report on the status of the relevant rights within their borders, noting impediments to ratification and areas where assistance may be required.
Date: Adopted 18 June 1998.
ULR: http://www.un-documents.net/dfprw.htm (last visited 13 December 2012).

94. Declaration on Human Rights in Islam: See **Cairo Declaration on Human Rights in Islam**.

95. Declaration on Occupational Health For All
Description: International human rights proclamation adopted at the Second Meeting of the World Health Organization Collaborating Centers in Occupational Health, to address the rapid changes in working life affecting occupational health. The Declaration recognizes that health at work is a priority issue, and provides measures for employers, governments and international actors to insure a healthy working life.
Date: Adopted 14 October 1994.
Citation: UN Doc. WHO/OCH/94.1.
URL: http://www.who.int/occupational_health/publications/declaration/en/index.html (last visited 13 December 2012).

96. Declaration on Social and Legal Principles relating to the Protection and Welfare of Children, with Special Reference to Foster Placement and Adoption Nationally and Internationally
Description: International human rights proclamation adopted by resolution of the United Nations General Assembly as universal principles to be taken into account in cases where procedures are instituted relating to foster placement or adoption of a child, either nationally or internationally. The Declaration provides guidance

regarding family and child welfare in general and foster family care, as well as adoption.
Date: Adopted 3 December 1986.
Citation: UN Doc. A/RES/41/85.
URL: http://www.un.org/documents/ga/res/41/a41r085.htm (last visited 13 December 2012).

97. **Declaration on the Elimination of All Forms of Intolerance and of Discrimination Based on Religion or Belief**
    Description: International human rights proclamation adopted by resolution of the United Nations General Assembly for the speedy elimination of discrimination in matters of religion and beliefs. The Declaration calls for States to take measures to prevent and eliminate such intolerance in all its manifestations.
    Date: Adopted 25 November 1981.
    Citation: UN Doc. A/RES/36/55.
    URL: http://www.un-documents.net/a36r55.htm (last visited 13 December 2012).

98. **Declaration on the Elimination of Violence Against Women**
    Description: International human rights proclamation adopted by resolution of the United Nations General Assembly as a statement of the rights to be applied to ensure the elimination of violence against women in all its forms. The Declaration serves as a commitment by States and the international community to pursue appropriate means to eliminate violence against women.
    Date: Adopted 20 December 1993.
    Citation: UN Doc. A/RES/48/104.
    URL: http://www.un-documents.net/a48r104.htm (last visited 13 December 2012).

99. Declaration on the Elimination of Violence Against Women in the ASEAN Region
    Description: International human rights proclamation adopted by the Association of Southeast Asian Nations. The Declaration aims at strengthening regional co-operation and coordination to eliminate violence against women in the ASEAN region.
    Date: Adopted 30 June 2004.
    URL: http://www.asean.org/16189.htm (last visited Sept 25, 2011).

100. **Declaration on the Protection of All Persons from Being Subjected to Torture and Other Cruel, Inhuman, or Degrading Treatment or Punishment**
     Description: International human rights proclamation adopted by

resolution of the United Nations General Assembly. The Declaration defines and condemns torture and other cruel, inhuman or degrading treatments or punishments. It precedes the Convention Against Torture and Other Cruel, Inhuman or Degrading Treatment or Punishment of 10 December 1984.
Date: Adopted 9 December 1975.
Citation: UN Doc. A/RES/30/3452.
URL: http://www.un-documents.net/dpptcidt.htm (last visited 13 December 2012).

101. **Declaration on the Right of Peoples to Peace**
Description: International human rights proclamation adopted by resolution of the United Nations General Assembly, proclaiming that peoples have a sacred right to live without war, and declaring that the preservation of this right constitutes a fundamental obligation of each State.
Date: Adopted 12 November 1984.
Citation: UN Doc. A/RES/39/11.
URL: http://www.un-documents.net/a39r11.htm (last visited 13 December 2012).

102. **Declaration on the Rights of Indigenous Peoples**
Description: International human rights proclamation adopted by resolution of the United Nations General Assembly, recognizing that indigenous individuals are entitled without discrimination to all human rights recognized in international law, in addition to collective rights. The Declaration provides a standard of achievement to be pursued by States.
Date: Adopted 13 September 2007.
Citation: UN Doc. A/RES/61/295.
URL: http://www.un-documents.net/a61r295.htm (last visited 13 December 2012).

103. **Declaration on the Rights of Persons Belonging to National or Ethnic, Religious and Linguistic Minorities**
Description: International human rights proclamation adopted by resolution of the United Nations General Assembly to ensure a more effective implementation of international human rights agreements with regard to the rights of national or ethnic, religious and linguistic minorities. The Declaration calls for States to protect the existence and identity of such minorities.
Date: Adopted 18 December 1992.
Citation: UN Doc. A/RES/47/135.

URL: http://www.un.org/documents/ga/res/47/a47r135.htm (last visited 13 December 2012).

104. **Declaration Relative to the Universal Abolition of the Slave Trade**
 Description: First international statement to condemn slavery, adopted in 1815 at the Congress of Vienna by the Anti-Slavery Society, the first international non-governmental organization, which was focused on ending the Atlantic slave trade. The Declaration was the basis of over 300 multilateral and bilateral agreements passed between 1815 and 1957 implemented to suppress slavery.
 Date: Adopted 8 February 1815.
 Citation: 63 C.T.S. 473.

105. Draft Declaration of Principles on Human Rights and the Environment: See **Draft Declaration of Principles on Human Rights and the Environment**.

106. ECOSOC Resolution 728F
 Description: Resolution of the United Nations Economic and Social Council, recognizing that the Commission on Human Rights has no power to take any action in regard to any complaints concerning human rights.
 Date: Adopted 30 July 1959.
 Citation: E.S.C. Res. 728F (XXVIII), UN Doc. E/3290.
 URL: http://www1.umn.edu/humanrts/procedures/728f.html (last visited 13 December 2012).

107. ECOSOC Resolution 1235
 Description: Resolution of the United Nations Economic and Social Council, granting the Human Rights Commission and the Sub-Commission on Prevention of Discrimination and Protection of Minorities explicit powers to examine information relevant to gross violations of human rights.
 Date: Adopted 6 June 1967.
 Citation: E.S.C. Res. 1235 (XLII), UN Doc. E/4393.
 URL: http://www1.umn.edu/humanrts/procedures/1235.html (last visited 13 December 2012).

108. ECOSOC Resolution 1503 Procedure for dealing with communications relating to violations of human rights and fundamental freedoms
 Description: Resolution of the United Nations Economic and Social Council, granting the Sub-Commission on Prevention of Discrimination and Protection of Minorities the power to appoint

a Working Group to consider all human rights communications in private meetings and to bring to the attention of the Sub-Commission those communications which appear to reveal a consistent pattern of gross and reliably attested violations of human rights.
Date: Adopted 27 May 1970.
Citation: E.S.C. Res. 1503 (XLVIII), UN Doc. E/4832/Add.1.
URL: http://www.unhchr.ch/Huridocda/Huridoca.nsf/TestFrame/9fb315fdda618e28802567d000550d12?Opendocument (last visited 13 December 2012).

109. English Bill of Rights of 1689: See An Act Declaring the Rights and Liberties of the Subject and Settling the Succession of the Crown.

110. **European Charter on Water Resources**
Description: Recommendation of the Committee of Ministers of the Council of Europe to Member States. The Charter sets forth principles to be applied within national policies, including sustainable development, due regard for the needs of present and future generations, equitable and reasonable use of water resources in the public interest and protection of the aquatic ecosystems and wetlands.
Date: Adopted 17 October 2001.
Citation: Rec(2001)14E.
URL: https://wcd.coe.int/wcd/ViewDoc.jsp?id=231615&Site=COE (last visited 13 December 2012).

111. **European Code of Social Security**
Description: International human rights instrument adopted by Member States of the Council of Europe to encourage members to develop and harmonize their systems of social security. The Code establishes minimum standards of social security in areas such as medical care, sickness, unemployment, old-age, employment injury, family and maternity benefits. A Revised European Code of Social Security has been opened for signature which has not yet entered into force.
Date: Adopted 16 April 1964 (entered into force 17 March 1968); Revised 6 November 1990 (not entered into force).
Citations: E.T.S. 048; Revised Code: E.T.S. 139.
URLs: http://conventions.coe.int/Treaty/en/Treaties/Html/048.htm (last visited 13 December 2012); Revised Code: http://conventions.coe.int/Treaty/en/Treaties/Html/139.htm (last visited 13 December 2012).

112. **[European] Convention for the Protection of Human Rights and Fundamental Freedoms**
Description: International human rights instrument, known as the European Convention of Human Rights, adopted by Member States of the Council of Europe as a first step for the collective enforcement of certain of the rights Stated in the Universal Declaration of Human Rights of 10 December 1948. The Convention recognizes a number of fundamental freedoms and civil and political rights, and establishes the European Court of Human Rights.
Date: Adopted 4 November 1950 (entered into force 3 September 1953).
Citation: E.T.S. 005.
URL: http://conventions.coe.int/Treaty/en/Treaties/html/005.htm (last visited 5 February 2012).

113. **European Convention for the Prevention of Torture and Inhuman or Degrading Treatment or Punishment**
Description: International human rights instrument adopted by Member States of the Council of Europe to strengthen the protection of persons deprived of their liberty against torture and inhuman or degrading treatment or punishment, by preventive, non-judicial means. The Convention establishes a Committee, which shall, by means of visits, examine the treatment of persons deprived of their liberty.
Date: Adopted 26 November 1987 (entered into force 1 February 1989).
Citation: E.T.S. 126.
URL: http://conventions.coe.int/Treaty/en/Treaties/Html/126.htm (last visited 13 December 2012).

114. European Convention on the Suppression of Terrorism
Description: International instrument adopted by Member States of the Council of Europe to ensure that the perpetrators of acts of terrorism do not escape prosecution and punishment. The Convention relies mainly on the measure of extradition to achieve this result.
Date: Adopted 27 January 1977 (entered into force 4 August 1978).
Citation: E.T.S. 090.
URL: http://conventions.coe.int/Treaty/en/Treaties/html/090.htm (last visited 13 December 2012).

115. **European Social Charter**
Description: International instrument adopted by Member States of the Council of Europe to improve the standard of living and social

well-being of European urban and rural populations. The Charter addresses many economic and social human rights, such as the right to work, to just conditions of work, to safe and healthy working conditions, to a fair remuneration, to social security, the right to organize and to bargain collectively, as well as the rights of specifically protected groups.
Date: Adopted 18 October 1961 (entered into force 26 February 1965).
Citation: E.T.S. 035.
URL: http://conventions.coe.int/Treaty/en/Treaties/html/035.htm (last visited 13 December 2012).

116. First Optional Protocol to the International Covenant on Civil and Political Rights: See **Optional Protocol to the International Covenant on Civil and Political Rights.**

117. Forced Labour Convention of 1930: See Convention concerning Forced or Compulsory Labour, as Modified; see also, **International Labor Organization Forced Labor Conventions (ILO Conventions Nos. 29 and 105).**

118. Framework For Action to Meet Basic Learning Needs
Description: The Framework For Action derives from the World Declaration on Education for All, adopted by the World Conference on Education for All. It was intended as a reference for governments, international organizations, aid agencies and non-governmental organizations in formulating their own plans of action for implementing the Declaration. The Framework For Action identifies priorities at the national, regional, and world levels and provides indicative phases of implementation for the 1990s.
Date: Adopted 9 March 1990.
Citation: Final Report of the World Conference on Education for All: Meeting Basic Learning Needs, Jomtien, Thailand, 5–9 March 1990, appendix II.
URL: http://www.un-documents.net/jomteinf.htm (last visited 13 December 2012).

119. French Declaration of the Rights of Man and of the Citizen: See **French Declaration of the Rights of Man and of the Citizen**.

120. General Framework Agreement for Peace in Bosnia and Herzegovina
Description: International instrument agreed upon by the Republic of Bosnia and Herzegovina, the Republic of Croatia and the

Federal Republic of Yugoslavia, in Dayton, United States, and formally signed in Paris, to put an end to the war in Bosnia. The parties endorsed the arrangements that had been made concerning the establishment of a Commission on Human Rights and a Commission on Refugees and Displaced Persons, which are detailed in Annexes 6 and 7 to the Agreement.
Date: Adopted 14 December 1995.
URL: http://www.ohr.int/dpa/default.asp?content_id=380 (last visited 13 December 2012).

121. Geneva Convention I for the Amelioration of the Condition of the Wounded and Sick in Armies in the Field
Description: International human rights instrument defining basic principles for the protection of victims in cases of armed conflict or occupation, and retaining the red cross on a white ground as the emblem of the Medical Service of armed forces. The Convention represents the fourth version of the Geneva Convention on the wounded and sick after those adopted in 1864, 1906 and 1929.
Date: Adopted 12 August 1949 (entered into force 21 October 1950).
Citation: 75 U.N.T.S. 31, UN Doc. 970.
URL: http://www.un-documents.net/gc-1.htm (last visited 13 December 2012).

122. **Geneva Convention II for the Amelioration of the Condition of Wounded, Sick and Shipwrecked Members of Armed Forces at Sea**
Description: International human rights instrument defining basic principles for the protection of wounded and sick members of armed forces at sea. The Convention adapts the main protections of the First Geneva Convention to combat at sea, and replaces the 1907 Hague Convention for the Adaptation to Maritime Warfare of the Principles of the Geneva Convention.
Date: Adopted 12 August 1949 (entered into force 21 October 1950).
Citation: 75 U.N.T.S. 85, UN Doc. 971.
URL: http://www.un-documents.net/gc-2.htm (last visited 13 December 2012).

123. **Geneva Convention III relative to the Treatment of Prisoners of War**
Description: International human rights instrument defining basic principles for the protection of prisoners of war. The Convention covers the labor of prisoners of war, their financial resources, the relief they receive and the judicial proceedings instituted against them. It provides that prisoners of war shall be released and repatriated without delay after the cessation of active hostilities.

Date: Adopted 12 August 1949 (entered into force 21 October 1950).
Citation: 75 U.N.T.S. 135, UN Doc. 972.
URL: http://www.un-documents.net/gc-3.htm (last visited 13 December 2012).

124. **Geneva Convention IV relative to the Protection of Civilian Persons in Time of War**
Description: International human rights instrument defining basic principles for the protection of civilians in cases of armed conflict or occupation. The Convention provides for the protection of populations against certain consequences of war, and sets forth regulations governing the status and treatment of foreigners on the territory of a party to a conflict and that of civilians in occupied territory.
Date: Adopted 12 August 1949 (entered into force 21 October 1950).
Citation: 75 U.N.T.S. 287, UN Doc. 973.
URL: http://www.un-documents.net/gc-4.htm (last visited 12 December 2012).

125. **Geneva Conventions of 1949**: See also **Protocol I Additional to the Geneva Conventions of 12 August 1949, and relating to the Protection of Victims of International Armed Conflicts; Protocol II Additional to the Geneva Conventions of 12 August 1949, and relating to the Protection of Victims of Non-International Armed Conflicts**.

126. Geneva Declaration of the Rights of the Child
Description: International proclamation adopted by the League of Nations, recognizing that mankind owes to children the best that it has to give, and accepting as a duty of the international community to give children the means necessary to their development, to attend to their basic needs and to protect them from exploitation, among other commitments.
Date: Adopted 26 September 1924.
Citation: League of Nations O.J. Spec. Supp. 21, at 43.
URL: http://www.un-documents.net/gdrc1924.htm (last visited 13 December 2012).

127. Guidelines for Action on Children in the Criminal Justice System
Description: International standards adopted by resolution of the United Nations Economic and Social Council to provide a framework for the implementation of the Convention of the Rights of the Child and to assist States Parties to the Convention and related instruments. The Guidelines set forth national and international measures that should be taken in the area of juvenile justice to

further the rights of children in contact with criminal justice systems and provide safeguards for the protection of child victims and witnesses.
Date: Adopted 21 July 1997.
Citation: UN Doc. E/RES/1997/30.
URL: http://www.un.org/documents/ecosoc/res/1997/eres1997-30.htm (last visited 13 December 2012).

128. Guidelines for the Alternative Care of Children
Description: International standards adopted by resolution of the United Nations General Assembly to enhance the implementation of the Convention on the Rights of the Child and other relevant international instruments regarding the protection and well-being of children deprived of parental care or who are at risk of being so. The Guidelines call upon States to strengthen families and prevent the separation of children from their families. They provide that poverty should never be a reason for separation, and that decisions surrounding care must be made in the best interests of the child. When alternative care is needed, the Guidelines provide for key standards that should be met in every State.
Date: Adopted 24 February 2010.
Citation: UN Doc. A/RES/64/142.
URL: http://www.unicef.org/protection/alternative_care_Guidelines-English.pdf (last visited 13 December 2012).

129. Guidelines for the Implementation of the Universal Declaration on the Human Genome and Human Rights
Description: International standards adopted by resolution of the United Nations Educational, Scientific and Cultural Organization General Conference to supplement the Universal Declaration on the Human Genome and Human Rights of 11 November 1997. The Guidelines seek to identify the tasks devolving on different actors in the implementation of the Declaration and the modalities of action for their achievement. Among the tasks, the Guidelines identify the dissemination of the principles set forth in the Declaration, consciousness-raising, the exchange of studies and the establishment of relationships between actors.
Date: Adopted 29 October 1999.
Citation: UNESCO Doc. 30 C/Resolution 23.
URL: http://www.unesco.org/new/fileadmin/MULTIMEDIA/HQ/SHS/pdf/Guidelines-Genome_EN.pdf (last visited 13 December 2012).

130. Guidelines on the Role of Prosecutors
Description: International standards adopted by the Eighth United Nations Congress on the Prevention of Crime and the Treatment of Offenders to assist Member States in securing and promoting the effectiveness, impartiality and fairness of prosecutors in criminal proceedings. The Guidelines cover the qualifications, selection and training of prosecutors, their status, their freedom of expression and association, their role in criminal proceedings and disciplinary proceedings against them, among other aspects.
Date: Adopted 27 August–7 September 1990.
Citation: UN Doc. A/CONF.144/28/Rev.1 at 189.
URL: http://www2.ohchr.org/english/law/prosecutors.htm (last visited 13 December 2012).

131. Guiding Principles on Business and Human Rights for implementing the UN "Protect, Respect and Remedy" Framework
Description: International human rights standards endorsed by the United Nations Human Rights Council to enhance practices with regard to business and human rights, achieve tangible results for affected individuals and communities and overall contribute to a socially sustainable globalization. The Guiding Principles provide foundational and operational principles to implement the State duty to protect human rights, the corporate responsibility to respect human rights, and the need for access to an effective remedy.
Date: Adopted 6 July 2011.
Citation: UN Doc. A/HRC/17/31.
URL: http://www.ohchr.org/Documents/Issues/Business/A-HRC-17-31_AEV.pdf (last visited 13 December 2012).

132. Guiding Principles on Internal Displacement
Description: International human rights standards developed at the request of the United Nations Commission on Human Rights to address the specific needs of internally displaced persons worldwide. The Guidelines identify rights and guarantees relevant to the protection of displaced persons from forced displacement and to their protection and assistance during displacement and during return or resettlement.
Date: Adopted 11 February 1998.
Citation: E/CN.4/1998/53/Add.2.
URL: http://www.un-documents.net/gpid.htm (last visited 13 December 2012).

Appendix 215

133. Hague Conventions of 1899
     Description: Set of three Conventions, three Declarations and one Final Act adopted by the First Peace Conference of the Hague held in 1899. These international instruments aimed at promoting international peace through the regulation of various aspects of warfare, such as the use of certain projectiles and explosives. The Final Act was signed but not ratified, and therefore has no binding force.
     Date: Adopted 29 July 1899.
     URL: http://www.icrc.org/ihl.nsf/TOPICS?OpenView (last visited 13 December 2012).

134. Hague Conventions of 1907
     Description: Set of 14 Conventions, one Declaration, and one Final Act adopted by the Second Peace Conference of The Hague, held in 1907. These international instruments aimed at further promoting peace and at limiting the development of armament through the regulation of various aspects of warfare. The Final Act and the twelfth Convention were signed but not ratified, and therefore have no binding force.
     Date: Adopted 18 October 1907.
     URL: http://www.icrc.org/ihl.nsf/TOPICS?OpenView (last visited 13 December 2012).

135. **Handbook on Procedures and Criteria for Determining Refugee Status under the 1951 Convention and the 1967 Protocol relating to the status of Refugees**
     Description: International guidelines adopted by the United Nations High Commissioner for Refugees for the guidance of contracting States' government officials concerned with the determination of refugee status under the 1951 Convention and 1967 Protocol relating to the status of Refugees. The Handbook provides interpretations of certain terms contained in the international instruments, including under the inclusion clauses, cessation clauses and exclusion clauses, and analyzes distinctive refugee cases.
     Date: Adopted 1979, reedited January 1992.
     Citation: UN Doc. HCR/IP/4/Eng/REV.2.
     URL: http://www.unhcr.org/3d58e13b4.html (last visited 13 December 2012).

136. **Inter-American Convention Against Terrorism**
     Description: International instrument adopted by members of the Organization of American States to prevent, punish and eliminate terrorism. States Parties agree to strengthen their co-operation

and to adopt necessary measures, in the respect of the rule of law, human rights and fundamental freedoms. The Convention expressly provides that any person taken into custody pursuant to this instrument shall be guaranteed fair treatment, including the enjoyment of all rights and guarantees in conformity with international human rights law.
Date: Adopted 3 June 2002 (entered into force 10 July 2003).
Citation: O.A.S.T.S. A-66.
URL: http://www.oas.org/juridico/english/treaties/a-66.html (last visited 13 December 2012).

137. **Inter-American Convention on Forced Disappearance of Persons**
Description: International human rights instrument adopted by members of the Organization of American States to help prevent, punish and eliminate the forced disappearance of persons in the Western Hemisphere. States Parties committed to not practice, permit, or tolerate forced disappearances, to punish those persons who commit or attempt to commit this crime and to co-operate with one another to achieve the treaty's purpose.
Date: Adopted 9 June 1994 (entered into force 28 March 1996).
Citation: O.A.S.T.S. A-60.
URL: http://www.oas.org/juridico/english/treaties/a-60.html (last visited 13 December 2012).

138. Inter-American Convention on International Traffic in Minors
Description: International human rights instrument adopted by members of the Organization of American States to prevent and punish the international traffic in minors, and regulate its civil and penal aspects. The Convention organizes international co-operation to achieve the effective protection of the best interests of all human beings below the age of 18.
Date: Adopted 18 March 1994 (entered into force 15 August 1997).
Citation: O.A.S.T.S. B-57.
URL: http://www.oas.org/dil/treaties_B-57_Inter-American_Convention_on_International_Traffic_in_Minors.htm (last visited 13 December 2012).

139. Inter-American Convention on the Elimination of All Forms of Discrimination Against Persons with Disabilities
Description: International human rights instrument adopted by members of the Organization of American States, reaffirming that persons with disabilities have the same human rights and fundamental freedoms as other persons, and mandating that Member

States undertake to adopt the legislative, social, educational, labor-related or other measures needed to eliminate discrimination against persons with disabilities and to promote their full integration into society.
Date: Adopted 8 June 1994 (entered into force 14 September 2001).
Citation: O.A.S.T.S. A-65.
URL: http://www.oas.org/juridico/english/sigs/a-65.html (last visited 13 December 2012).

140. Inter-American Convention on the Granting of Civil Rights to Women
    Description: International human rights instrument adopted by members of the Organization of American States, resolving to grant to women the same civil rights that men enjoy.
    Date: Adopted 2 May 1948, (entered into force 17 March 1949).
    Citation: O.A.S.T.S. A-45, 1438 U.N.T.S. 51, UN Doc. 24374.
    URL: http://www.oas.org/juridico/english/treaties/a-45.html (last visited 13 December 2012).

141. Inter-American Convention on the Granting of Political Rights to Women
    Description: International human rights instrument adopted by members of the Organization of American States, agreeing that the right to vote and to be elected to national office shall not be denied or abridged by reason of sex.
    Date: Adopted 2 May 1948 (entered into force 17 March 1949).
    Citation: O.A.S.T.S. A-44, 1438 U.N.T.S. 63, UN Doc. 24375.
    URL: http://www.oas.org/juridico/english/treaties/a-44.html (last visited 13 December 2012).

142. [Inter-American] Convention on the Nationality of Women
    Description: International human rights instrument adopted at the Seventh International Conference of American States. The States Parties agreed that there shall be no distinction based on sex as regards nationality, in their legislation or in their practice.
    Date: Adopted 26 December 1933 (entered into force 29 August 1934).
    URL: http://www.oas.org/en/cim/docs/CNW%5BEN%5D.pdf (last visited 13 December 2012).

143. Inter-American Convention on the Prevention, Punishment and Eradication of Violence Against Women
    Description: International human rights instrument adopted by

members of the Organization of American States to prevent, punish and eliminate acts based on gender which causes death or physical, sexual or psychological harm or suffering to women, whether in the public or the private sphere. The Convention sets forth protected rights of women, duties of State Parties, and Inter-American mechanisms of protection.
Date: Adopted 9 June 1994 (entered into force 5 March 1995).
Citation: O.A.S.T.S. A-61.
URL: http://www.oas.org/juridico/english/treaties/a-61.html (last visited 13 December 2012).

144. **Inter-American Convention to Prevent and Punish Torture**
Description: International human rights instrument adopted by members of the Organization of American States to prevent and punish any act intentionally performed whereby physical or mental pain or suffering is inflicted on a person for purposes of criminal investigation, as a means of intimidation, as personal punishment, as a preventive measure, as a penalty, to obliterate the personality of the victim, to diminish his physical or mental capacities, or for any other purpose.
Date: Adopted 9 December 1985 (entered into force 28 February 1987).
Citation: O.A.S.T.S. A-51.
URL: http://www.oas.org/juridico/english/treaties/a-51.html (last visited 13 December 2012).

145. Inter-American Declaration of Principles on Freedom of Expression
Description: International human rights proclamation adopted by the Inter-American Commission on Human Rights, recognizing freedom of expression in all its forms and manifestations as a fundamental and inalienable right of all individuals. The Declaration also affirms the right to access information, and the right of social communicators to keep their sources of information and notes confidential.
Date: Adopted 19 October 2000.
URL: http://www.iachr.org/declaration.htm (last visited 13 December 2012).

146. **Inter-American Democratic Charter**
Description: International human rights instrument adopted by the General Assembly of the Organization of American States to clarify provisions set forth in the Organization's founding documents on the preservation and defense of democratic institutions. The

Charter reaffirms the peoples of the Americas' right to democracy and governments' obligation to promote and defend it.
Date: Adopted 11 September 2001.
Citation: OEA/SerP/AG/Res.1.
URL: http://www.oas.org/charter/docs/resolution1_cn_p4.htm (last visited 13 December 2012).

147. International Agreement for the Suppression of the White Slave Traffic, as Amended by Protocol
Description: International human rights instrument obligating the States Parties to establish or name a national authority responsible for the coordination of all information relative to the procuring of women or girls for immoral purposes abroad, and for direct communication with similar authorities established in other States.
Date: Convention adopted 18 May 1904 (entered into force 18 July 1905); Protocol adopted 9 May 1949 (entered into force 21 June 1951).
Citation: 92 U.N.T.S. 19, UN Doc. 1257.
URL: http://treaties.un.org/doc/Publication/UNTS/Volume%2092/volume-92-I-1257-English.pdf (last visited 13 December 2012).

148. International Convention Against the Taking of Hostages
Description: International instrument adopted by resolution of the United Nations General Assembly to develop international co-operation between States in devising and adopting effective measures for the prevention, prosecution and punishment of all acts of taking of hostages as manifestations of international terrorism. The Convention aims at protecting the right to life, liberty and security of persons.
Date: Adopted 17 December 1979 (entered into force 3 June 1983).
Citation: 1316 U.N.T.S. 205, UN Doc. 21931.
URL: http://treaties.un.org/doc/db/Terrorism/english-18-5.pdf (last visited 13 December 2012).

149. International Convention on the Protection and Promotion of the Rights and Dignity of Persons with Disabilities: See **Convention on the Rights of Persons with Disabilities**.

150. International Convention for the Suppression of Acts of Nuclear Terrorism
Description: International instrument adopted by the United Nations General Assembly to enhance international co-operation between States in devising and adopting measures for the prevention of acts of nuclear terrorism and for the prosecution and punishment

of their perpetrators. Any person taken into custody pursuant to the Convention shall be guaranteed fair treatment, including enjoyment of all rights and guarantees in conformity with the international law of human rights.
Date: Adopted 13 April 13, 2005 (entered into force 7 July 2007).
Citation: 2445 U.N.T.S. 89, UN Doc. A/RES/59/290.
URL: http://www.un-documents.net/icsant.htm (last visited 13 December 2012).

151. International Convention for the Suppression of Terrorist Bombings
Description: International instrument adopted by resolution of the United Nations General Assembly to enhance international co-operation among States in devising and adopting effective and practical measures for the prevention of acts of terrorism and for the prosecution and punishment of their perpetrators. Any person taken into custody pursuant to the Convention shall be guaranteed fair treatment, including enjoyment of all rights and guarantees in conformity with the international law of human rights.
Date: Adopted 15 December 1997 (entered into force 23 May 2001).
Citation: 2149 U.N.T.S. 256, UN Doc. A/RES/52/164.
URL: http://treaties.un.org/doc/db/Terrorism/english-18-9.pdf (last visited 13 December 2012).

152. **International Convention for the Suppression of the Financing of Terrorism**
Description: International instrument adopted by resolution of the United Nations General Assembly to enhance international co-operation among States in devising and adopting effective measures for the prevention of the financing of terrorism, as well as for its suppression through the prosecution and punishment of its perpetrators. Any person taken into custody pursuant to the Convention shall be guaranteed fair treatment, including enjoyment of all rights and guarantees in conformity with the international law of human rights.
Date: Adopted 12 September 1999 (entered into force 10 April 2002).
Citation: 2178 U.N.T.S. 197, UN Doc. A/RES/54/109.
URL: http://www.un.org/law/cod/finterr.htm (last visited 13 December 2012).

153. International Convention for the Suppression of the Traffic in Women and Children, as Amended by Protocol
Description: International human rights instrument obligating State

Parties to take all measures to discover, prosecute and punish persons engaged in the traffic of children of both sexes.
Date: Convention adopted 30 September 1921 (entered into force 15 June 1922); Protocol adopted 12 November 1947 (entered into force 24 April 1950).
Citation: 53 U.N.T.S. 39, UN Doc. 771.
URL: http://treaties.un.org/doc/Publication/UNTS/Volume%2053/volume-53-I-771-English.pdf (last visited 13 December 2012).

154. **International Convention for the Suppression of the Traffic in Women of Full Age, as Amended by Protocol**
Description: International human rights instrument providing that whoever, in order to gratify the passions of another person, has procured, enticed or led away even with her consent, a woman or girl of full age for immoral purposes to be carried out in another country, shall be punished. The Convention provides for the sharing of relevant information between contracting parties, such as records of convictions.
Date: Convention adopted 11 October 1933 (entered into force 24 August 1934); Protocol adopted 12 November 1947 (entered into force 24 April 1950).
Citation: 53 U.N.T.S. 49, UN Doc. 772.
URL: http://treaties.un.org/doc/Publication/UNTS/Volume%2053/volume-53-I-772-English.pdf (last visited 13 December 2012).

155. **International Convention for the Suppression of the White Slave Traffic, as Amended by Protocol**
Description: International human rights instrument providing that any person who, to gratify the passions of others, has hired, abducted or enticed, even with her consent, a woman or a girl who is a minor, for immoral purposes, shall be punished. The same applies under the Convention to traffic involving women of full age by fraud or by the use of violence, threats, abuse of authority, or any other means of constraint.
Date: Convention adopted 4 May 4; Protocol adopted 4 May 1949 (entered into force 14 August 1951).
Citation: 98 U.N.T.S. 102, UN Doc. 1358.
URL: http://treaties.un.org/doc/Publication/UNTS/Volume%2098/volume-98-I-1358-English.pdf (last visited 13 December 2012).

156. **International Convention on the Elimination of All Forms of Racial Discrimination**
Description: International human rights instrument adopted by

resolution of the United Nations General Assembly to implement the principles embodied in the United Nations Declaration on the Elimination of All Forms of Racial Discrimination of 20 November 1963. The Convention imposes obligations on State Parties and provides for the establishment of a Committee on the Elimination of Racial Discrimination.
Date: Adopted 21 December 1965 (entered into force 4 January 1969).
Citation: 660 U.N.T.S. 195, UN Doc. A/6014 at 47.
URL: http://www.un-documents.net/icerd.htm (last visited 13 December 2012).

157. International Convention on the Protection of All Persons from Enforced Disappearance
Description: International human rights instrument adopted by resolution of the United Nations General Assembly, affirming the right not to be subjected to any form of deprivation of liberty by persons acting with the authorization or acquiescence of the State, followed by a refusal to acknowledge the deprivation of liberty or by concealment of the fate or whereabouts of the disappeared person. The Convention also affirms the right of relatives to know the truth about the circumstances of an enforced disappearance and the fate of the disappeared person.
Date: Adopted 12 January 2007 (entered into force 23 December 2010).
Citation: UN Doc. A/61/177.
URL: http://www2.ohchr.org/english/law/disappearance-convention.htm (last visited 13 December 2012).

158. International Convention on the Protection of Rights of All Migrant Workers and Members of Their Families
Description: International human rights instrument adopted by resolution of the United Nations General Assembly to protect persons engaged in a remunerated activity in a State of which they are not a national, as well as family members of such persons. The Convention addresses the basic human rights and some social and economic rights of migrant workers and family members who are documented or in a regular situation.
Date: Adopted 18 December 1990 (entered into force 1 July 2003).
Citation: 2220 U.N.T.S. 3, UN Doc. A/RES/45/158.
URL: http://www.un-documents.net/icpramw.htm (last visited 13 December 2012).

159. International Covenant on Civil and Political Rights (ICCPR)
Description: International human rights instrument adopted by resolution of the United Nations General Assembly, providing for the rights of all peoples to self-determination, to life, to freedom from torture and slavery, to be treated with humanity in case of deprivation of liberty, to leave any country and to a fair trial, among other rights. The Covenant establishes a Human Rights Committee to monitor the implementation of the treaty.
Date: Adopted 16 December 1966 (entered into force 23 March 1976).
Citation: 999 U.N.T.S. 171, UN Doc. A/RES/21/2200.
URL: http://www.un-documents.net/iccpr.htm (last visited 13 December 2012).

160. International Covenant on Economic, Social and Cultural Rights (ICESCR)
Description: International human rights instrument adopted by resolution of the United Nations General Assembly, providing for the rights of all peoples to self-determination, to work in just and favorable conditions, to form and join trade unions, to social protection, to an adequate standard of living, to the highest attainable standard of physical and mental health, to education, and to take part in cultural life, among other rights. The Covenant establishes a reporting mechanism to the Secretary-General of the United Nations and to the Economic and Social Council.
Date: Adopted 16 December 1966 (entered into force 3 January 1976).
Citation: 993 U.N.T.S. 3, UN Doc. A/RES/21/2200
URL: http://www.un-documents.net/icescr.htm (last visited 13 December 2012).

161. International Declaration on Human Genetic Data
Description: International proclamation adopted by resolution of the United Nations Educational, Scientific and Cultural Organization General Conference to ensure the respect of human dignity and the protection of human rights and fundamental freedoms in the collection, processing, use and storage of human genetic and proteomic data and the biological samples from which they are derived. The Declaration sets forth procedures for such collection and use, and establishes ethical principles such as non-discrimination based on genetic and proteomic data and consent to the collection, confidentiality, and sharing of benefits resulting from the use of the data.
Date: Adopted 16 October 2003.

224 *Dictionary of international human rights law*

Citation: UNESCO Doc. 32 C/Resolution 22.
URL: http://portal.unesco.org/en/ev.php-URL_ID=17720&URL_DO=DO_TOPIC&URL_SECTION=201.html (last visited 13 December 2012).

162. International Labour Conference Conventions: See the database of the International Labour Organization, which contains a series of instruments on international labor standards and work-related human rights, including the **International Labor Organization Convention of 1948 concerning Freedom of Association and Protetction of the Right to Organize**
URL: http://www.ilo.org/ilolex/english/convdisp1.htm (last visited 13 December 2012).

163. Johannesburg Principles on National Security, Freedom of Expression and Access to Information
Description: International standards adopted by a group of experts in international law, national security and human rights to promote a clear recognition of the limited scope of restrictions on freedom of expression and freedom of information that may be imposed in the interest of national security, and to discourage governments from using the pretext of national security to place unjustified restrictions on the exercise of these freedoms.
Date: Adopted 1 October 1995.
Citation: UN Doc. E/CN.4/1996/39.
URL: http://www.article19.org/data/files/pdfs/standards/joburgprinciples.pdf (last visited 13 December 2012).

164. League of Nations Slavery Convention: See **Slavery, Servitude, Forced Labour and Similar Institutions and Practices Convention**.

165. Lisbon, Treaty of: See Treaty of Lisbon.

166. London Agreement: See **Agreement for the Prosecution and Punishment of the Major War Criminals of the European Axis**.

167. Maputo Protocol: See **Protocol to the African Charter on Human and Peoples' Rights on the Rights of Women in Africa**.

168. Mexico City Declaration on Cultural Policies
Description: International declaration adopted by the World Conference on Cultural Policies, agreeing on an international definition of culture and on principles that should govern cultural policies. The Declaration acknowledges many facets of culture and addresses cultural identity; the cultural dimension of development;

culture and democracy; cultural heritage; artistic and intellectual creation and art education; the relationship of culture with education, science and communication; planning, administration and financing of cultural activities; as well as international cultural co-operation.
Date: Adopted 6 August 1982.
URL: http://portal.unesco.org/culture/en/files/12762/11295421661 mexico_en.pdf/mexico_en.pdf (last visited 13 December 2012).

169. Nairobi Forward-looking Strategies for the Advancement of Women
Description: International plan of action adopted by the World Conference to Review and Appraise the Achievements of the United Nations Decade for Women. The Forward-looking Strategies reaffirm the international concern regarding the status of women and provide a framework for renewed commitment by the international community to the advancement of women and the elimination of gender-based discrimination.
Date: Adopted 26 July 1985.
Citation: UN Doc. A/CONF.116/28/Rev.
URL: http://www.un-documents.net/nflsaw.htm (last visited 13 December 2012).

170. Norms on the Responsibilities of Transnational Corporations and Other Business Enterprises with Regard to Human Rights
Description: International standards adopted by the United Nations Sub-Commission for the Promotion and Protection of Human Rights as a guide to corporate social responsibility. The Norms set out the responsibilities of transnational corporations and other business enterprises with regard to human rights and labor rights, and provide guidelines for companies in conflict zones.
Date: Adopted 13 August 2003.
Citation: UN Doc. E/CN.4/Sub.2/2003/12/Rev.2.
URL: http://www.unhchr.ch/huridocda/huridoca.nsf/%28Symbol%29/E.CN.4.Sub.2.2003.12.Rev.2.En (last visited 13 December 2012).

171. Nuremberg Charter: See **Charter of the International Military Tribunal of 8 August 1945**.

172. Optional Protocol to the Convention on the Rights of Persons with Disabilities
Description: International human rights instrument supplementing the Convention on the Rights of Persons with Disabilities of 13 December 2006. The Optional Protocol recognizes the competence

of the Committee on the Rights of Persons with Disabilities to receive and consider communications from individuals who claim to be victims of a violation of the Convention.
Date: Adopted 13 December 2006 (entered into force 3 May 2008).
Citation: 2515 U.N.T.S. 3, UN Doc. A/RES/61/106.
URL: http://www.un-documents.net/a61r106.htm (last visited 13 December 2012).

173. Optional Protocol to the Convention on the Rights of the Child on a communications procedure
Description: International human rights instrument adopted by resolution of the United Nations General Assembly to provide an enforcement mechanism to the Convention on the Rights of the Child of 20 November 1989. States Parties to this Protocol recognize the competence of the Committee on the Rights of the Child to receive and examine complaints alleging violations of rights under the Convention or its first two additional protocols by States Parties to this third Protocol.
Date: Adopted 19 December 2011 (not entered into force).
Citation: UN Doc. A/RES/66/138.
URL: http://www.un.org/Docs/asp/ws.asp?m=A/RES/66/138 (last visited 13 December 2012).

174. **Optional Protocol to the Convention on the Rights of the Child on the Involvement of Children in Armed Conflicts**
Description: International human rights instrument adopted by resolution of the United Nations General Assembly to complement the Convention on the Rights of the Child of 20 November 1989. The Protocol aims at increasing the protection of children from direct involvement in armed hostilities and from recruitment into armed forces.
Date: Adopted 25 May 2000 (entered into force 18 January 2002).
Citation: 2173 U.N.T.S. 222, UN Doc. A/RES/54/263.
URL: http://www.un-documents.net/opcrccac.htm (last visited 13 December 2012).

175. Optional Protocol to the Convention on the Rights of the Child on the Sale of Children, Child Prostitution and Child Pornography
Description: International human rights instrument adopted by resolution of the United Nations General Assembly to complement the Convention on the Rights of the Child of 20 November 1989. The Protocol obligates States Parties to take measures in

order to guarantee the protection of children against traffic for the purpose of the sale of children, child prostitution and child pornography.
Date: Adopted 25 May 2000 (entered into force 12 February 2002).
Citation: 2173 U.N.T.S. 222, UN Doc. A/RES/54/263.
URL: http://www.un-documents.net/opcrcsc.htm (last visited 13 December 2012).

176. **Optional Protocol to the International Covenant on Civil and Political Rights**
Description: International human rights instrument adopted by resolution of the United Nations General Assembly to enable the Human Rights Committee to receive and consider communications from individuals claiming to be victims of violations of rights set forth in the International Covenant on Civil and Political Rights of 16 December 1966.
Date: Adopted 16 December 1966 (entered into force 23 March 1976).
Citation: 999 U.N.T.S. 171, UN Doc. A/RES/21/2200.
URL: http://www.un-documents.net/iccpr-op.htm (last visited 13 December 2012).

177. **Optional Protocol to the International Covenant on Economic, Social and Cultural Rights**
Description: International human rights instrument adopted by resolution of the United Nations General Assembly to enable the Committee on Economic, Social and Cultural Rights to receive and consider communications from individuals claiming to be victims of violations of rights set forth in the International Covenant on Economic, Social and Cultural Rights of 16 December 1966.
Date: Adopted 10 December 2008 (not entered into force).
Citation: UN Doc. A/RES/63/117.
URL: http://www2.ohchr.org/english/law/docs/A.RES.63.117_en.pdf (last visited 13 December 2012).

178. Ottawa Charter for Health Promotion
Description: International human rights agreement adopted by the First International Conference on Health Promotion to achieve health for all by the year 2000 and beyond. The Charter defines the process of health promotion, provides practical actions to promote health, commits the Conference participants to a strong public health alliance and calls on the World Health Organization and

other international organizations to advocate the promotion of health and to support countries in setting up programs for health promotion.
Date: Adopted 26 November 1986.
Citation: UN Doc. WHO/HPR/HEP/95.1.
URL: http://www.who.int/healthpromotion/conferences/previous/ottawa/en/ (last visited 13 December 2012).

179. Ottawa Convention: See Convention on the Prohibition of the Use, Stockpiling, Production and Transfer of Anti-Personnel Mines and on their Destruction.

180. Pacific Charter of Human Rights
Description: Draft of international human rights instrument adopted by States of Oceania to reinforce and complement the protection of rights under the domestic law of Pacific jurisdictions. The Charter recognizes individual civil, political, economic, social and cultural rights, as well as collective rights of Peoples, and sets forth correlating duties. It also provides for the establishment of a Pacific Human Rights Commission.
Date: Draft adopted 17 May 1989 (not entered into force).
URL: http://pacific.ohchr.org/docs/Draft_Pacific_Charter_Memoranda.pdf (last visited 13 December 2012).

181. Pact of San José: See **American Convention on Human Rights**.

182. Palermo Convention: See United Nations Convention Against Corruption.

183. **Paris Minimum Standards of Human Rights Norms in a State of Emergency**
Description: International standards adopted by the 61st Conference of the International Law Association, and intended to govern the declaration and administration of states of emergency that threaten the life of a nation. The Standards set forth the non-derogable basic human rights and freedoms to which individuals remain entitled even during states of emergency.
Date: Adopted 1 September 1984.
Citation: Reprinted in Richard B. Lillich, *Current Developments, The Paris Minimum Standards of Human Rights Norms in a State of Emergency*, 79 Am. J. Int'l L. 1072 (1985).
URL: http://www.uio.no/studier/emner/jus/humanrights/HUMR5503/h09/undervisningsmateriale/ParisMinimumStandards.pdf (last visited 13 December 2012).

Appendix 229

184. Paris Principles on National Human Rights Institutions: See **Principles relating to the Status of National Institutions**.

185. Plan of Implementation of the World Summit on Sustainable Development
    Description: International plan of action adopted by the World Summit on Sustainable Development, reaffirming the fundamental principles of the Rio Declaration on Environment and Development of 14 June 1992 and Agenda 21. Ten years after their adoption, the Plan of Implementation further builds on the achievements made since the Conference on Environment and Development to expedite the realization of the remaining goals.
    Date: Adopted 4 September 2002.
    Citation: UN Doc. A/CONF.199/20.
    URL: http://www.un-documents.net/jburgpln.htm (last visited 13 December 2012).

186. Principles and Guidelines on Children Associated with Armed Forces or Armed Groups
    Description: International standards known as the Paris Principles, developed by the United Nations Children's Fund and endorsed by States to support and promote good practices on the disarmament, demobilization and reintegration of all children associated with armed groups. The Paris Principles are based on the 1997 Cape Town Principles and Best Practices on the Prevention of Recruitment of Children into the Armed Forces and on Demobilization and Social Reintegration of Child Soldiers in Africa.
    Date: Adopted February 2007.
    URL: http://www.un.org/children/conflict/_documents/parisprinciples/ParisPrinciples_EN.pdf (last visited 13 December 2012).

187. Principles and Best Practices on the Protection of Persons Deprived of Liberty in the Americas
    Description: International standards adopted by the Inter-American Commission on Human Rights as an input to the process of drafting an Inter-American Declaration on the rights, duties and care of persons under any form of detention or imprisonment. The Principles recognize the right to human treatment, non-discrimination, personal liberty, legality and due process of law, among others.
    Date: Adopted 13 March 2008.
    Citation: OEA/Ser/L/V/II.131 doc. 26.
    URL: http://www.cidh.oas.org/Basicos/English/Basic21.a.Principles

%20and%20Best%20Practices%20PDL.htm (last visited 13 December 2012).

188. **Principles for the Protection of Persons with Mental Illness and the Improvement of Mental Health Care**
Description: International standards adopted by resolution of the United Nations General Assembly, recognizing basic rights and fundamental freedoms of persons with a mental illness. The Principles set forth several rights of persons receiving mental health care and provide a framework of safeguards for the involuntary treatment of patients with a mental illness.
Date: Adopted 17 December 1991.
Citation: UN Doc. A/RES/46/119.
URL: http://www.un-documents.net/pppmi.htm (last visited 13 December 2012).

189. **Principles of Medical Ethics relevant to the Role of Health Personnel, particularly Physicians, in the Protection of Prisoners and Detainees Against Torture and Other Cruel, Inhuman or Degrading Treatment or Punishment**
Description: International standards adopted by resolution of the United Nations General Assembly, as a framework for the medical care of prisoners and detainees. The Principles provide for the equal treatment of all persons regardless of their status as prisoners or detainees, and for the accountability of medical personnel engaging in acts contravening medical ethics.
Date: Adopted 18 December 1982.
Citation: UN Doc. A/RES/37/194.
URL: http://www.un.org/documents/ga/res/37/a37r194.htm (last visited 13 December 2012).

190. **Principles on Human Rights and the Environment**
Description: Declaration drafted by an international group of experts on human rights and environmental protection. The Declaration sets forth general principles, including the human right to a secure and healthy environment and the right to an environment adequate to meet the needs of the present generation without impairing the rights of future generations to meet their needs.
Date: Draft adopted 16 May 1994 (not entered into force).
Citation: In Report of the UN Special Rapporteur on Human Rights and the Environment, E/CN.4/Sub.2/1994/9, Annex I.
URL: http://www.unhchr.ch/Huridocda/Huridoca.nsf/0/eeab2b693

7bccaa18025675c005779c3?Opendocument (last visited 13 December 2012).

191. Principles on National Security and Right to Information: See **Johannesburg Principles on National Security, Freedom of Expression and Access to Information.**

192. **Principles on the Effective Prevention and Investigation of Extra-Legal, Arbitrary and Summary Execution**
Description: International standards adopted by resolution of the United Nations Economic and Social Council to prevent extralegal, arbitrary and summary execution, and insure that cases of such practices be investigated and prosecuted. The Principles are intended for members of the executive and legislative bodies of Governments, law enforcement and criminal justice officials, military personnel, lawyers and the public in general.
Date: Adopted 24 May 1984.
Citation: UN Doc. E/RES/1989/65.
URL: http://www.un-documents.net/1989-65.htm (last visited 13 December 2012).

193. **Principles relating to the Status of National Institutions**
Description: International standards adopted by resolution of the United Nations General Assembly to guide the establishment and functioning of national institutions for the promotion and protection of human rights. The Principles include guidance on the definition of the competence and responsibilities of national institutions, and on maintaining their independence and pluralism.
Date: Adopted 20 December 1993.
Citation: UN Doc. A/RES/48/134.
URL: http://www.un.org/documents/ga/res/48/a48r134.htm (last visited 13 December 2012).

194. Programme of Action of the World Summit for Social Development
Description: International recommendations adopted at the World Summit for Social Development, outlining policies, actions and measures to implement the principles and fulfill the commitments enunciated in the Copenhagen Declaration on Social Development. The Programme recommends actions to create, in a framework of sustained economic growth and sustainable development, a national and international environment favorable to social development, to eradicate poverty, to enhance productive employment and reduce unemployment and to foster social integration.
Date: Adopted 14 March 1995.

Citation: UN Doc. A/CONF.166/9.
URL: http://www.un-documents.net/poa-wssd.htm (last visited 13 December 2012).

195. **Protocol I Additional to the Geneva Conventions of 12 August 1949, and relating to the Protection of Victims of International Armed Conflicts**
Description: The First Protocol to the Geneva Conventions of 12 August 1949 brought several innovations. In particular, the Protocol broadened the definition of international conflicts, extended the protection of the Conventions to civilian medical personnel, equipment and supplies and to civilian units and transports, and redefined armed forces and combatants.
Date: Adopted 8 June 1977 (entered into force 7 December 1978).
Citation: 1125 U.N.T.S. 3, UN Doc. 17512.
URL: http://www.un-documents.net/gc-p1.htm (last visited 13 December 2012).

196. **Protocol II Additional to the Geneva Conventions of 12 August 1949, and relating to the Protection of Victims of Non-International Armed Conflicts**
Description: The Second Protocol to the Geneva Conventions of 12 August 1949 extended the essential rules of the law of armed conflicts to internal wars between a State Party's armed forces and dissident armed groups that exercise such control over a part of its territory as to enable them to carry out sustained and concerted military operations. The Protocol does not apply to situations of internal disturbances and tensions, such as riots or sporadic acts of violence.
Date: Adopted 8 June 1977 (entered into force 7 December 1978).
Citation: 1125 U.N.T.S. 609, UN Doc. 17513.
URL: http://www.un-documents.net/gc-p2.htm (last visited 13 December 2012).

197. **Protocol Against the Smuggling of Migrants by Land, Sea and Air, supplementing the United Nations Convention against Transnational Organized Crime**
Description: International human rights instrument adopted by resolution of the United Nations General Assembly to prevent and combat the smuggling of migrants. It provides for the criminalization of such smuggling, with the establishment of aggravating circumstances when the lives or safety of migrants are endangered

or when the smuggling involves inhuman or degrading treatment, including exploitation.
Date: Adopted 11 November 2000 (entered into force 28 January 2004).
Citation: 2241 U.N.T.S. 507, UN Doc. A/RES/55/25.
URL: http://www.un-documents.net/uncatoc.htm (last visited 13 December 2012).

198. **Protocol for the Suppression of Unlawful Acts Against the Safety of Fixed Platforms Located on the Continental Shelf**
    Description: International instrument supplementary to the Convention for the Suppression of Unlawful Acts Against the Safety of Maritime Navigation of 10 March 1988. The Protocol extends the protections against unlawful acts under the Convention to offenses committed on board or against fixed platforms such as artificial islands or structures permanently attached to the sea bed for the purpose of exploration, exploitation of resources or other economic purposes.
    Date: Adopted 10 March 1988 (entered into force 1 March 1992).
    Citation: 1678 U.N.T.S. 201, UN Doc. 29004.
    URL: http://treaties.un.org/doc/db/Terrorism/Conv9-english.pdf (last visited 13 December 2012).

199. **Protocol for the Suppression of Unlawful Acts of Violence at Airports Serving International Civil Aviation**
    Description: International instrument supplementary to the Convention for the Suppression of Unlawful Acts against the Safety of Civil Aviation of 23 September 1971. The Protocol adds provisions to the Convention in order to deal with acts endangering the safety of persons at airports serving international civil aviation. It will be superseded by the Convention on the Suppression of Unlawful Acts Relating to International Civil Aviation of 10 September 2010, if it enters into force.
    Date: Adopted 24 February 1988 (entered into force 6 August 1989).
    Citation: 1589 U.N.T.S. 474, UN Doc. 14118.
    URL: http://treaties.un.org/doc/db/Terrorism/Conv7-english.pdf (last visited 13 December 2012).

200. **Protocol of Amendment to the Charter of the Organization of American States**
    Description: International instrument adopted by members of the Organization of American States to forge a new dynamism for the inter-American system. The Protocol provides for the establishment

of an Inter-American Commission on Human Rights, to promote the observance of human rights and to serve as a consultative organ. According to the Protocol, the structure, competence, and procedure of this Commission shall be determined by an inter-American convention on human rights.
Date: Adopted 27 February 1967 (entered into force 27 February 1970).
Citation: O.A.S.T.S. B-31, 721 U.N.T.S. 324, UN Doc. 1609.
URL: http://www.oas.org/dil/treaties_B-31_Protocol_of_Buenos_Aires.htm (last visited 13 December 2012).

201. Protocol of Buenos Aires: See **Protocol of Amendment to the Charter of the Organization of American States**.

202. Protocol of San Salvador: See Additional Protocol to the American Convention on Human Rights in the Area of Economic, Social and Cultural Rights.

203. Protocol of the Court of Justice of the African Union
Description: International instrument supplementing the Constitutive Act of the African Union of 11 July 2000. The Protocol was adopted by Member States of the African Union to establish the Court of Justice of the African Union. The measures of this Protocol were replaced by the Protocol on the Statute of the African Court of Justice and Human Rights of 1 July 2008, which has not yet entered into force.
Date: Adopted 11 July 2003 (entered into force 11 February 2009).
URL: http://www.au.int/en/sites/default/files/PROTOCOL_COURT_OF_JUSTICE_OF_THE_AFRICAN_UNION.pdf (last visited 13 December 2012).

204. Protocol on the Statute of the African Court of Justice and Human Rights
Description: International human rights instrument adopted by Member States of the African Union to create the African Court of Justice and Human Rights. This Court merges the African Court on Human and Peoples' Rights established by the Protocol to the African Charter on Human and Peoples' Rights on the Establishment of an African Court on Human and Peoples' Rights of 9 June 1998 and the Court of Justice of the African Union established by the Constitutive Act of the African Union into a single institution. This Protocol also replaces the Protocol of the Court of Justice of the African Union of 11 July 2003.
Date: Adopted 1 July 2008 (not entered into force).

URL: http://www.au.int/en/sites/default/files/PROTOCOL_STATUTE_AFRICAN_COURT_JUSTICE_AND_HUMAN_RIGHTS.pdf (last visited 13 December 2012).

205. **Protocol relating to the Status of Refugees**
 Description: International instrument supplementing the Convention relating to the Status of Refugees of 28 July 1951. The Protocol extended the definition of refugee to cover any person who meets the definition under the Convention, irrespective of the dateline of 1 January 1951.
 Date: Adopted 31 January 1967 (entered into force 4 October 1967).
 Citation: 606 U.N.T.S. 267, UN Doc. 8791.
 URL: http://www.un-documents.net/prsr.htm (last visited 13 December 2012).

206. **Protocol Supplementary to the Convention for the Suppression of Unlawful Seizure of Aircraft**
 Description: International instrument adopted at the International Conference on Air Law, and supplementing the Convention for the Suppression of Unlawful Seizure of Aircraft of 16 December 1970. The Protocol adds a provision stating that any person taken into custody pursuant to the Convention shall be guaranteed fair treatment, including the enjoyment of all rights and guarantees in conformity with international human rights law.
 Date: Adopted 10 September 2010 (not entered into force).
 Citation: ICAO Doc. 9959.
 URL: http://legacy.icao.int/DCAS2010/restr/docs/beijing_protocol_multi.pdf (last visited 13 December 2012).

207. **Protocol to Prevent, Suppress and Punish Trafficking in Persons, Especially Women and Children, supplementing the United Nations Convention Against Transnational Organized Crime**
 Description: International human rights instrument adopted by resolution of the United Nations General Assembly to protect persons who are vulnerable to trafficking. It provides for the criminalization of trafficking in persons, for the assistance of victims of such trafficking and for the co-operation of States Parties in order to meet those objectives.
 Date: Adopted 11 November 2000 (entered into force 25 December 2003).
 Citation: 2237 U.N.T.S. 319, UN Doc. A/RES/55/25.
 URL: http://www.un-documents.net/uncatoc.htm (last visited 13 December 2012).

208. **Protocol to the African Charter on Human and Peoples' Rights on the Establishment of the African Court on Human and Peoples' Rights**
Description: International human rights instrument adopted by Member States of the Organization of African Unity to establish an African Court on Human and Peoples' Rights and govern its organization, jurisdiction and functioning. According to the Protocol, the Court is to complement the functions of the African Commission on Human and Peoples' Rights in enforcing the African Charter on Human and Peoples' Rights.
Date: Adopted 9 June 1998 (entered into force 25 January 2004).
Citation: OAU/LEG/EXP/AFCHPR/PROT (III).
URL: http://www.au.int/en/content/protocol-african-charter-human-and-peoples-rights-establishment-african-court-human-and-peop (last visited 13 December 2012).

209. **Protocol to the African Charter on Human and Peoples' Rights on the Rights of Women in Africa**
Description: International human right instrument adopted by Member States of the African Union to eliminate discrimination and harmful practices against women, and promote the rights of women in Africa. The Protocol includes provisions on civil and political rights, economic, social and cultural rights, marriage, the protection of women in armed conflicts and reproductive rights.
Date: Adopted 11 July 2003 (entered into force 25 November 2005).
Citation: CAB/LEG/66.6.
URL: http://www.au.int/en/content/protocol-african-charter-human-and-peoples-rights-rights-women-africa (last visited 13 December 2012).

210. Protocol to the American Convention on Human Rights to Abolish the Death Penalty
Description: International human rights instrument adopted by members of the Organization of American States to consolidate the practice of not applying the death penalty in the Americas. States Parties may not apply the death penalty in their territory to any person subject to their jurisdiction. No reservations may be made to the Protocol.
Date: Adopted 8 June 1990 (entered into force in accordance with Article 4).
Citation: O.A.S.T.S. A-53.
URL: http://www.oas.org/juridico/english/treaties/a-53.html (last visited 13 December 2012).

211. Recommendation on the Safeguarding of Traditional Culture and Folklore
Description: International recommendations adopted by the General Conference of the United Nations Educational, Scientific and Cultural Organization, as guidelines to safeguard folklore. The Recommendation defines folklore, provides for its conservation, preservation, dissemination, and protection and for the cooperation of Member States in carrying out folklore development, revitalization programs and research.
Date: Adopted 15 November 1989.
Citation: UNESCO Doc. 25C/Resolutions, at 238.
URL: http://www.un-documents.net/folklore.htm (last visited 13 December 2012).

212. **Rio Declaration on Environment and Development**
Description: International proclamation adopted by the United Nations Conference on Environment and Development to establish a new and equitable global partnership between States, key sectors of societies and people, and to work towards international agreements which respect the interests of all and protect the integrity of the global environmental and developmental system.
Date: Adopted 14 June 1992.
Citation: UN Doc. A/CONF.151/26/Rev.1 (Vol. I) at 3.
URL: http://www.un-documents.net/rio-dec.htm (last visited 13 December 2012).
See also: Agenda 21.

213. Riyadh Guidelines: See United Nations Guidelines for the Prevention of Juvenile Delinquency.

214. **Rome Declaration on World Food Security**
Description: International proclamation adopted at the World Food Summit, organized in 1996 by the United Nations Food and Agriculture Organization. The Declaration reaffirmed the right of everyone to have access to safe and nutritious food. Heads of State and Government committed to make national and international efforts to guarantee food security.
Date: Adopted 13 November 1996.
Citation: UN Doc. WFS 96/REP.
URL: http://www.un-documents.net/rome-dec.htm (last visited 27 March 2012).
See also: World Food Summit Plan of Action.

215. **Rome Statute of the International Criminal Court**
Description: International instrument establishing an independent, permanent International Criminal Court with jurisdiction over the crime of genocide, crimes against humanity, war crimes and the crime of aggression. The Statute establishes the court's structure and functioning, and defines the first three types of crimes over which the court shall have jurisdiction.
Date: Adopted 17 July 1998 (entered into force 1 July 2002).
Citation: 2187 U.N.T.S. 3, UN Doc. A/CONF.183/9.
URL: http://www.un-documents.net/icc.htm (last visited 13 December 2012).

216. **Safeguards Guaranteeing Protection of the Rights of Those Facing the Death Penalty**
Description: International standards adopted by resolution of the United Nations Economic and Social Council to protect the rights of persons facing capital punishment. Among other protections, the Safeguards provide that, in countries that have not abolished it, the death penalty should be only used for the most serious crimes, and only for persons older than 18 at the time of the commission of the crime.
Date: Adopted 25 May 1984.
Citation: UN Doc. E/1984/50.
URL: http://www2.ohchr.org/english/law/protection.htm (last visited 13 December 2012).

217. Sankey Declaration: See **A Declaration of the Rights of Man**.

218. **Second Optional Protocol to the International Covenant on Civil and Political Rights, Aiming at the Abolition of the Death Penalty**
Description: International human rights instrument adopted by resolution of the United Nations General Assembly as an international commitment to abolish the death penalty, complementing the International Covenant on Civil and Political Rights. No reservation is admissible to the Protocol.
Date: Adopted 15 December 1989 (entered into force 11 July 1991).
Citation: 1642 U.N.T.S. 414, UN Doc. A/RES/44/128.
URL: http://www.un.org/documents/ga/res/44/a44r128.htm (last visited 13 December 2012).

219. **Single European Act**
Description: International instrument adopted by the members of the European Union, amending the Treaty establishing the European Economic Community of 1957. The Act reaffirms the

members' commitment to fundamental rights and adds provisions permitting the European Community to protect and improve the quality of the environment, to contribute towards protecting human health and to ensure a prudent and rational utilization of natural resources.
Date: Adopted 17 February 1986 (entered into force 1 July 1987).
Citation: OJ L 169 of 29.6.1987.
URL: http://ec.europa.eu/economy_finance/emu_history/documents/treaties/singleuropeanact.pdf (last visited 13 December 2012).

220. **Siracusa Principles on the Limitation and Derogation Provisions in the International Covenant on Civil and Political Rights**
    Description: International interpretative principles adopted by the United Nations Economic and Social Council, to reflect the state of international law with respect to the limitation clauses and provisions for derogation to the International Covenant on Civil and Political Rights in situations of public emergency.
    Date: Adopted 28 September 1984.
    Citation: UN Doc. E/CN.4/1985/4.
    URL: http://www.unhcr.org/refworld/pdfid/4672bc122.pdf (last visited 13 December 2012).

221. **Slavery, Servitude, Forced Labour and Similar Institutions and Practices Convention**
    Description: International human rights instrument adopted by the League of Nations and first defining slavery as "the status or condition of a person over whom any or all of the powers attaching to the right of ownership are exercised". The Convention obligates the contracting parties to prevent and suppress the slave trade and to bring about the complete abolition of slavery in all its forms.
    Date: Adopted 25 September 1926 (entered into force 9 March 1927).
    Citation: 60 L.N.T.S. 253.
    URL: http://www1.umn.edu/humanrts/instree/f1sc.htm (last visited 13 December 2012).
    See also: **Supplementary Convention on the Abolition of Slavery, the Slave Trade, and Institutions and Practices Similar to Slavery**.

222. **Special Proclamation, Establishment of an International Military Tribunal for the Far East**
    Description: Proclamation of the Supreme Commander for the Allied Powers, made in 1946 and providing that there shall be established an International Military Tribunal for the Far East. The

Tribunal was to try those persons charged with offenses including crimes against peace after World War II.
Date: Adopted 19 January 1946.
Citation: T.I.A.S. 1589.
URL: http://www.ibiblio.org/hyperwar/PTO/IMTFE/IMTFE-A4.html (last visited 13 December 2012).

223. Standard Minimum Rules for the Treatment of Prisoners
Description: International standards adopted by resolutions of the United Nations Economic and Social Council to set out what is generally accepted as being good principle and practice in the treatment of prisoners and the management of detention institutions. The Rules cover various aspects such as the separation of prisoners, accommodation, medical services and discipline. They also provide specifically for different categories of prisoners, such as convicted inmates and untried prisoners.
Date: Adopted 31 July 1957; Amended 13 May 1977.
Citations: UN Doc. E/3048 and UN Doc. E/5988.
URL: http://www2.ohchr.org/english/law/treatmentprisoners.htm (last visited 13 December 2012).

224. Statute of the Inter-American Commission of Human Rights
Description: International human rights instrument adopted by the General Assembly of the Organization of American States, organizing the Inter-American Commission on Human Rights. The Statute provides for the membership, structure, powers, and functioning of the Commission.
Date: Adopted October 1979 (entered into force November 1979).
Citation: OEA/Ser.P/IX.0.2/80, Vol. 1 at 88.
URL: http://www.cidh.oas.org/Basicos/English/Basic17.Statute%20of%20the%20Commission.htm (last visited 13 December 2012).

225. Statute of the Inter-American Court of Human Rights
Description: International human rights instrument adopted by the General Assembly of the Organization of American States, organizing the Inter-American Court of Human Rights. The Statute provides for the jurisdiction, composition, structure, and functioning of the Court.
Date: Adopted October 1979 (entered into force 1 January 1980).
Citation: OEA/Ser.P/IX.0.2/80, Vol. 1 at 98.
URL: http://www.corteidh.or.cr/estatuto.cfm (last visited 13 December 2012).

Appendix 241

226. Stockholm Declaration on the Human Environment: See **Declaration of the United Nations Conference on the Human Environment**.

227. **Supplementary Convention on the Abolition of Slavery, the Slave Trade, and Institutions and Practices Similar to Slavery**
Description: International human rights instrument adopted by a United Nations Conference of Plenipotentiaries to augment the 1926 Slavery, Servitude, Forced Labour and Similar Institutions and Practices Convention. The Supplementary Convention was designed to intensify national efforts and international co-operation towards the abolition of slavery and similar practices.
Date: Adopted 7 September 1956 (entered into force 30 April 1957).
Citation: 226 U.N.T.S. 3, UN Doc. 3822.
URL: http://treaties.un.org/doc/Publication/UNTS/Volume%2026 6/volume-266-I-3822-English.pdf (last visited 13 December 2012).

228. Tokyo Convention: See Convention on Offences and Certain Other Acts Committed On Board Aircraft.

229. Treaties of Westphalia
Description: Series of two peace treaties signed in 1648 in Osnabrück and Münster, Germany, ending the Thirty Years' War and involving the Holy Roman Emperor, France, Sweden and their respective allies. The Treaties redesigned national boundaries within Europe and are considered to have originated the international system of States and the modern concept of sovereign statehood.
Date: Adopted 24 October 1648.
Citation: *Instrumentum Pacis Monasteriensi*; *Instrumentum Pacis Osnabrugensis*.
URL: http://germanhistorydocs.ghi-dc.org/pdf/eng/87.%20Peace Westphalia_en.pdf [excerpts] (last visited 13 December 2012).

230. **Treaty Establishing the European Economic Community**: See Treaty on the Functioning of the European Union.

231. Treaty of Lisbon
Description: International instrument adopted by Member States of the European Union, and amending two fundamental treaties of the Union: the Treaty on European Union and the Treaty establishing the European Community. The Treaty of Lisbon opened the way for the Union to seek accession to the Convention on the Protection of Human Rights and Fundamental Freedoms of 4 November 1950, and guaranteed the rights, freedoms and principles set out

in the Charter of Fundamental Rights of the European Union of 7 December 2000.
Date: Adopted 13 December 2007 (entered into force 1 December 2009).
Citation: OJ C 306 of 17.12.2007.
URL: http://eur-lex.europa.eu/JOHtml.do?uri=OJ:C:2007:306:SOM:EN:HTML (last visited 13 December 2012).

232. **Treaty of Maastricht**: See Treaty on European Union.

233. Treaty of Rome: See Treaty on the Functioning of the European Union.

234. Treaty on European Union
Description: International instrument adopted by the members of the European Union to mark a new stage in the process of European integration. The Treaty reaffirms the members' attachment to the principles of liberty, democracy, respect for human rights and fundamental freedoms, and as amended by the Treaty of Lisbon of 13 December 2007, it provides for the accession of the Union to the Convention on the Protection of Human Rights and Fundamental Freedoms of 4 November 1950, and provides that the Union recognizes the rights, freedoms and principles set out in the Charter of Fundamental Rights of the European Union of 7 December 2000.
Date: Adopted 7 February 1992 (entered into force 1 November 1993).
Citation: OJ C 191 of 29.07.1992.
URL: http://eur-lex.europa.eu/en/treaties/dat/11992M/htm/11992M.html; http://eur-lex.europa.eu/LexUriServ/LexUriServ.do?uri=OJ:C:2010:083:0013:0046:EN:PDF [consolidated version] (last visited 13 December 2012).

235. **Treaty on the Functioning of the European Union**
Description: International instrument adopted in 1957 as the Treaty establishing the European Economic Community, to lay the foundations of a union among the peoples of Europe. It has been amended multiple times and was renamed 'Treaty on the Functioning of the European Union' (TFEU) by the Treaty of Lisbon of 13 December 2007. As amended, the TFEU provides for the accession of the Union to the Convention on the Protection of Human Rights and Fundamental Freedoms of 4 November 1950, and expresses the members' attachment to the fundamental social rights set out in the European Social Charter of 18 October 1961

Appendix 243

and in the Community Charter of the Fundamental Social Rights of Workers of 9 December 1989.
Date: Adopted 25 March 1957 (entered into force 1 January 1958).
Citation: OJ C 83 of 30.3.2010.
URL: http://eur-lex.europa.eu/LexUriServ/LexUriServ.do?uri=OJ:C:2010:083:0047:0200:en:PDF [consolidated version] (last visited 13 December 2012).

236. Twenty Guiding Principles for the Fight Against Corruption
Description: International principles adopted by the Committee of Ministers of the Council of Europe, which considers corruption as a serious threat to the basic principles and values of the Council of Europe, undermining the confidence of citizens in democracy, eroding the rule of law, constituting a denial of human rights and hindering social and economic development. The Principles therefore recommend the implementation of certain measures in domestic legislations and practices to fight corruption.
Date: Adopted 6 November 1997.
Citation: Res. (97) 24.
URL: https://wcd.coe.int/ViewDoc.jsp?id=593789 (last visited 13 December 2012).

237. United Nations Convention Against Corruption
Description: International instrument adopted by resolution of the United Nations General Assembly to prevent and combat corruption more efficiently. The Convention recognizes the seriousness of the threats posed by corruption to the stability and security of societies, undermining the institutions and values of democracy, ethical values and justice and jeopardizing sustainable development and the rule of law.
Date: Adopted 31 October 2003 (entered into force 14 December 2005).
Citation: 2349 U.N.T.S. 41, UN Doc. A/RES/58/4.
URL: http://www.un-documents.net/a58r4.htm (last visited 13 December 2012).

238. **United Nations Convention Against Transnational Organized Crime**
Description: International instrument adopted by resolution of the United Nations General Assembly to promote international co-operation in preventing and combating transnational organized crime more effectively. The Convention mandates the criminalization of criminal activities of organized criminal groups,

money-laundering and corruption, organizes extradition and provides for mutual legal assistance.
Date: Adopted 10 November 2000 (entered into force 29 September 2003).
Citation: 2225 U.N.T.S. 209, UN Doc. A/RES/55/25.
URL: http://www.un-documents.net/uncatoc.htm (last visited 13 December 2012).
See also: Protocol Against the Smuggling of Migrants by Land, Sea and Air, supplementing the United Nations Convention against Transnational Organized Crime; **Protocol to Prevent, Suppress and Punish Trafficking in Persons, Especially Women and Children, supplementing the United Nations Convention Against Transnational Organized Crime**.

239. United Nations Declaration on Human Cloning
Description: International human rights proclamation adopted by the United Nations General Assembly to prevent the potential dangers of human cloning to human dignity. The Declaration calls upon Member States to prohibit all forms of human cloning and the application of genetic engineering techniques inasmuch as they are incompatible with human dignity and the protection of human life.
Date: Adopted 23 March 2005.
Citation: UN Doc. A/RES/59/280.
URL: http://www.un.org/Docs/asp/ws.asp?m=A/RES/59/280 (last visited 13 December 2012).

240. United Nations Declaration on the Elimination of All Forms of Racial Discrimination
Description: International human rights proclamation adopted by the United Nations General Assembly, affirming the necessity of speedily eliminating racial discrimination throughout the world and of securing understanding of and respect for the dignity of the human person. The Declaration also affirms the necessity of adopting national and international measures, including teaching, education and information, to achieve those ends.
Date: Adopted 20 November 1963.
Citation: UN Doc. A/RES/18/1904.
URL: http://www.un-documents.net/a18r1904.htm (last visited 13 December 2012).

241. United Nations Guidelines for the Prevention of Juvenile Delinquency
Description: International standards known as the Riyadh

Guidelines, adopted by resolution of the United Nations General Assembly to prevent juvenile delinquency pursuant to a child-centered orientation. The Guidelines recommend adopting preventive policies facilitating the socialization and integration of young persons. They also recommend funding social services and enacting specific laws and procedures to promote and protect the rights and well-being of all young persons.
Date: Adopted 14 December 1990.
Citation: UN Doc. A/RES/45/112.
URL: http://www.un.org/documents/ga/res/45/a45r112.htm (last visited 13 December 2012).

242. United Nations Millennium Declaration
Description: International human rights proclamation adopted by resolution of the United Nations General Assembly, recognizing a collective responsibility to uphold the principles of human dignity, equality and equity at the global level, and affirming States' commitment to peace, security and disarmament, development and poverty eradication, environmental protection, democracy and good governance and protection of the vulnerable.
Date: Adopted 8 September 2000.
Citation: UN Doc. A/RES/55/2.
URL: http://www.un-documents.net/a55r2.htm (last visited 13 December 2012).

243. United Nations Rules for the Protection of Juveniles Deprived of Their Liberty
Description: International standards adopted by resolution of the United Nations General Assembly to address the conditions and circumstances under which persons under the age of 18 are being deprived of their liberty worldwide. The Rules affirm that juvenile justice systems should uphold the rights and safety of juveniles and use imprisonment as a last resort. They also address several issues such as juveniles under arrest or awaiting trial, the management of juvenile facilities, and specific human rights of juveniles in detention.
Date: Adopted 14 December 1990.
Citation: UN Doc. A/RES/45/113.
URL: http://www.un.org/documents/ga/res/45/a45r113.htm (last visited 13 December 2012).

244. United Nations Rules for the Treatment of Women Prisoners and Non-custodial Measures for Women Offenders
Description: International standards adopted by resolution of the

Third Committee of the United Nations General Assembly to address the particular needs of female offenders. The Rules supplement the Standard Minimum Rules for the Treatment of Prisoners of 31 July 1957. They cover the general management of institutions for women deprived of liberty, prisoners under sentence, prisoners under arrest or awaiting trial, the treatment of juvenile female prisoners, as well as the application of non-custodial sanctions and measures for women offenders, among other topics.
Date: Adopted 6 October 2010.
Citation: UN Doc. A/C.3/65/L.5.
URL: http://www.un.org/Docs/journal/asp/ws.asp?m=A/C.3/65/L.5 (last visited 13 December 2012).

245. United Nations Standard Minimum Rules for Non-custodial Measures
Description: International standards known as the Tokyo Rules, adopted by resolution of the United Nations General Assembly to address the increasing prison population and prison overcrowding worldwide. The Rules promote the use of non-custodial measures and provide minimum safeguards for persons subject to alternatives to imprisonment at the pre-trial, trial and post-sentencing stages.
Date: Adopted 14 December 1990.
Citation: UN Doc. A/RES/45/110.
URL: http://www2.ohchr.org/english/law/tokyorules.htm (last visited 13 December 2012).

246. **United Nations Standard Minimum Rules for the Administration of Juvenile Justice**
Description: International standards known as the Beijing Rules, adopted by resolution of the United Nations General Assembly as a guide to amend existing national legislation, policies and practices. The Rules recognize that the young, owing to their early stage of human development, require particular care, assistance and legal protection. They address many aspects of the administration of juvenile justice, including investigation, prosecution, adjudication, disposition and juvenile institutions.
Date: Adopted 29 November 1985.
Citation: UN Doc. A/RES/40/33.
URL: http://www.un.org/documents/ga/res/40/a40r033.htm (last visited 13 December 2012).

247. Universal Declaration of Human Rights
Description: International declaration adopted by resolution of

the United Nations General Assembly as a common standard of achievement for all peoples and all nations. The Declaration sets forth a number of human rights and fundamental freedoms, to the end that everyone shall strive to promote respect for these rights and to secure their universal and effective recognition and observance.
Date: Adopted 10 December 1948.
Citation: UN Doc. A/RES/3/217A (III).
URL: http://www.un-documents.net/a3r217a.htm (last visited 13 December 2012).

248. Universal Declaration on Bioethics and Human Rights
Description: International human rights proclamation adopted by resolution of the United Nations Educational, Scientific and Cultural Organization General Conference to provide guidance with regard to ethical issues related to medicine, life sciences and associated technologies as applied to human beings. To guarantee human dignity, human rights and fundamental freedoms, the Declaration establishes a series of principles such as consent to medical intervention, respect for human vulnerability, non-discrimination, promotion of health, and sharing of benefits resulting from scientific research.
Date: Adopted 19 October 2005.
Citation: UNESCO Doc. 33C/Resolution 36.
URL: http://portal.unesco.org/en/ev.php-URL_ID=31058&URL_DO=DO_TOPIC&URL_SECTION=201.html (last visited 13 December 2012).

249. **Universal Declaration on Cultural Diversity**
Description: International human rights proclamation adopted by resolution of the United Nations Educational, Scientific and Cultural Organization General Conference to ensure the preservation and promotion of the fruitful diversity of cultures. The Declaration analyzes cultural diversity and pluralism, affirms cultural rights as an integral part of human rights and provides for the protection and promotion of culture.
Date: Adopted 2 November 2001.
Citation: UNESCO Doc. 31C/Resolution 25, Annex I.
URL: http://www.un-documents.net/udcd.htm (last visited 13 December 2012).

250. Universal Declaration on the Eradication of Hunger and Malnutrition
Description: International human rights proclamation adopted by

the World Food Conference and endorsed by the United Nations General Assembly as a way to resolve the world food problem within the broader context of development and international economic co-operation. The Declaration affirms that every person has the inalienable right to be free from hunger and malnutrition and that their eradication is a common objective of the international community.
Date: Adopted 6 November 1974; Endorsed 17 December 1974.
Citations: UN Doc. E/CONF.65/20 at 1; UN Doc. A/RES/3348 (XXIX).
URL: http://www2.ohchr.org/english/law/malnutrition.htm (last visited 13 December 2012).

251. **Universal Declaration on the Human Genome and Human Rights**
Description: International human rights proclamation adopted by resolution of the United Nations Educational, Scientific and Cultural Organization General Conference and endorsed by the General Assembly. The Declaration affirms that research on the human genome and resulting applications should fully respect human dignity, human rights, and the prohibition of all forms of discrimination based on genetic characteristics.
Date: Adopted 11 November 1997; Endorsed 9 December 1998.
Citation: UNESCO Doc. 29C/Resolution 16.
URL: http://www.un-documents.net/udhghr.htm (last visited 13 December 2012).

252. **Vienna Convention on Consular Relations**
Description: International instrument on consular relations, privileges and immunities, adopted to ensure the efficient performance of their functions by consular posts on behalf of their respective States. The Convention provides for the operation of consulates, outlines the functions of consular agents and addresses the privileges and immunities granted to consular officials when posted to a foreign country.
Date: Adopted 24 April 1963 (entered into force 19 March 1967).
Citation: 596 U.NT.S. 261.
URL: http://untreaty.un.org/ilc/texts/instruments/english/conventions/9_2_1963.pdf (last visited 13 December 2012).

253. **Vienna Convention on Diplomatic Relations**
Description: International instrument on diplomatic intercourse, privileges and immunities, adopted to ensure the efficient performance of the functions of diplomatic missions, as representing States.

Appendix 249

The Convention provides a framework for the establishment, maintenance and termination of diplomatic relations and diplomatic missions, and sets out special rules to enable those missions to act without fear of coercion or harassment and to communicate securely with their sending governments.
Date: Adopted 18 April 1961 (entered into force 24 April 1964).
Citation: 500 U.N.T.S. 95.
URL: http://untreaty.un.org/ilc/texts/instruments/english/conventions/9_1_1961.pdf (last visited 13 December 2012).

254. **Vienna Convention on the Law of Treaties**
Description: International instrument codifying previously existing customary law in order to promote the maintenance of international peace and security, the development of friendly relations and the achievement of co-operation among nations. The Convention only applies to treaties concluded between States, and excludes those involving international organizations.
Date: Adopted 23 May 1969 (entered into force 27 January 1980).
Citation: 1155 U.N.T.S. 331.
URL: http://untreaty.un.org/ilc/texts/instruments/english/conventions/1_1_1969.pdf (last visited 13 December 2012).

255. **Vienna Declaration and Programme of Action**
Description: International declaration adopted by the World Conference on Human Rights to increase efforts of international co-operation and solidarity in human rights endeavors. The Declaration and Programme of Action reaffirm the commitment of the international community to strengthen and further implement the body of human rights constructed on the foundation of the Universal Declaration of Human Rights of 1948.
Date: Adopted 25 June 1993.
Citation: UN Doc. A/CONF.157/23.
URL: www.un-documents.net/ac157-23.htm (last visited 13 December 2012).

256. Westphalia, Treaties of: See **Treaties of Westphalia**.

257. **World Declaration on Education for All**
Description: International human rights proclamation adopted by the United Nations World Conference on Education for All to promote basic education of children, youths and adults. Recalling that education is a fundamental right, the Declaration provides an expanded vision of, and a renewed commitment to, basic education of all people.

250 *Dictionary of international human rights law*

Date: Adopted 9 March 1990.
Citation: *Final Report of the World Conference on Education for All: Meeting Basic Learning Needs*, Jomtien, Thailand, 5–9 March 1990, appendix I.
URL: http://www.un-documents.net/jomtien.htm (last visited 13 December 2012).
See also: Framework For Action to Meet Basic Learning Needs.

258. World Food Summit Plan of Action
Description: Along with the Rome Declaration on World Food Security, the World Food Summit Plan of Action sought to lay the foundations to food security, at the individual, household, national, regional and global levels. The Plan of Action breaks down the commitments set forth in the Declaration in several detailed objectives and recommendations. See **World Food Summit**
Date: Adopted 17 November 1996.
Citation: UN Doc. WFS 96/REP.
URL: http://www.un-documents.net/wfs-poa.htm (last visited 13 December 2012).

259. **Yogyakarta Principles**
Description: International standards adopted by a group of international human rights experts as a universal guide to human rights. The Principles address a broad range of binding human rights standards and their application to issues of sexual orientation and gender identity.
Date: Adopted 9 November 2006.
URL: http://www.yogyakartaprinciples.org/principles_en.htm (last visited 13 December 2012).